Series in Explorations in Social Holiness

The goal of this Series in Explorations in Social Holiness is to gather a number of thinkers together and allow them to think through various aspects of what the doctrine of holiness looks like as a social phenomenon. The question this series poses is "What makes a community holy?" In order to answer such a question, the series draws from biblical scholars, historians, theologians, philosophers, and any others who want to explore the idea of social holiness. This series arises from the holiness tradition and is rooted therein. The approach to social holiness embraced in the series comes from being part of the holiness movement. The series, though, asks the holiness movement to expand its bounds beyond the focus on the personal and move toward the social. In so doing, holiness theology can open the way of rethinking the nature of what it means to be church.

A caveat must be made. Within this series, social holiness is not an endorsement of any specific political affiliation. Rather, the series asks its contributors and readers to engage Christian communities in a way that opens aspects of its holiness. More times than not, this approach necessitates interacting with various "social problems" that exist. The authors in this series offer ways of approaching such problems from different angles and foci, at times disagreeing with one another. The goal, though, is to consistently imagine the way that a community may be holy.

The first book in this series is entitled *Holy Imagination: Rethiinking Social Holiness*. The goal of this book is to imagine social holiness, an aspect of the doctrine of holiness often neglected. The proposed project offer ways of thinking about holiness as a social manifestation that moves beyond the individual. This is not another attempt to "reclaim" the doctrine of holiness nor is it an attempt to make the doctrine "relevant" for a postmodern generation. The project is for historians to capture and tell the story of persons driven by the impulse of social holiness; for biblical scholars to decipher the meaning of texts and the ways they have been (mis)appropriated in regards to social holiness; and for theologians to examine how social holiness transforms our understandings of traditional theology. The ultimate goal is to create a social holiness imagination; thus no essay in this volume will simple focus on social holiness as a concept in and of itself, but will rather contribute to the construction of a way of thinking that embraces social holiness as part and parcel of what it means to think about holiness.

—Nathan Crawford, Jonathan Dodrill, and David Wilson, Series Editors

Holy Imagination

Rethinking Social Holiness

Edited by

Nathan Crawford
Jonathan Dodrill
David Wilson

Series in Explorations in Social Holiness

EMETH PRESS
www.emethpress.com

Holy Imagination: Rethinking Social Holiness

Copyright © 2015 Nathan Crawford

Printed in the United States of America on acid-free paper. All rights reserved. No part of this book may be reproduced, or stored in a retrieval system or transmitted in any form or by any means, electronic, mechanical, photocopying, recording, scanning or otherwise, except as permitted by the 1976 United States Copyright Act, or with the prior written permission of Emeth Press. Requests for permission should be addressed to: Emeth Press, P. O. Box 23961, Lexington, KY 40523-3961   http://www.emethpress.com.

Library of Congress Cataloging-in-Publication Data

Holy imagination : rethinking social holiness / edited by Nathan Crawford, Jonathan Dodrill, David Wilson.
    pages cm. -- (Series in explorations in social holiness)
  ISBN 978-1-60947-087-6 (alk. paper)
  1. Holiness. 2. Christian sociology. 3. Change--Religious aspects--Christianity. 4. Communities--Religious aspects--Christianity. 5. Methodist Church. 6. Wesley, John, 1703-1791. I. Crawford, Nathan, editor.
  BT767.H735 2014
  234'.8--dc23
                          2014042253

Photo on Front Cover
This painting by Richard Douglas depicts a young John Wesley giving his coat to a poor man. Used by Permission

Table of Contents

Introduction: Reimagining Holiness / 1

Chapter 1: Enfolding Others: Social Holiness in the Bible and Biblical Interpretation / 11
    Karen Winslow

Chapter 2: Social Holiness in James and 1 Peter / 29
    Abson Joseph

Chapter 3: Reclaiming Holisitic Salvation: A Continuing Wesleyan Agenda / 41
    Randy L. Maddox

Chapter 4: Kenosis not Control: The Social Holiness of Chicago's Urban Missions / 55
    Jonathan Dodrill

Chapter 5: The Evolution of Social Ministry in The Salvation Army / 73
    Roger Green

Chapter 6: Peaceful Pentecost: The Pentecostal Pacifist Tradition for Contemporary Political Praxis and Theology / 95
    AJ Swoboda

Chapter 7: Speaking Truth to Power—With a Twist: Reenvisioning the Task of Theology and the Academy / 113
    Joerg Rieger

Chapter 8: Understanding The Social Structure of Sin: *Han* and the Example of Racism / 127
    Nathan Crawford

Chapter 9: Zionism and the Subversion of Justice / 139
    Barry E. Bryant

Chapter 10: "In the City, for the City": Re-Membering Roots and Discovering What it Means to be Our Full Selves and Good Neighbors in Southeast Portland / 161
    Cassie Trentaz

About the Contributors / 175

Introduction: Reimagining Holiness

"The gospel of Christ knows of no religion, but social; no holiness, but social holiness."[1]

"Christianity is essentially a social religion ... to turn it into a solitary religion, is indeed to destroy it. ... I mean not only that it cannot subsist so well, but that it cannot subsist at all, without society—without living and conversing with other [people]. ... Not that we can in anywise condemn the intermixing solitude or retirement with society. ... Yet such retirement must not swallow up all our time."[2]

These two quotes from John Wesley are often used to point to the fact that Methodist and Holiness theologies should be concerned with the social aspects of salvation. As Randy Maddox' essay in this volume suggests though, such an appeal is somewhat unwarranted since it takes the quotes out of context. But, as Maddox also makes apparent, the quotes still point to a broader, more holistic understanding of salvation within the corpus of John Wesley than we often give him credit for, especially those of us coming from or working within the holiness tradition.[3]

In this volume, we offer a collection of essays that seek to rethink various aspects of the doctrine of holiness in a social way. While this has been done at times before, there has been a major lack in regards to the actual spelling out of the doctrine of social holiness. In this introduction to the volume, let us briefly do four things. First, we offer a critique of those coming from the holiness tradition and their lack of thought on the subject of social holiness. Second, we show where the holiness tradition has a way of opening up the doctrine of social holiness through the idea of the ethical and moral. Third, we make a constructive attempt to define holiness in light of the Most Holy, the Triune God, making holiness a reflection of the community that exists within the

---

[1] John Wesley, *Hymns and Sacred Poems* (1739), Preface, §5, *The Works of John Wesley*, third edition, ed. Thomas Jackson, vol. 14, (London: John Mason, 1829), 321.

[2] John Wesley, Sermon 24, "Sermon on the Mount, IV," §§ I.1-4 in *Sermons I*, ed. Albert C. Outler, vol. 1 of *The Bicentennial Edition of the Works of John Wesley* (Nashville: Abingdon Press, 1984), 533-534.

[3] For another account of the holistic understanding of salvation in Wesley, see Theodore Runyon, "Introduction: Wesley and the Theologies of Liberation," in *Sanctification and Liberation*, ed. Theodore Runyon (Nashville: Abingdon, 1981), 9-48, esp. 44-47.

Godhead. Last, we detail the contents of the rest of the book in order to offer a guide to the way in which this volume seeks to rethink the idea of holiness.

I. Critique

For two of the editors of this text, Laurence Wood's "The Wesleyan View" in the volume *Christian Spirituality: Five Views on Sanctification*, edited by Donald L. Alexander, was one of our first forays into the world of academic, systematic holiness theology, especially around the idea of entire sanctification.[4] Wood's account is a clear articulation of the doctrine of holiness as it is usually conceived within holiness theologies. However, within that articulation, Wood is also typical in his lack of dealing with the social nature of salvation for Methodist and holiness theologies.[5] While Wood clearly and acutely describes the process of entire sanctification for the individual, he leaves out an understanding of salvation as social.

This is not to single Wood out, though, since his understanding is quite reflective of the general understanding of holiness and sanctification within the holiness movement.[6] In fact, if one were to go through some of the main journals articulating holiness theology—such as the journal of the Wesleyan Theological Society, the *Wesleyan Theological Journal*, or the *Asbury Journal*—it is easy to notice a stunning lack of articulation of the social aspect of salvation. Mostly, if such a social aspect to salvation and holiness is dealt with, it is done so in a historical way, articulating the way that certain people in the history of the movement have understood and acted in a way that underscores a social dimension to salvation. Representative of the type of article that is in this vein is Woodrow W. Whidden's "Eschatology, Soteriology, and Social Activism in

---

[4] Laurence W. Wood, "The Wesleyan View," in *Christian Spirituality: Five Views on Sanctification*, ed. Donald L. Alexander (Downer's Grove: IVP Academic, 1989), 95-118. In a conversation with Wood, the editors discovered that he did have a section on social holiness in his article, but that the editor of the volume said it needed to be removed. From this, we can surmise that even people and groups outside of the Methodist and Holiness traditions place an identity on the movements that is "otherworldly" and pietistic.

[5] Another notable failure to deal with the social dimension of salvation occurs in Thomas C. Oden, *John Wesley's Scriptural Christianity: A Plain Exposition of His Teaching on Christian Doctrine* (Grand Rapids: Zondervan, 1994).

[6] I (Crawford) would even say that aspects of Wood's holiness theology do open up into a broader understanding of social holiness. I would argue this is especially true of his "Pentecostal" emphasis, drawing from the work of John Fletcher [See, Laurence W. Wood, *The Meaning of Pentecost in Early Methodism: Rediscovering John Fletcher as John Wesley's Vindicator and Designated Successor* (Lanham: Scarecrow Press, 2002)]. However, Wood's thought does not ever go into a detailed understanding or articulation of social holiness.

Four Mid-Nineteenth Century Holiness Methodists."[7] In his article, Whidden aims to show a lack of consensus among holiness Methodists in regard to how eschatology affects their understanding of social salvation. He wants to counter the idea that postmillennialism leads to a social understanding of holiness. He points to three of these holiness Methodists as being postmillennial, eschatologically, while focusing on the personal, soteriologically. The other holiness Methodist eschews this, but the point is clear: social holiness and salvation is not necessarily an assumed consequence within a more social, postmillennial eschatology.

By underscoring the personal over the social, holiness theology opens itself to only articulating the personal aspects of salvation, even if and when we try to do otherwise. This is quite apparent in Henry W. Spaulding III's article "Practicing Holiness: A Consideration of Action in the Thought of John Wesley."[8] Spaulding writes the article to articulate how Wesley calls for action to be coupled with inward experience in order to participate in real Christianity, while also showing how Wesley provides the framework for such action.[9] This would seem to imply a "social" aspect as needed, since action is usually coupled with action for someone or something; or, action becomes a sort of solipsistic movement that only benefits "me." But, Spaulding does not take this social aspect into consideration in his understanding of Wesley's call to action. He wants to show that for the Wesleyan-holiness tradition, "action engenders character and character frames action."[10] The idea of a rightly ordered faith leading to rightly ordered action is important for Spaulding's understanding. There is a distinct lack of communal ordering for Spaulding here, only to be found in the way that one is part of a tradition.[11] Again, though, the focus is still on the one, the person, as part of a larger whole instead of the way that the larger functions to shape individuals. We see this clearly as Spaulding focuses on Wesley's understanding of self in order to articulate the nature of action for a Wesleyan-holiness theology.[12] He tries to emphasize the doxological side of the formation of the self, but the emphasis is still on the way that one chooses to act, the "singleness and purity of intention" of the individual, moral agent.[13] Spaulding tries to move out of such an individual, personal focus on action by talking of participation, namely one's participation leading to having real

---

[7] Woodrow W. Whidden, "Eschatology, Soteriology, and Social Activism in Four Mid-Nineteenth Century Holiness Methodists," *Wesleyan Theological Journal* 29 (1994), 92-109.

[8] Henry W. Spaulding III, "Practicing Holiness: A Consideration of the Action in the Thought of John Wesley," *Wesleyan Theological Journal* 40, no. 1 (2005), 110-137.

[9] Ibid., 111.
[10] Ibid., 118.
[11] Ibid., 118-120.
[12] See especially, Ibid., 129.
[13] Ibid., 131 and 134.

Christianity and the "character of a Methodist."[14] However, Spaulding's failure is that he does not articulate the nature of Methodism as community first, as a social institution that is seeking purity and holiness. Had he done so, he would have been able to then move to the way that this shapes individuals. Rather, his focus on the self and how the self makes decisions for action only further entrenches Methodist theology within the bounds of individual, personal holiness to the neglect of the social.

The emphasis on the personal over the social is perhaps best seen in the thought of Kenneth Collins. Collins emphasizes the idea that John Wesley always taught and adhered to an instantaneous, personal experience of entire sanctification.[15] This emphasis on the personal eventually leads to Collins' understanding that even social acts, like giving to the poor, are still about personal salvation. This personal salvation can be "my own" or it can be about "evangelism" and helping those who are shown mercy to see Christ. In either way the idea is that works are done for soteriological reasons and not out of the attempt to perfectly love our neighbor. For Collins, Wesley's understanding says that good works are done by the individual and are tied to the moral law. Collins argues that Wesley ties human good works to the moral law because good works serve as preparation for the final judgment one faces after death. Good works prepare a person to account for one's adherence to the moral law of God.[16] We see then a strong emphasis on the personal nature of salvation at work in Collins.

Collins emphasizes the personal so heavily that he even argues that Wesley's ministry to the poor is primarily about saving the souls of the poor. In a footnote, Collins states, "With the notable exception of slavery, Wesley, as an eighteenth century thinker, was hardly aware of the institutional and structural dimensions of sin." He goes on, in the same footnote, to say that Wesley's concern for the poor is useful today, though, because it demands a love of God and neighbor to go along with social analysis.[17] This reverberates in Collins' treatment of Wesley's thoughts on the rich. Instead of offering critique of the rich as rich, Collins' Wesley sees richness as leading to certain types of sin, like greed, inordinate desires, and nonreliance upon God. The rich, then, must look after the poor by giving all they can as a move to look after their own souls so that their souls will not be corrupted.[18] For Collins, Wesley exhorts people to give because "dispensing wealth improved the spiritual state of the giver as well as the temporal condition of the receiver."[19] Part of the reason the rich do give,

---

[14] Ibid., 133.

[15] For an example, see Kenneth J. Collins, *The Scripture Way of Salvation: The Heart of John Wesley's Theology* (Nashville: Abingdon, 1997); see also his *The Theology of John Wesley: Holy Love and the Shape of Grace* (Nashville: Abingdon, 2007).

[16] Collins, *The Scripture Way of Salvation*, 198-200.

[17] Kenneth J. Collins, "The Soteriological Orientation of John Wesley's Ministry to the Poor," *Wesleyan Theological Journal* 36, no. 2 (2001), 36, n.97.

[18] Ibid., 17.

[19] Ibid., 25.

though, is also to help "save the souls" of the poor, so that they are simultaneously improving temporal conditions as well as helping the spiritual state of poor people.[20] For Collins, salvation is purely tied to the state of one's soul and insuring that oneself is in the good graces of God. While Collins' focus on aspects of Wesley—most notably his emphasis on the cultivation of the holy tempers—is good, his overall decision to place the person, the individual, over the social is a mistake. Also, Collins' account seems to eschew love of neighbor in that loving neighbor is almost always done for one's own sake—the only reason the rich give to the poor is so that they can fulfill moral law and move further along in their own salvation. This is not love, but self-interest and seems to be antithetical to the nature of love as the Gospels (and Wesley) describe.

II. A Brief Respite

In holiness theologies, we find that there is an intentional focus on the personal, often to the detriment of the social, especially in regards to soteriology. This leads to an inability to think about the nature of salvation as social or to understand the aspects of holiness as a social doctrine. However, holiness theologies find a brief respite when they turn to the idea of ethics. We already saw how Collins wants to see salvation as being personal, yet tries to include actions important to Wesley, like giving to the poor. While Collins does an inadequate job of connecting ethical action with the nature of salvation—mainly by ignoring the social dimension—he is typical in that he turns to ethics in order to pursue the social aspects of the doctrine of holiness and sanctification.

Melvin Dieter does a much better job of showing the connection between holiness and ethical concerns. This is because he views "faith working by love" as "the ultimate hermeneutic for understanding God's entire plan of salvation."[21] He argues that Wesley's consistent, overriding concern was for the restoration of the moral image of God, manifested in love and purity, to humanity.[22] This occurs in overcoming systemic sin. However, Dieter continues to understand this overcoming of systemic sin in a personal way, in that he argues that God's grace in entire sanctification brings one out of such systems in order to fully love God and neighbor.[23] This grace, though, activates the believer to do the work of God, to love and live in purity.[24] The activation of grace is done within the individual, but the individual joins others to work together for the fulfilling and restoring of God's structures. People become a corporate witness to the saving grace of Christ in our world.[25] The essence of sanctification, then, is love, extended outward, fulfilling the law on the basis of faith

---

[20] Ibid., 26-27.
[21] Melvin E. Dieter, "The Wesleyan Perspective," in Melvin E. Dieter, et al., *Five Views on Sanctification* (Grand Rapids: Zondervan, 1987), 13.
[22] Ibid., 16.
[23] Ibid., 17.
[24] Ibid., 20-21.
[25] Ibid., 32.

through the grace of God. This fulfillment of the law is worked out by the individual, along with others to spur one another on to holiness.[26]

Dieter and others find a way of thinking through the social nature of salvation by focusing on the ethical in the practice of holiness.[27] In fact, Dieter says, "[Wesley's] distinctive contribution was his conviction that true biblical Christianity finds its highest expression and ultimate test of authenticity in the practical and ethical experience of the individual Christian and the church and only secondarily in doctrinal and propositional definition."[28] The ethical shows the practice of Christianity, most evident in the way that we act towards others. Dieter says that this is a focus for the New Testament, which he believes articulates a strong emphasis on the ethical as "[t]he sanctified are to demonstrate the holiness and love, or character, of their God to whom they are consecrated."[29] The ethical provides an important place to see the work of God in the lives of people among people.

Dieter believes that holiness theology can have such an intermingling of the ethical and soteriological because of the fact that God's grace is an "active principle." When God's grace is worked out in and through a saving faith, it is active as it actively works to change the hearts of people into something more akin to the image of God.[30] God's grace *does* something to people. The Christian life is the working out of the grace of God in works of love; thus, Christianity is not concerned with an inner spirituality alone, but an inner spirituality that is manifest in works of love towards others.[31] The activity of God in human lives creates activity by the human lives.

From this, Dieter believes that Wesley's entire hermeneutic for understanding God's plan of salvation is "faith working by love."[32] Faith, worked out in love, is the goal of the human life. Wesley believed in a teleological nature to salvation, with God's plan of salvation being ruled by a desire to restore the human heart to God's own image.[33] This is ultimately ethical, since love demands some sort of action. Love does not exist without the action that accompanies it, without the action of some moral being. Thus, the action of love is for all purposes ethical. From this, Dieter can say that "the essence of sanctification is love in action."[34]

---

[26] Ibid., 27.

[27] In addition to Dieter, "The Wesleyan Perspective," see also Laurence K. Mullen, "Holy Living—the Adequate Ethic," *Wesleyan Theological Journal* 14, no. 2 (Fall 1979), 82-95.

[28] Dieter, "The Wesleyan Perspective," 11-12.

[29] Ibid., 30.

[30] Ibid., 20-21.

[31] Ibid., 27.

[32] Ibid., 13.

[33] Ibid., 15. See also Clarence L. Bence, "Processive Eschatology: A Wesleyan Alternative," *Wesleyan Theological Journal* 14, no. 1 (Spring 1979), 45-57.

[34] Ibid., 27.

While Dieter, and others, open the path for thinking about social holiness, they also have two major weaknesses with their approach. First, theologians in the holiness tradition are often overly focused on the personal nature of ethics and social thought. They approach ethics, even social ethics, as an individual making individual choices that lead to individual changes that hopefully change social structures. To this point, Dieter even talks of how the remedy for "systematic sinfulness," i.e., social sin, is actually entire sanctification, "a *personal*, definitive work of God's sanctifying grace by which the war within one*self* might cease and the heart be fully released from rebellion into wholehearted love for God and others."[35] If the approach to holiness is merely personal, then there is no hope for the social. Only when we believe that the social can be changed by God's grace through God's entire community working together can social holiness really take place.

The second major weakness in this type of approach to social holiness is that there is a lack of understanding as to how social practices can lead to social change, which can also change people. There is an underlying assumption that one first needs to be justified and regenerated and on the way to sanctification to participate in the social grace God gives. However, for Wesleyan-Methodist thinkers, God's grace is always operative in one's life, as well as in the world. Thus, anytime that a person or community is doing the good or acting in love, they are acting and participating in the grace of God. The social practices that many do—feeding the hungry, freeing the oppressed, pursuing peace, helping the homeless and hurting, etc.—are times of participation in God, even if the person does not know it. Dieter et al. seem to miss the fact that these times are "graced" moments that can lead to richer and purer salvation. They want to develop an inner spirituality that leads to outward works; instead, the movement goes both ways.

III. A Trinitarian Holiness

The approach to social holiness taken in this book begins from a Trinitarian perspective. The idea is that the God who Christians worship is already a perfect community, three co-equal, co-eternal beings, living together in perfect harmony and peace, mutually giving of one to another in and through perfect self-giving love. This is often referred to as the "Social Trinity."[36] By approaching social holiness through the doctrine of the Trinity, holiness takes on the idea of actually reflecting God in the world. No longer is holiness about an individual's actions, but about mirroring the image of the Triune God through

---

[35] Ibid., 17, emphasis mine.
[36] For a representational understanding of social Trinitarian thought, see Wolfhart Pannenberg, *Systematic Theology: Volume I*, trans. Geoffrey Bromiley (Grand Rapids: Wm. B. Eerdmans, 1991); Jurgen Moltmann, *The Trinity and the Kingdom*, trans. Margaret Kohl (Minneapolis: Fortress, 1993); and Stanley Grenz, *Theology for the Community of God* (Grand Rapids: Wm. B. Eerdmans, 1994).

community. The community's work and action, in social settings, is as important to holiness as is inner piety or individual action.

Leon O. Hynson opens a Trinitarian approach to social holiness.[37] He does so through a focus on pneumatology. While he still stays within the area of ethics in his articulation of social holiness, his use of pneumatology makes his thought thoroughly Trinitarian. He finds the interpenetrative nature of the three persons of Godhead in their work together as an example and *modus operandi* for Christian social thought and action. Here, we follow his approach to articulate a more Trinitarian way of thinking social holiness.

Hynson and the editors of this book agree that the type of holiness practiced in the Kingdom of God here on earth should reflect the holiness of the Triune God. This holiness is a communal holiness that includes four parts: it is Christian, evangelical, social, and spiritual. The Christian aspect of social holiness, for Hynson, derives from the fact that the work and ministry of the Holy Spirit is always Christocentric, meaning it spreads the work and ministry inaugurated by Jesus Christ. The evangelical nature of social holiness comes from the idea that the Holy Spirit continues to bear witness to the Good News of the Triune God reconciling the world to Godself in and through the work and mission of Jesus Christ. The ethics of the Spirit of Hynson is social because it is a holiness always involved in a community. The Holy Spirit is always part of the perfect community of the Triune God and the Spirit reflects this in the Spirit's work towards the church and the world. The Spirit's work is to move both church and world closer to the unity and community found in the Trinitarian relations, hopefully moving both to image the life of God. Hynson says, "The Holy Spirit creates in the church a community of faith and through that community calls the world into that communion of faith and hope and love."[38] The spirituality of this social holiness comes from the fact that the Spirit moves us beyond the self so that we may participate in the life of the other, just as the Spirit participates in the life of the Father and Son in the Trinitarian relations. In this spiritual dimension, there is an emphasis on self-transcendence to a deep, abiding love of the other, love of neighbor.[39]

The type of holiness that is Christian, evangelical, social, and spiritual is dependent upon the work of the Holy Spirit to connect us to God. The Holy Spirit connects us to God through the Spirit's work and mission in the church universal. The church is a place of transformation, both personal and social. The church helps each person that enters the community to move into a deeper love of God, offering a role to play in the work of God's kingdom on earth and through eternity. But, the church is also a social institution whose work and mission is to transform the world, the whole world. The church asks us to participate in its activity to perform acts of holiness in the world for the transformation of the world.[40]

---

[37] Leon O. Hynson, "The Church and Social Transformation: An Ethics of the Spirit," *Wesleyan Theological Journal* 11 (1976), 49-61.
[38] Ibid., 52.
[39] Ibid., 53.
[40] Ibid., 56.

The question of what work the church should do for the transformation of the world now comes to the fore. This has been argued about for centuries, even millennia. The answer that Hynson points to is that social holiness looks like the holiness that Jesus practiced. The church takes on the work and mission of Jesus as the Spirit empowers it. Hynson believes the community formed by the Spirit—the church—is a "spiritual community [becoming] a transforming community for [humanity], dedicated to [humanity], challenging and transforming [the human's] spirit."[41] As the Spirit works in and through the church, the church performs the work Jesus Christ performed. This work confronts the social and systemic sin that so troubles society. The work of the spirit calls us into the "world where slaveries of economics, human indignity and oppression, poverty, and disease, hold persons under purgations as severe as the medieval fires were portrayed."[42] The church goes into the places no one else to go to "set the captives free," to act like Christ, eating with sinners, tax collectors, prostitutes, the lame, etc. The church echoes the work and mission of Christ by being the Christ to the world, shining the light of Jesus where it seems darkness reigns. This is the culmination of a Trinitarian approach to social holiness.

IV. Holiness Reimagined

In light of the above proposals, this book is an attempt to fill the noticeable lack of thought and theology relating to the doctrine of social holiness. We approach the topic from a Trinitarian perspective but elaborate on the doctrine more, taking it in different directions, sometimes disagreeing with one another. However, this volume is a start to the discussion that must surround the social nature to the doctrine of holiness.

The following essays are arranged in a fairly straightforward order. The first part of the book covers the way in which the biblical texts speak to social holiness. Beginning with the Old Testament is the essay by Karen Winslow. In her argument, she makes the case that an understanding of social holiness within the Old Testament must be predicated upon the relationship that Israel has with the Other(s). She acknowledges that this is usually seen to be a relationship of neglect—in that, Israel tries to stay away from any Other(s)—but then shows how Israel also interacts with the Other(s) and how this is encouraged throughout the Old Testament. Abson Joseph continues this strain of thought in his essay on the New Testament. He focuses on the books of James and 1 Peter and argues that within them holiness is caught up with ideas of purity and perfection. These are ultimately communal ideas in these epistles (and, really, in the whole of the New Testament) as they follow the witness already given to them in the Old Testament. Joseph's reading of James and 1 Peter of-

---

[41] Ibid., 56.
[42] Ibid., 55.

fers a way of thinking about social holiness that is in line with the way Winslow's account of holiness in the Old Testament. In both, we find a commitment to holiness as a social phenomenon.

Second, we tackle the question of social holiness as a doctrine developed in history. First, we have Randy L. Maddox' article on John Wesley. Herein he makes the argument that Wesley understands holiness and salvation in a holistic way that encompasses human emotions, the human body, the social elements of society and, ultimately, results in an emphasis on a "new creation." Next, Jonathan Dodrill explores the way in which two Chicago urban missions in the Progressive Era perform the task of social holiness in a "kenotic" way, by critiquing material wealth and power structures, giving these up to be with and to serve the poor and oppressed. Roger Green continues to explore the historical side of social holiness by examining the way in which the doctrine functioned in the social ministry of the Salvation Army and how the ministry evolved to include a strong component of social salvation. AJ Swoboda offers the final essay in the section on history by detailing the relationship of pacifism to Pentecostalism in the 20th century. Notably, Swoboda shows the pacifist leanings of early Pentecostals and then examines why pacifism declines in the Pentecostal tradition. Through this collection of historical essays we find the underpinnings for the action and ministry of social holiness.

In the last section, we present four essays that deal with social holiness in its contemporary manifestation. We begin with an essay by Joerg Rieger, who argues against a contextual theology that simply allows each context to exist side-by-side with each other. Instead, he offers a way of thinking that is embodied in the life of a community but then challenges the community and other communities, tying his work to the workers' movements around Dallas. Nathan Crawford continues this trajectory by analyzing the structural nature of sin in relation to racism. He ultimately uses the Korean concept of *han* as a way of navigating structural sin in a way to counter such. Barry Bryant offers an essay that details the way in which social holiness speaks to the current crisis between Israel and Palestine. He argues that for one concerned with social holiness, the beginning point is by doing justice to and with the Palestinian as a way of countering the oppressive structures they currently exist within.

1

Enfolding Others: Social Holiness in the Bible and Biblical Interpretation

Karen Strand Winslow

Without truth telling there is no peacemaking[1]

I. Introduction

Whereas social holiness takes many forms throughout the Scriptures, the treatment of the Other, the non-Israelite or non-Jew, is the concern of this chapter.[2] When we examine the story of Israel and God in the Bible—ever intertwined, we find tensions that must be faced regarding Israel—and God's— relationships to Others, those persons constructed as not-Israel in the Bible. The Bible supplies a mixed account of how Israel treated Others, and, in some troubling places, this must be extended to God, in that Israel is portrayed as acting on God's orders. The encounters between Israel and Others, as described in the Bible, either embody or undermine social holiness, righteousness, and justice, broadly speaking.

In this chapter, I examine the correspondence and conflict between holiness and Othering, between set apart to be distinct from Others and set apart to serve and bless Others. I point out that Others in the Bible, as elsewhere, are textually and socially constructed, then illustrate the tension in the Bible regarding insider-outsider relations, a crucial site for embodying social holiness.[3]

---

[1] Jean Zaru, "Biblical Teachings and the Hard Realities of Life," in *Hope Abundant: Third World and Indigenous Women's Theology*, Kwok Pui-Ian, ed. (Maryknoll, New York: Orbis Books, 2010), 136.

[2] I capitalize "Others" to indicate the groups and individuals textually depicted as "not Israel." These Others encounter Israel as outsiders in various, instructive ways. Sometimes persons within Israel are textually marginalized or Othered, such as women or people from other tribes. In lower case, "others" refers to any persons distinguished from "us," the dominant group or the producers of the texts.

[3] Textual construction reflects social construction by the writers and their group, but one is not identical with the other.

This entails discussing the meaning of holiness/*qadosh* and how it gathers substance as the biblical story unfolds, requiring the social behaviors that embody justice/*mishpat*, righteousness/*tsedakah*, and mercy/*hesed*. Thus, I show that holiness/*qadosh* is the resulting state of having been set apart: the person or thing has been set apart/*qadash*, for a purpose.

After recognizing the reasons given for Israel's distinctiveness from surrounding cultures (holiness), I turn to the texts that show some Others presented as models for faithfulness and lauded for preserving Israel. At this juncture, we must examine the texts that show Others as set aside, designated as *herem* (God's possession alone) and thus destroyed. We shall see that *herem* is used in the Bible, along with *qadosh*, to mean a state of being set apart, but to a radically different end. I conclude by affirming *qadosh*, holiness as way by which God's people demonstrate justice and righteousness in order to represent God as they seek to embrace Others and proclaim an era of release—a Jubilee.

Perspectives on the authoritative nature of Scripture and certain interpretations of Scripture must be problematized here, for invaders throughout history have used biblical *herem* texts to oppress Others and take their land. In so doing, I rely upon Jean Zaru of Palestine, who is among the global community of scholars who have experienced marginalization by dominant forces in their cultures and from their faith and scholarly communities. Post-colonial biblical interpreters such as Zaru and Richard Horsley eloquently confess the hazards of deploying authoritative texts and interpretations to conquer, confiscate, and oppress. They join other scholars who critique abusive reading and interpretive processes.[4] As Zaru writes:

> While generations of religious people have derived profit and pleasure from the retelling of biblical stories, victims of oppression—including especially women from global communities of faith—pose fundamental moral questions with regard to understanding God, God's dealings with humankind, and human behavior. Many of these biblical traditions have been deployed in support of violent oppressive actions in a wide variety of contexts. In the spirit of contemporary moral discourse, it is a matter of grave concern that the Bible has been used and is still being used by many as a rod of colonialism, oppression, and the domination of women.... The problem is not only with the interpretation of the text but also with the way in which many understand the Bible as holding all the authority of the word of God. Yet the Word of God is much more than that. The Bible is a history of people's experiences of God and of how these people perceived God, but it is not the whole reality of God.[5]

I use Zaru's bold statement at the outset of this paper to emphasize what Wesleyans consider a vital foundation of biblical interpretation. Scripture points to God and witnesses to God's dynamic activity and interactions with people; Scripture recounts the story of God incarnate, Jesus Christ. However, Scripture is not, in itself, divine. It is a multivalent library, representing many

---

[4] Richard A. Horsley, "Submerged Biblical Histories and Imperial Biblical Studies," in *The Postcolonial Bible*, R. S. Sugirtharajah, ed. (Sheffield: Sheffield University Press, 1998), 152-173.

[5] Zaru, "Biblical Teachings,"131.

human voices as they instruct, inspire, preach, and make sense of their encounters with God, their history, and their traditions. They continuously cry: Remember and be grateful; remember and be obedient!

In this great pedagogical treatise, the Bible, Others are sometimes the foil for God's people representing how Israel should not live. The Bible's Others illustrate the results of idolatry, forgetting, and ingratitude. Yet, as already noted, there are stunning exceptions that do the opposite: Others show Israel how anyone, anywhere can walk with God in faithfulness and how Israel should live before God. They shame Israel by their faithfulness, determination, wits, and/or awe of God.

A passage that governs this discussion of mostly Old Testament texts is Luke 4:16-30. The incident described there sets the theme and foreshadows the rest of Luke's gospel. At the outset of Jesus' ministry, he pointed out to his fellow Nazarenes that, in their sacred traditions, Others—people known to be not-Israel—received demonstrable acts of healing, justice, mercy, and blessing. After reading Isa 61:1-2, Jesus reminded them that the LORD used both Elijah and Elisha to help foreigners, members of nations who were Israel's enemies.[6] This proved controversial. Had Jesus referenced Scriptural traditions about captive Israel triumphing over oppressors, his neighbors would have continued to laud him. Instead they attempted to rush him over a cliff (Luke 4:16-30)![7] The fact that both sorts of stories are in the Bible—Israel overcoming Others and Israel blessing Others— represents the canon's tension regarding "us"

---

[6] Isaiah 61:1-2: The spirit of the Lord God is upon me, because the Lord has anointed me; he has sent me to bring good news to the oppressed, to bind up the broken-hearted, to proclaim liberty to the captives, liberation to the imprisoned; to proclaim a year of the Lord's favor, and a day of vindication by our God (NRSV, 1989).

[7] Luke 4:16-30: When he came to Nazareth, where he had been brought up, he went to the synagogue on the Sabbath day, as was his custom. He stood up to read, and the scroll of the prophet Isaiah was given to him. He unrolled the scroll and found the place where it was written: "The Spirit of the Lord is upon me, because he has anointed me to bring good news to the poor. He has sent me to proclaim release to the captives and recovery of sight to the blind, to let the oppressed go free, to proclaim the year of the Lord's favor." And he rolled up the scroll, gave it back to the attendant, and sat down. The eyes of all in the synagogue were fixed on him. Then he began to say to them, "Today this scripture has been fulfilled in your hearing." All spoke well of him and were amazed at the gracious words that came from his mouth. They said, "Is not this Joseph's son?" He said to them, "Doubtless you will quote to me this proverb, 'Doctor, cure yourself!' And you will say, 'Do here also in your hometown the things that we have heard you did at Capernaum.' " And he said, "Truly I tell you, no prophet is accepted in the prophet's hometown. But the truth is, there were many widows in Israel in the time of Elijah, when the heaven was shut up three years and six months, and there was a severe famine over all the land; yet Elijah was sent to none of them except to a widow at Zarepheth in Sidon. There were also many lepers in Israel in the time of the prophet Elisha, and none of them was cleansed except Naaman the Syrian." When they heard this, all in the synagogue were filled with rage. They got up, drove him out of the town, and led him

and "them," insiders and outsiders. And yet Jesus, in an inaugural moment in the text, did *not* tell a story about Israel triumphing over others, but a story about Elijah and Elisha helping Others.

II. Israel and Others

The biblical narrative explains the origins of Others within accounts of Israel's genesis and in relation to Israel. Early on, we see that the text constructs Insiders (Israel) and Outsiders (Others) over against each other. Although Israel and Others have their origins in common, as Genesis narratives and genealogies show, they are separated from Others as the story moves forward (Gen 10-12).[8] This is *Israel's* story, and the writers are Jews or their ancestors; they construct the text that constructs Israel and Others.

For example, Genesis narratives describe the formation of Israel, Edom, Moabites, Ammonites, and Midianites as descendant of Terah, Abraham's father (Gen 12, 19, 25). As the story proceeds throughout the Pentateuch and beyond, it recounts affiliations and conflicts between Israelites and their erstwhile relatives. Israel also encountered the peoples whose connections to Israel are pre-Abrahamic, going back to the sons of Noah whose descendants spread over the face of the land, separated by geography, culture and language (Gen 9-11, see especially 9:18-27). In both cases, all of these are defined as Other to Israel who alone descended from Jacob/Israel and experienced slavery in and deliverance from Egypt. Later Jews, as we shall see when we turn to the book of Ezra, wished to define a Jew as one a Babylonian exile.

On the other hand, biblical narratives show that shared experiences, faith in Israel's god, and/or a desire to join Israel brought Others into Israel and coalesced people who were not descended from Abraham (Gen 38; 41:45, 48; Exod 2-4; 12:38; Josh 2; 8; 24; Num 10, Ezra 6; Ruth, and etc.). In either case, by defining Others through traditions about origins, Israel defined itself.[9] From the Torah, we hear how God encountered the Jews' ancestors and Others (e.g. Hagar, Gen 16, 21; Zipporah, Exod 2-4; 18; Hobab, Num 10; and *passim*). We learn God's thoughts concerning Others in the Prophets (e.g. Amos 5:8-9). We watch how God in the flesh treated Others in the New Testament (e.g. Mk 7:24-30). From Scripture, we learn how to weigh and interpret the portions of

---

to the brow of the hill on which their town was built, so that they might hurl him off the cliff. But he passed through the midst of them and went on his way (NRSV, 1989).

[8] Israel was united to or joined by Others through marriage, kinship rites, faith confessions, shared experiences, and permeable boundaries.

[9] See Karen Strand Winslow, "Ethnicity, Exogamy, and Zipporah," *Women in Judaism* (Spring 2006), Online Interdisciplinary Journal; idem, *Jewish and Christian Memories of Moses' Wives: Ethnicity and Exogamous Marriage* (New York: Edwin Mellen Press, 2005); idem and Luke Winslow, "Ezra's 'Holy Seed': Marriage and COMMunities of Others in the Bible," presentation at Religion and Communication Association Conference, Nov 15, 2012, Orlando.

Scripture that depict Others as a threat to be avoided or ruined. And we learn the purpose for Israel's distinctiveness, the meaning of Israel's holiness.

III. Holiness in the Bible

Wesley used the term "social holiness" to advocate Christians living righteously in community. Wesley wrote, "Directly opposite to this [the approach of the desert mystics] is the gospel of Christ. Solitary religion is not to be found there. "Holy solitaries" is a phrase no more consistent with the gospel than holy adulterers. The gospel of Christ knows no religion, but social; no holiness but social holiness."[10] In the Bible, holiness is always social, always connected to human communities, always relational; even when it is used to describe Israel's God. The Bible shows that Israel's God, who is called holy, continuously interacts and interferes with humans, encountering people in various ways to shape and use them, to sanctify them, to set them apart for service. Human encounters with God sometimes leave the woman or man stunned by the numinous quality of God's holiness (Isa 6:1-5), but often they are depicted as responding simply and naturally, as a man would speak to his peer (Exod 33:11; Exod 3-4, 32; Num 14; and etc.).

God's holiness is sometimes considered something that belongs to God alone. God is "wholly other" from humans and completely beyond human comprehension.[11] However, biblical writers connect divine holiness to people and things. A holy God happens and humans respond with awe; they experience God and God's holiness and report on the contact. The primary characters of the Bible are people who see God and live.[12] Furthermore, God's holiness is revealed and transmitted to humans. God's holiness may be unique, but it is not inimitable! In fact, God requires such imitation. "For I am the LORD your God; sanctify yourselves therefore, and be holy, for I am holy" (Lev 11:44); "Speak to all the congregation of the people of Israel and say to them: You shall be holy, for I the LORD your God am holy" (Lev 19:1-2). This command is cited in 1 Peter 1:15-16: "Instead, as he who called you is holy, be holy yourselves in

---

[10] John Wesley, *The Works of John Wesley: Volume XIV: Preface to Poetical Works* (Grand Rapids: Hendrickson Publishers, 1991), 321. Many of Wesley's followers use the term "social holiness" to mean caring for the poor, which Wesley's life also exemplified.

[11] One example will suffice. According to Matt Slick of http://carm.org/dictionary-wholly-other, "the term 'wholly other' is used in Christian theology to describe the difference between God and everything else. God, the Christian God, is completely different than all other things that exist. God can be described by essential properties such as holiness, immutability, etc. Matt Slick, "Wholly Other," *Christian Apologetics & Research Ministry*, Feb. 1, 2013, http://carm.org/ dictionary-wholly-other. We must ask how we, as finite creatures, can relate to the "wholly other," infinite God. .

[12] Many biblical characters experience theophanies or direct words from the LORD, beginning with Adam and continuing with Cain, Abraham, Hagar, Sarah, Rebekah, Jacob, Moses, the elders (Exod 24), Joshua, Manoah's wife, and prophets.

all your conduct; [16] for it is written, 'You shall be holy, for I am holy.'" This will be expanded upon further below.

God's holiness is associated with God's glory in Isa 6:3. "And one [seraph] called to another and said: 'Holy, holy, holy is the LORD of hosts; the whole earth is full of his glory.'" God's weighty, spectacular, frightening, and humbling glory fills the entire world, a world that humans inhabit (see Exod 19:10-13, 16-24). God's glory is God's holiness made manifest. Thus, even at its farthest remove, God's holiness has something to do with humans who live in the world that God's glory fills. God's holiness touches us, and we, like Isaiah, know it.[13] Not only this, but one of God's names, "the Holy One of Israel" (Isa 1:4), connects God's holiness to a community. We cannot understand God's dynamic and holy nature except as members of communities who were brought into being by God. Thus God's holiness has relational and social aspects. Although God's holiness is unique to God, it is a revealed, shared, and relational holiness.

For example, in addition to expressing the awesome, fearful, wonderful, and numinous quality of God's holiness (Gen 32, Exod 34, and Judg 13), biblical writers claim that people and things were made holy. They include the reasons and means by which this was accomplished. People and things were sanctified, literally *set apart from* other people and things *for service to* the community of Israel and to all the families of the world. Blessing Others was God's purpose for directing Abraham to leave his home at the beginning of Israel's story.

> Now the LORD said to Abram, "Go from your country and your kindred and your father's house to the land that I will show you. I will make of you a great nation (Hebrew: *goy*), and I will bless you, and make your name great, so that you will be a blessing. I will bless those who bless you, and the one who curses you I will curse; and in you all the families of the earth shall be blessed (Gen. 12:1-3).

Whereas social holiness pertains to living in a community that is set apart by encounters with and conformity to God holiness, which is similar to Wesley's use of the term; it also includes the outcome, the purpose for which God established and deployed the community: blessing and service, as Gen 12:1-3 so aptly shows. Furthermore, in Exod 19:5-6 the LORD spoke to Israel: "Now therefore, if you obey my voice and keep my covenant, you shall be my treasured possession out of all peoples, for all the earth is mine; but you shall be to me a kingdom of priests and a holy nation."

Just as God set apart Israel, so also Israel was required to continually and intentionally regard God as holy and the source of their own holiness. Intentionally setting God apart, according to both narrative and law sections of the Torah, meant honoring and revering God by obeying covenantal commands,

---

[13] Isa 6:5-6: And I said: "Woe is me! I am lost, for I am a man of unclean lips, and I live among a people of unclean lips; yet my eyes have seen the King, the LORD of hosts!" Then one of the seraphs flew to me, holding a live coal that had been taken from the altar with a pair of tongs. The seraph touched my mouth with it . . ."

many of which concerned justice, righteousness, and mercy. In this way, holiness gathers substance. As the biblical story unfolds, Israel's holiness is manifested as justice *mishpat*, righteousness *tsedakah*, and mercy *hesed*, all of which are social. Early in Abraham's walk with God, we find this account regarding Abraham's influence upon the potential destruction of Sodom and Gomorrah.

> The Lord said, "Shall I hide from Abraham what I am about to do, seeing that Abraham shall become a great and mighty nation, and all the nations of the earth shall be blessed in him?[19] No, for I have *chosen* him, that he may charge his children and his household after him to keep the way of the Lord *by doing righteousness and justice*; so that the Lord may bring about for Abraham what he has promised him" (Gen 18:17-19, NRSV; my italics).

The selection of Abraham eventuated in setting apart his offspring, sanctifying them for special service. But even before they came into existence, their purpose is *to do* righteousness and justice. God's people were required to live like God lives in order to experience and represent God's ways to others/Others (Lev 20:26; Deut 26:19).[14] The consecrated group, office, individual, or thing does not exist to be served, but to serve. This is what we understand about God, taking in the wholeness of the biblical witness, the sustained message of the canon and its collections. As it is with God so it must be with Israel.

Biblical social holiness, that which is mandatory of God's people in their dealings with each other (insiders to Israel) and Others (outsiders to Israel), is based upon God's nature and actions, as some have observed.[15] The overall story of the Bible illustrates that when people live justly, with righteousness, love, and mercy toward others, they demonstrate the holiness of God. This is what is usually understood as "social holiness" (communal/shared separa-

---

[14] See Matt 11:5: "the blind receive their sight, the lame walk, the lepers are cleansed, the deaf hear, the dead are raised, and the poor have good news brought to them; Ps 146:7-8: "who executes justice for the oppressed; who gives food to the hungry. The LORD sets the prisoners free; the LORD opens the eyes of the blind. The LORD lifts up those who are bowed down; the LORD loves the righteous; Ps 146:7, 8. See also Isa 42:7, 49:8, 9, 58:6.

[15] See the recent chapter by Kelsie Gayle Job and Frank Anthony Spina, "Holiness in the Old Testament," in *Holiness as a Liberal Art*, Daniel Castelo, ed. (Eugene: Wipf and Stock, 2012), 20-29. Furthermore, in his plenary address to the 2013 Wesleyan Theological Society Meeting (Seattle, WA, Mar 23), Thomas Dozeman demonstrated the different perspectives on human holiness held by the Deuteronomistic (D) and the Priestly (P) writers. In Deut, people were holy (separated) and justified through divine speech to all the people. In Deut, social holiness—ethics—protects cultic holiness from the contamination of the world and provides justification. For the Priestly writer, cultic holiness is not transferred to the people, but social holiness (ethics) perfects the transfer of holiness to the people. D and P agree that God makes people holy. Dozeman said that D would disagree with Wesley who said there is no [private] holiness; it must be communal. P would agree with Wesley: social holiness perfects cultic holiness.

tion), although this is something of an oxymoron, turned paradox, for, although holiness means set apart, it must be expressed to and through human communities. And not only among the people of Israel but by them to Others.

Nonetheless, for Israel to have substance and content, for them to embody God's ways, they must exist, be identifiable, and survive as a separate people group. Otherwise, Israel would not exist to demonstrate the ways of God to Others. Tracing the necessity for boundaries around Israel will help us to see how their set-apartness/holiness, was essential to their continued existence.

IV. Israel Separated from Others

In Lev 20:26, the LORD spoke to Israel: "You shall be holy to me; for I the LORD am holy, and I have separated you from the other peoples to be mine." Here we see that Israel's consecration—their holiness—meant separation from Others, that God's people, who will be taught how to be holy, are intentionally distinct from Others. To be consecrated persons (Israel, priests, Nazirites) or things (tabernacle, temple and its furnishings) are differentiated from other people or things that belong to the "common" or "profane" category.[16] Consecrated or holy has no meaning if those so designated act or are used in the same way as everyone and everything else. Without selection, election, proscriptions, unique experiences, instructions—torah—from Yahweh, we would have no story about people living before God, learning God's ways, and bringing salvation, wholeness and hope to the world. A few examples of the value of separation from the biblical text are in order.

Let us examine some imagined contingencies within the world of the story. If Isaac had married a neighbor girl, instead of Rebekah, Israel would have been assimilated into the Hittites or other Canaanites (Gen 23-4). If Jacob's sons had moved into Shechem and intermarried and shared resources, they would have become Shechemites, not Israelites (Gen 34; although their violence was not condoned by Jacob or the writer).[17] If the progeny of Jacob had not been abhorrent to the Egyptians and thus isolated in Goshen, they may have become Egyptians (Gen 45:17; 46:28-34).[18]

Subsequent stories indicate the risk that Israel could have been lost entirely had they been absorbed into the land and culture of the Canaanites (Josh-

---

[16] These terms are merely labels for that which has not been designated as holy and they do not imply sinfulness or immorality. However, some people and things belong to a category that is on the other end of the continuum: ḥerem. See Richard D. Nelson, "Ḥerem and the Deuteronomic Social Conscience," in *Deuteronomy and Deuteronomic Literature; Festschrift C. H. W. Brekelmans*, M. Vervenne and J. Lust, ed. (Leuven: University Press, 1997), 39-54.

[17] However, Simeon and Levi captured the women of Shechem and took them into their family encampment before moving on (Gen 34:5-31).

[18] Notice that Joseph married an Egyptian and this two famous sons, eponymous ancestors of the Joseph tribes were half Egyptian! (Gen 41:45-52).

Judg), Assyrians (2 Kgs 17), Babylonians (2 Kgs 25, Jeremiah), Greeks (1-2 Maccabees), or Romans (New Testament period). Israel's task was to survive and an identifiable people group who lived before the LORD in righteousness and justice. They were to convey the meaning of holiness by how they lived. The message they embodied by surviving as Israel would have ended if they had assimilated into surrounding cultures and lost their identity and their stories.

Following Israel's story in which they were always at risk, "the fewest of all peoples" (Deut 7:7), shows that Israel could not have survived without land or identifying marks and practices that distinguished them from Others. Nonetheless, we must also recognize the Scriptures' emphasis on the faith of Outsiders, as well as the benefits that the *goyim*, the nations, brought to Israel.[19] Social holiness goes both ways in the biblical text; individuals and nations of the world blessed Israel.

V. Others Preserved Israel

Israel's story shows that, as nascent Israel grew and developed into a distinct and known people, Others nurtured, served, and preserved them. Outsiders expanded, enriched, and were enfolded into Israel. The Bible is laden with examples of intermarriage from Judah (his first Canaanite wife, then Tamar who gave him sons, Gen 38); Joseph (Asenath, mother of Ephraim and Manasseh Gen 41:45; 48) to Moses, Naomi's sons, Boaz, David, and Esther.[20] These marriages produced offspring that built up Israel. Any proscriptions against intermarriage were based upon Israel's proneness to idolatry and apostasy. For example, Joshua's generation was not allowed to intermarry with Canaanites in the central cities, the same ḥerem Canaanites they were supposed to "utterly destroy" (Deut 7:2-4).

In addition, the biblical story includes numerous positive examples of outsider women preserving Israel apart from bearing children. Pharaoh's daughter saved Moses from death as a baby (Exod 1:5-10). And in Exod 4:24-26, we learn that Zipporah, by circumcising her son, saved Moses' life from the LORD's attempt to kill him. Zipporah was a Midianite *woman* who demonstrated the significance of circumcision for Israel's males. Even Moses' life was in danger for failing to bring his son into Israel in this way. The only other named circumcisers in the Bible are Abraham and Joshua.[21] Other outsiders confessed faith in the LORD and acted with loyalty to Israel (Jethro, Exod 18; Rahab, Josh 2; Ruth). These narratives intentionally challenge Israel to be as faithful as these outsiders.

Egypt was a place of sustenance for Abraham's household and all of Jacob's sons and their families when there was famine in Canaan. Some of Egypt's kings allowed Israel to flourish, giving Joseph's brothers jobs, the best of the

---

[19] See Frank A. Spina, *The Faith of the Outsider Faith of the Outsider: Exclusion and Inclusion in the Biblical Story* (Grand Rapids: Eerdmans, 2005).

[20] Solomon was strictly rebuked for his idolatry, which the writer associates with his building shrines to the gods of his many wives (1 Kgs 11; Neh 13: 23-27).

[21] See Karen Strand Winslow, *Early Jewish*, 19-97.

land, and other provisions so that they grew and thrived (Gen 46-47) and this is remembered in Deut 10:19: "You shall also love the stranger, for you were strangers in the land of Egypt;" and Deut 23: 7-8: ". . . You shall not abhor any of the Egyptians, because you were an alien residing in their land. The children of the third generation that are born to them may be admitted to the assembly of the Lord."

These sometimes overlooked accounts must be central to any discussion of Israel's relationship to Others in the Bible. As pointed out above, the library of the Bible does not speak with one voice in this regard. Others are included and admired, but sometimes Others are denigrated, even harmed. The difference in treatment was not a matter of bloodlines (although in some cases it was connected to their location and their related desire to curse or tempt Israel as in Num 22-25). The Others who are marked as heroines or heroes expressed faith in Israel's god and/or saved and nurtured Israel, in sharp contrast to Others who led Israel to apostasy and idolatry (Num 25), or who gathered to fight Israel (Num 21-21-36; Josh 5). Others who confessed faith in the LORD or preserved Israel are held up as exemplary.[22]

On one level, it should come as no surprise that different views on Others exist, given that the Bible is a collection of books and genres that convey meanings for, of, and by different people, under changing circumstances over a long period of time. An ancient Jewish library should contain multiple human expressions of Israel's story about Israel. On another level, a witness in Scripture about violence against Others must be recognized as a problem that demonstrating the multi-voice/multi-valency of Scripture regarding Others will not resolve.

Thus, it is time to turn to biblical texts that depict dispossession, war, vengeance, and exclusivity. The question remains: how could a God of justice, righteousness, not to mention mercy and compassion, command violence against Others by people who were being trained in holiness? As noted above, the Others who were under the ban of *ḥerem* could have led Israel to apostasy, but this is an indictment of Israel's weakness. Was there not another way to procure a place for Israel to live and thrive? Many have asked that question. I wonder here if the *ḥerem* texts that command the destruction of whole cities are literary examples of what Kevin Lowery describes when he writes: "History is strewn with atrocities that have been committed in God's name."[23] The next

---

[22] The friendly Midianites of Exod 2,4,18 and Num 10 performed rites of hospitality, covenant making, communion, and service. Hostile Moabites in Num 25 (Midianites in ch 31) led Israel to apostasy through ritual acts of sex, sacrifice, and eating. See the discussion in Winslow, *Early Jewish,* 2005, 88-97.

[23] Kevin Twain Lowery, "Ethics as Relational," in *Relational Theology Issues and Implications,* Brint Montgomery, Thomas J. Oord and Karen Strand Winslow, eds. (Eugene: Wipf and Stock; published in association with Point Loma Nazarene University Press 2012), 90. Lowery goes on to say: "Many problems arise when people fail to recognize the relational nature of ethics. It is even worse when they use God's

section explores the notion of *ḥerem* as it appears in the Bible and considers how it compares and contrasts with *qadosh*, holiness.

VI. Others under the Ban of *Ḥerem*

As we examine the extreme form of Othering represented by the ban of *ḥerem*, we must keep in mind the command found in Lev 19:34 concerning outsiders who lived among the Israelites: "You shall love the alien as yourself." Deuteronomy is also filled with such directives that protect outsiders to Israel.[24] These directives are identifying marks of Israel that are *behavioral*, not genetic or biological.[25] Many commands that mark or define Israel are just, loving, and merciful *actions* that show concern for aliens, widows, orphans, strangers, sojourners—Others. They show what God is like, what God likes, what God can do through people.

Other commands seem morally neutral, indicating unique ways Israel marked itself out as distinct from greater nations in order to survive (food laws, circumcision, worship rituals). And yet Israel was also given orders to destroy Others, namely, actions associated with the Deuteronomistic ban of *ḥerem*. In these cases, Israel's distinction came at a price to the Others who lived in certain areas of Canaan.[26] Israel carved out a place (under divine, Mosaic, or priestly command) by destroying Others (Deut 7:1-2; 20:16-18; Josh 6; 10, esp. v 40; 1 Sam 15). Whereas Israel was set apart—*qadosh*— for service and blessing, certain Canaanite Others were set apart under the ban of *ḥerem* for destruction.

As Richard Nelson explains, for Israel and surrounding nations, the term *ḥerem* meant destruction of things and people to whom it was applied because

---

name to justify immoral acts, because they become too self-assured and refuse to listen to reason."

[24] For example, Deut 10:17: "The Lord your God is God of gods and Lord of lords, the great God, mighty and awesome, who is not partial and takes no bribe, [18]who executes justice for the orphan and the widow, and who loves the strangers, providing them food and clothing. [19]You shall also love the stranger, for you were strangers in the land of Egypt." See also Deut 24:10-22.

[25] To disabuse Jews of the notion that being the seed of Abraham privileged his listeners, John the Baptist said: "Do not presume to say to yourselves, 'We have Abraham as our ancestor'; for I tell you, God is able from these stones to raise up children to Abraham (Matt 3:9). This is not a New Testament. innovation, as I have shown above.

[26] Those first subjected to *ḥerem* were the Canaanites who gathered troops to fight against Israel (Josh 5; 10:1-42).These battles were the result of Israel's pact with Gibeon to protect them. Gibeon was one of the central cities (and under the ban), but they deceived Israel into promising protection. When the Gibeonites were threatened by other kings and armies from the central hill country, they appealed to Israel, who fought for them, and, in this way gained access to the central region. So there is a bit of a twist to the story in Joshua; Israel was fighting for a city that was supposed to be *ḥerem*.

these things must not be used by humans. In Israel's case, ḥerem items were Yahweh's unalienable property.[27] Persons could not be slaves and cattle could not be deployed by ordinary humans for any purpose.[28] In contrast, the spoil from *non-ḥerem* battles included virgins—Midianite Others—who were counted and given to priests (Num 31), or taken captive and then married (Deut 21:10-14).

These anti-Other commands that appear relatively early in Israel's story (canonically speaking), when they were a tribal confederation, are joined by incidents from much later, which are associated with past ḥerem peoples. The book of Ezra recounts Shecaniah and Ezra's attempt to expel wives from the restored Jewish community of Persian Yehud, indigenous women to whom the Jews were legally bound (Ezra 9-10). To inflame Ezra's anger over the "intermarriage," the officials told him that the returned male Jews "had not separated themselves from," they had "mixed with" the peoples of the land. The officials labeled these wives who had not been among the exiles of Babylon: "Canaanites, Hittites, Perizzites, Jebusites, Ammonites, Moabites, Egyptians, and Amorites" (Ezra 9:1-2).

The first four nations had disappeared from history (and had been under the ban of ḥerem in Deut-Josh). However, the last four were the returned Jews' neighbors and some had probably intermarried with the Jews left behind in Judah, now Persian Yehud. The officials used the first four historically impossible labels to compare marriage in the restoration period to the dangers of assimilation with ḥerem people groups from the conquest period (Ezra 9:1-2). In this way, the officials Othered the wives, who were indigenous women of the land of Judah, descendants of Judahites left behind or mixed with those brought in from other places during the exile. As James Kugel notes, the purpose of aligning the latter four real people groups with the first four extinct groups is to claim that Deuteronomy's bans on intermarriage must surely apply to the living "non-Israel" peoples of the restoration period. This is clearly not Deuteronomy's view concerning the latter four people groups.[29] After I turn to the studies of Mark Brett and Yair Hoffman who suggest historical settings that gave rise to these texts, I will conclude with a discussion of the hermeneutical questions.

---

[27] Nelson, "Ḥerem," 39-54.

[28] In some texts, ḥerem land or items were claimed by priests (Num 18:14; Ezek 44:29). The core meaning of ḥerem is not destruction, working out a war vow, religious justification for total war, or sacrifice, according to Nelson. Instead it means belonging to the gods, as in ḥerem to Yahweh (Lev 27:28-29; Micah 4:13; Josh 6:17; and in the Mesha inscription line 17). It is a "cultural map category," See Nelson, "Ḥerem," 43-47, and *passim*.

[29] James Kugel, "The Holiness of Israel and the Land in Second Temple Times," *Texts, Temples and Traditions: A Tribute to Menahem Haran*, Michael Fox, et al., eds. (Winona Lake: Eisenbrauns, 1996), 21-32; 24.

Mark Brett (following other scholars) sees Deuteronomy as an example of "'discursive hybridity': a mix of literary conventions and transformations located in a web of mimicry (appropriating forms of the dominant culture) and ideological contestation."[30] He goes on to apply mimetic desire to Deuteronomy, noting how it turns these around, urging Israel *not* to imitate, *not* to learn or be taught the detestable ways of those other nations (Deut 18:9; 20:17-18). This is followed by the legal discourse of ḥerem, "the exclusion of near rivals," who are on an "ambiguous margin," made to be more foreign because the "Deuteronomic authors wish to inscribe boundaries of exclusive loyalty to Yahweh." The conflicts were more civil than foreign. For example, the ḥerem banning of Israelites disloyal to Yahweh in Deut 13 is the same as that of Canaanites in Deut 20. Syncretists (those in the community who worship Yahweh *and* other gods, perhaps refugees from the north) are scapegoated and Othered.

Brett associates the ḥerem texts with the Assyrian crisis of the seventh century that claimed the northern kingdom and Josiah's reform, during which priests of northern high places were the only ones slaughtered (2 Kgs 23:5, 20, 24; compare 23:8-9). "There is no evidence that the Deuteronomic reform led to mass killings." However, Brett continues, "it is the reception of these texts in Christian tradition which has yielded the most violent consequences, notably when Christian hermeneutics was wedded to colonialism."

In another vein, Yair Hoffman argues that the practice of ḥerem of Canaanites was depicted by the Persian period author of Joshua in order to make irrelevant and anachronistic any association of women of the land (wives of previously exiled male Jews) with Canaanite people groups, as the officials speaking to Ezra attempted to do (Ezra 9:1-2).[31] Since these nations were utterly destroyed by Joshua, exclusivist post-exilic Jews should not use them in their attempt to expel these women from the Jewish community. According to Hoffman, ḥerem was a notion deployed to mitigate concerns over legal ties with indigenous residents of Yehud against the use of Othering ethnic labels, since those Others, no longer exist.

Hoffman's view can be critiqued on a number of levels. Since Deuteronomy and Joshua are foundational for Israel's self-understanding and covenant relationship with God, their prohibitions against intermarriage and the stories of destruction do not help the cause of the Jews accused of intermarriage with woman compared to peoples under the ḥerem ban. Even if these people groups were extinct, they, and the supposed current counterparts are utterly Othered by these texts. So to use them as ethnic slurs against the wives of Jews from

---

[30] Mark Brett, "Genocide in Deuteronomy," *Seeing Signals, Reading Signs: The Art of Exegesis*, Mark A. O'Brien and Howard N. Wallace, eds. (London: T & T Clark, 2004), 75-89.

[31] Yair Hoffman, "The Deuteronomistic Concept of the Ḥerem," *Zeitschrift für die Alttestamentliche Wissenschaft* 111, no. 2 (1999): 196-210.

Babylon would have a deleterious effect.[32] In addition, the practices of these "foreigners" are only said to be "like" those of the Canaanites (Ezra 9:1). Nonetheless, Hoffman's point that what may have once been construed as relevant was now irrelevant must be taken. If such Othering was irrelevant then, as shown by the inclusive stories mentioned here and many others, how much more so now.

Whether historical or not, these *ḥerem* passages textually express violence toward Others based on cultural identity and geography. This polarity lies in tension with expressions of Israel's role to function as priests to the world, to serve, love, and to bless others/Others, a manifestation of God's holiness that we call social holiness. As noted above, blessing the families of the land was the reason Abraham and Sarah were called apart. Out of love for the entire world, God sent his son (John 3:16-17). Furthermore, the Scriptures consistently insist that holiness means loving friends, strangers, and enemies alike (Lev 19:1-2, 34; 1 Kgs 18; 2 Kgs 5; Luke 25:10-37; Matt 22:34-40; Mark 12:28-34; 1 Pet 1:15-16, and etc.). Since both *ḥerem* and *qadosh* are associated with Othering, being set apart to the LORD (see again Lev 27:28-33) and yet are manifested so differently, should we tolerate the tension of ancient notions enfolded within timeless principles of compassion to strangers? Or should we set *ḥerem*, aside while keeping *qadosh*?

VII. Conclusions

These *ḥerem* and expulsion passages are rife with theological meanings and hermeneutical implications that continue to be discussed in useful and useless ways.[33] In any case, these Scriptures clearly express an anti-Other stance that is based on some kind of reality in social or textual history—all texts emerge from

---

[32] Hoffman perceives a moral conflict between *ḥerem* and Deuteronomy's call to love the stranger/alien (*ger*). But the resident alien of Deut is a worshipper of Yahweh and has settled into the community of Israel—they are assimilated. The treatment of the resident alien is a concern of Jer 7:6, Ezek 14:7 as well. Mark Brett finds Hoffman's argument useful, not in terms of composition, but of reception, wondering why Ezra 9-10 fails to mention women proselytes, such as Rahab of Jericho. Hoffman would say that story was written to counter and undermine Ezra's ideology of ethnicity construction (politics of identity) and any other attempts to be exclusive of outsiders who wished to join Israel and worship Israel's god. See Brett, "Genocide in Deuteronomy," 79.

[33] Examples of useful expositions of Joshua and *ḥerem* are: Frank Anthony Spina, "Rahab and Achan: Role Reversals," in *The Faith of the Outsider*, 52-71; Nelson, "Ḥerem; Phillip D. Stern, *Biblical Ḥerem: A Window on Israel's Religious Experience* (Atlanta: Scholars Press, 1991); Karen Strand Winslow, "Mixed Marriage in Torah Narratives," in *Mixed Marriages Intermarriage and Group Identity in the Second Temple Period,* Christian Frevel, ed. (New York: T & T Clark International: *Series:* Library of Hebrew Bible/Old Testament Studies, *Volume* 547), 132-149.

a social context. They remain part of our Scriptures, even if Israel did not occupy all of the cities of Canaan mentioned in Joshua through bloody warfare,[34] or Joshua was written during the post-exilic period against Ezra 9:1-3 to indicate all of the traditional enemies of Israel were long gone,[35] or the husbands of "women of the land" preferred to expel Ezra over their wives and children.[36]

Tension will always remain in the great library of the Scriptures, for we cannot change it now. Our task as receivers and interpreters of biblical traditions, of the Bible as living Scripture for living faith communities, is to be discerning and discriminating. Some perspectives must be set aside or interpreted as theological teachings for Israel and the Church about the dangers of turning from the God of deliverance and holiness.[37]

Clearly, the biblical expressions of holiness *qadosh* for blessing and *ḥerem* for destruction or ritual use are not equally relevant for God's people.[38] *Ḥerem*, as an ancient concept, must reasonably and righteously be confined to the past, as a notion from the era of ancient history, when certain things and people were considered off limits to humans, set apart for the gods.[39] While *ḥerem* was intended to "prevent any human benefit communal or individual, from taking place,"[40] *qadosh* marked people who should become righteous and just, benefiting other families of the world.

---

[34] Some city states, such as Hazor show evidence of destruction in the 13th century B.C.E. (Josh 11:10-11); others, such as Jericho do not. See Amnon Ben-Tor, an excavator of Hazor, "Who Destroyed Hazor," *B.A.R.* 39:4 (2013): 26-36; E. Theodore Mullen Jr, *Narrative History and Ethnic Boundaries*, Semeia Studies (Atlanta: Scholars Press, 1993); idem, *Ethnic Myths and Pentateuchal Foundations*, Semeia Studies (Atlanta: Scholars Press, 1997); Israel Finkelstein and Neil Silberman, *The Bible Unearthed: Archaeology's New Vision of Ancient Israel and the Origin of Its Sacred Texts*, (New York: Free Press, 2001); W. G. Dever, *Who were the Israelites and Where Did They Come From?* (New York: Eerdman's Young Readers, 2003); Norman K. Gottwald, "Religious Conversion and the Societal Origins of Ancient Israel," in *Perspectives on the Hebrew Bible*, James L. Crenshaw, ed. (Macon, Georgia: Mercer University Press, 1988), 49-66; Peter Machinist, "Outsiders or Insiders: The Biblical View of Emergent Israel and Its Contexts," in *The Other in Jewish Thought and History: Constructions of Jewish Culture and Identity*, Laurence Silberstein and Robert Cohn, ed. (New York: New York University Press, 1994), 74-90.

[35] Hoffman, "The Deuteronomistic Concept of Ḥerem," 200-204.

[36] Joseph Blenkinsopp, *Ezra-Nehemiah*. Old Testament Library (Philadelphia: Westminster, 1988), 200; idem, *Judaism: The First Phase: The Place of Ezra and Nehemiah in the Origins of Judaism* (Grand Rapids: Eerdmans, 2009), 63-71; 80-84; 138-145.

[37] They were intended to be received this way by their producers and redactors who shaped the final form of the Bible.

[38] Lev 27:28-29; Num 18:14; Josh 6:19.

[39] Both Nelson and Stern show that *ḥerem* is the result of attempts to order out of chaos, to categorize various states that things could participate in or qualities they could take. As noted above, it coordinates with the state of holiness (Lev 27:28; Josh 6:19). Nelson, *Ḥerem*, 40-41; Stern, *Biblical Ḥerem*, 210-213; 218-226.

[40] Nelson, *Ḥerem*, 46-48.

The context of the Deuteronomy-Joshua ḥerem texts indicate their theological-*torah*-instructive nature to teach that just as outsiders to Israel can be under the ban, so also insiders can be expelled through disobedience. Likewise, outsiders such as Rahab and Gibeon—and indigenous Persian period women—can enter Israel, just as people of all nations are invited to worship Yahweh.[41] The issue regarding exclusion or inclusion, we learn, is about faith, obedience, desire, and wits, not ethnicity.[42]

We can and must affirm a two pronged holiness that includes: 1) behavioral boundaries that keep God's people from assimilating and being lost as representatives of God's ways; and 2) reaching out to embrace and serve Others, all others, both within and outside of faith communities. Furthermore, we can and must allow a rule of faith, a standard of interpretation, which we derive from the Bible to enervate texts about setting aside creatures of God's world for destruction. In whatever ways we interpret them theologically, historically ḥerem passages reflect a position—a notion, a superstition—that ancient Israel shared with other ancient peoples and re-presented in their texts.[43] In contrast, other texts from among the Scriptures show us the way of embrace without assimilation. As Luke's Jesus so clearly demonstrated by his inaugural reading and interpretation in Nazareth, holiness means releasing captives, healing, and restoring sight to the blind of all of the people of the world.

> The Spirit of the Lord is upon me, because he has anointed me to bring good news to the poor. He has sent me to proclaim release to the captives and recovery of sight to the blind, to let the oppressed go free, to proclaim a *Jubilee* —an era of freedom! (Luke 4:18-19)

I began this paper with Zaru's statement: "Without truth telling there is no peacemaking." This must be given its on-the-ground context: "Without truth telling there is no peacemaking. Can we have peace without self-determination and sovereignty? Without land and water that are essential for survival?" [44]

---

[41] The most adept theological interpretation involves noticing how the Canaanite Others escaped from the ban of ḥerem through faith and wits (Rahab and Gibeon). They "recognized" that Yahweh was life, health, and wisdom; something the Scriptures keep attempting to teach Israel! Furthermore, we learn from the books of Exodus and Numbers that Midianites could be assets or detriments to Israel, just as Israelites could remain aligned with the LORD or cut off. The consequence had nothing to do with ethnicity but rather with *behavior*, especially in regards to which gods they *ritually* allied themselves (see Num 25-31 and again the discussion in Winslow, *Early Jewish*, 88-97).

[42] The book of Ruth is a narrative way to show the loyalty exhibited by a *Moabite* woman to Israel's people and Israel's God. In this manner, it joins the many outsider women stories in the Torah who help Israel.

[43] People who could/would have practiced ḥerem would have had to have enough power and resources to do so. Israel shared the notion or concept of ḥerem, but may not have actually practiced it. When Israel was in such a position during the monarchy, ḥerem is not mentioned as resulting in destruction.

[44] Ibid., 136.

Zaru speaks for me and, I hope, most interpreters when she writes, "Justice and compassion are the central themes as I read the scriptures. God is a God of justice and compassion, not a God of war, vengeance, and exclusivity."[45]

Holiness, justice, truth-telling, righteousness, and peacemaking are ordinary, practical, social, and relational. And they must endure. They pursue life—the surviving and thriving before the Lord of all the peoples of the world. God loved the whole world so much that he gave his son, the one with whom he was one, that whoever believes on him should not perish, but have life and forever *leolam* in the world to come.

---

[45] Zaru, 124.

Chapter 2

Social Holiness in James and 1 Peter

Abson P. Joseph

Pure and undefiled worship in the presence of God the father is this: to care for orphans and widows in their distress, and to keep oneself from being defiled by the world. (James 1:27)

As obedient children no longer conforming to the passions you had during your time of ignorance, rather (conforming) after the image of the one who called you, you yourselves must become holy in all your conduct, because it is written: "You will be holy because I am holy." And since you call on a father who judges impartially each person according to his work, live with reverent fear during the time of your sojourn. (1 Peter 1:13-16)

I. Introduction

Holiness is rooted in the imagination, and finds its expression in social interaction and interpersonal relationships. Throughout Scripture, the people of God are urged to live in ways that honor God and testify about who he is to the world around them. They are invited to partake in God's holiness and to represent God faithfully. In what follows, I will demonstrate that the concept of holiness is intrinsically social in nature. Exhortations to holiness are framed in communal terms. They are designed to help the individual exhibit appropriate behavior within the community, on the one hand, for the sake of unity; and outside the community, on the other hand, because the individual represents the community in her interaction with the world. Further, they outline how the community as a whole is supposed to relate to the world.

The concept of holiness conveys the notion of separation and difference and the notion of ethical, moral excellence. It usually comes as an invitation or as a reminder to be different, to resist the pressures to conform to the outside world, and to display godly behavior because one belongs to the family of God. I propose that a reading of the epistles of James and 1 Peter can inform our discussion on and understanding of holiness as a social manifestation that moves beyond the individual. First, I will demonstrate why reading James and 1 Peter together is warranted; second, I will discuss two features present in the epistles that serve as evidence for the social rootedness of the concept of holiness; finally, I will use the instructions on "controlled speech" as an example to show how the movement from imagination to action in both epistles is further evidence that holiness is a socio-theological construct that needs not only to be understood but also performed as a communal endeavor.

II. Why Might We Read James and 1 Peter Together?

I propose that a discussion on what social holiness looks like from a scriptural perspective can benefit greatly from reading the epistles of James and 1 Peter together. Whereas each epistle has its peculiarities, there are several reasons why this approach is warranted; namely, they seem to be addressing a similar audience; there is an affinity in the language both authors used to address the situation their audience was facing; and there is internal evidence that the authors drew on common sources as basis of their exhortations.

Similar Audience: Existence in and Experience of Diaspora

The epistles of James and 1 Peter have similar audiences. James addresses his letter "to the twelve tribes in the *diaspora*..." (Jas. 1.1);[1] and Peter sends his epistle "to the elect strangers [living] in the *diaspora*..." (1 Pet. 1.1). The discussion about the composition of the audiences of James and 1 Peter focuses usually on whether they are made up primarily of Jewish Christians or primarily of Gentiles.[2] McCartney explains that scholars who hold to an early redaction of the letter by James tend also to argue for a Jewish audience.[3] In this context, "the twelve tribes of the diaspora" is understood as metaphor for the messianic Jewish communities living among non-messianic Jewish communities.[4] Those who claim that James is pseudepigraphal and written at a later date argue for an audience that is made up primarily of Gentiles Christians. There, the term "the twelve tribes" is being appropriated to describe Christianity, which has now replaced Israel as the locus of the people of God.[5] McCartney rightly highlights the possibility that James' audience was composed of Jewish and Gentile

---

[1] Biblical citations are the author's translation unless noted otherwise.

[2] For a discussion on the audience of James, see, e.g., Dan G. McCartney, *James*, BECNT (Grand Rapids: Baker, 2009), pp. 34-36. On 1 Peter, see my discussion in *A Narratological Reading of 1 Peter*, LNTS 440 (London: T&T Clark, 2012), pp. 26-29. See also, Richard Bauckham, *James*, NTR (London: Routledge, 1999), pp. 156-57.

[3] McCartney, *James*, p. 34

[4] See, e.g., Scot McKnight, *The Letter of James*, NICNT (Grand Rapids, Eerdmans: 2011), pp. 65-68; Ben Witherington, *Letters and Homilies for Jewish Christians: A Socio-Rhetorical Commentary on Hebrews, James, and Jude* (Downers Grove, IL: InterVarsity, 2007), pp. 417-19.

[5] McCartney, *James*, p. 34.

Christians and argues that James' focus is not the ethnicity of his audience, but the fact that they are like "Israel".⁶

In the case of 1 Peter, "strangers in the diaspora" begs the question of whether these people are literally displaced Christians throughout the Anatolian peninsula, or Christians who are at home, but find themselves on the fringes of society because of their commitment to Christ.7 The places mentioned in the introduction cover a vast geographical area. Therefore, it is safe to assume that the audience was heterogeneous and of diverse backgrounds. The author's overwhelming use of the OT, his identification of the audience with Israel, and the traditional view that Peter was the apostle to the Jews support the view that Peter's audience is comprised of Jewish Christians.8 Scholars who argue for a primarily Gentile audience find support for their views in the language that the author uses throughout the letter that implies a previous life of idolatrous practices (1 Pet. 1.14; 1.18; 2.10; 4.3-4).9 However, this language can also resonate with a Jewish audience given Israel's propensities for idolatry (e.g., Exod. 32.4; Lev. 17.7; Deut. 32.21; Jer. 8.19; Amos 5.25-27). As is the case for James, the audience's ethnicity is secondary. Their status as "marginal" trumps the importance of their being Jew or Gentile.10

In sum, James and 1 Peter's audiences are similar in so far as the authors are identifying their audience with Israel. They view and are encouraging their audience to see themselves as Israel in exile, which means "not at home", wherever they may be located geographically.¹¹ What is also clear, both statements contain similar theological significance and implications. In both letters, sufferings, a result of living in diaspora, take center stage. The call to holiness in James and 1 Peter is framed in the context of the audience's response to the sufferings they experience.

B. Affinity of Language

Another reason why we may read James and 1 Peter together is the affinity of language that is evident when holding the two epistles closely.¹² For example,

---

⁶ McCartney, *James*, p. 36.

⁷ See further, Joseph, *A Narratological Reading of 1 Peter*, pp. 26-27.

⁸ See, e.g., Ben Witherington, *A Socio-Rhetorical Commentary on 1-2 Peter*, LHHC, 2 (Downers Grove, IL: InterVarsity, 2007), pp. 27-28; Ramsey J. Michaels, *1 Peter*, WBC, 49 (Waco, TX: 1988), pp. xlix-lv. For a brief assessment, see Peter H. Davids, *The First Epistle of Peter*, NICNT (Grand Rapids: Eerdmans, 1990), pp. 8-9.

⁹ E.g. John H. Elliott, *Conflict, Community, and Honor: 1 Peter in Social-Scientific Perspective* (Eugene, OR: Wipf & Stock, 2007), p. 16; Leonhard Goppelt, *A Commentary on 1 Peter*, Ferdinand Hahn, ed.; John E. Aslup, trans. (Grand Rapids: Eerdmans, 1993), p. 6.

¹⁰ Joseph, *A Narratological Reading of 1 Peter*, p. 28.

¹¹ So also, McCartney, *James*, pp. 36-38.

¹² On the parallels between James and 1 Peter, see Bauckham, *James*, pp. 155-57; and also McCartney, *James*, pp. 52-53.

1. Similar language is used to describe the nature of the trials the audience faces (*peirasmōs*, Jas. 1.2, 12; 1 Pet. 1.7, 5.12). Trials are viewed as refining and educational; e.g., "the testing of your faith" (*tō dokimion humōn tēs pisteōs*, Jas. 1.3; 1 Pet. 1.7).[13] Trials are viewed as stemming from interpersonal conflicts; from outsiders who oppress and oppose their audience as those who blaspheme the name of God (Jas. 4.7; 1 Pet. 4.4). The epistles also promote a similar response to trials; namely, endurance. The verb *hupomēno*, and corresponding noun *hupomonē*, are attested in both epistles (Jas. 1.4, 12; 5.11; 1 Pet. 2.20). There are also conceptual affinities present. Both epistles encourage their audiences to experience joy in the midst of trials because trials are a means to a greater end; namely, perfection and honor (Jas. 1.2; 1 Pet. 1.7; 4.12-13).
2. While instructing their audience on how to live with one another, James and 1 Peter both use the imagery of "seeding" to describe the word and the salvific process. In James, the audience is exhorted to receive the "implanted word" as a means of salvation (Jas. 1.21). In 1 Peter, new birth is brought about from an imperishable seed, the living and abiding word of God (1 Pet. 1.23).
3. James and 1 Peter both urge their audiences to resist the devil (Jas. 4.7; 1 Pet. 5.8-9). In both contexts, this comes with a call to submit to God and to embody humility. In addition, the authors both use Prov. 3.34 as a basis for their exhortation (Jas. 1.9; 4.6; 1 Pet. 5.5).

C. Affinity of Sources

There is evidence that James and 1 Peter draw from similar sources and use them in similar contexts as bases for their message. Besides the use of Prov. 3.34, noted above, Prov.10.12 is quoted in Jas. 5.20 and 1 Pet. 4.8. Also, both epistles draw from Isaiah, "... The grass withers, the flower falls; but the word of our God remains forever" (Isa. 40:7-8). This is quoted almost *verbatim* in 1 Peter, the author only replaces "our God" with "the Lord" (1 Pet. 1.24). In James it occurs in the form of an allusion (Jas. 1.11-12). In both epistles, it is used as a basis for how members of God's family should treat one another. Further, Lev. 19.18 is part of the background of both letters. "...You must love your neighbor as yourself..." is echoed both in Jas. 2.8 and in 1 Pet. 1.22.

---

[13] In his discussion of the similarities between James and 1 Peter, McCartney sees here a distinction between the two. He proposes that in 1 Peter, trials are meaningful because of participation in the sufferings of Christ, whereas in James, they are meaningful because they build maturity and wholeness (*James*, p. 52-53). While this distinction is warranted in part, the language in the texts mentioned here convey a similar understanding of sufferings/trials as found in James. See Charles H. Talbert, *Learning Through Suffering: The Educational Value of Suffering in the New Testament and Its Milieu* (Collegeville, MN: Liturgical, 1991), pp. 42-57.

In addition, some instructions in both letters are reminiscent of Jesus' teaching (cf. Jas. 5.12 and Matt. 5.33-37; 1 Pet. 3.8-12 and Luke 6.27-28, Matt. 5.44-45). The scope of this discussion does not permit us to address source critical issues here. Suffice it to say that James and 1 Peter demonstrate awareness of the Jesus tradition and draw from it in crafting their exhortations.[14]

More could be said here, but in the context of our present discussion, the evidence supports the idea that James and 1 Peter can be read together given their understanding of their audience, the affinities of the language they use and sources they draw from as bases for their exhortation.

III. Envisioning Social Holiness through the Lens of James and 1 Peter

How is holiness depicted in James and 1 Peter? The authors root their discussion on holiness in the Old Testament.[15] As a result, their treatment of the concept bears resemblance with the way it was communicated in the OT. Further, the authors use familial language as "the fatherhood of God" and the "fellowship (literally brotherhood) of believers" as a socio-theological boundary marker to highlight the distinction between the family of God and the wider world, and use membership in God's household as the impetus for the call to holiness.

A. Holiness, Community, and the Old Testament

The call to holiness in James and 1 Peter is intrinsically communal in nature. James' treatment of the theme of holiness is grounded in part in his discussion of the concepts of purity and perfection.[16] There is general consensus

---

[14] For a discussion, see e.g., Bauckham, *James*, pp. 74-111; Patrick J. Hartin, "Call to be Perfect through Suffering (James 1:2-4): The Concept of Perfection in the Epistle of James and the Sermon on the Mount," *Biblica* 77, no. 4 (1996): 477-92; McCartney, *James*, pp. 49-52. See also, Reinhard Feldmeier, *The First Letter of Peter*; Peter H. Davids, trans. (Waco, TX: Baylor University Press, 2008), p. 186; Goppelt, *1 Peter*, pp. 230-32.

[15] See, e.g., Patrick J. Hartin, *A Spirituality of Perfection: Faith in Action in the Letter of James* (Collegeville, MN: Liturgical Press, 1999); John H. Elliott, *The Elect and the Holy: An Exegetical Examination of 1 Peter 2:4-10 and the Phrase basileion hierateuma* (Eugene, OR: Wipf & Stock, 1966).

[16] John H. Elliott has helpfully highlighted that (1) James discussion of wholeness happens on three interrelated levels: the personal, the social, and the cosmological; (2) the integrity or wholeness of the community and its members is portrayed as an essential feature of its holiness; and (3) that this holiness has both moral and social implications ("The Epistle of James in Rhetorical and Social Scientific Perspective: Holiness-Wholeness and Patterns of Replication," *BTB* 23 (1993): 71-81.

that the theme of perfection is central to James.[17] The use of *tēleios* (1:4, 17, 25, 3:2), *teleō* (2.8), and *teleioō* (2.22) is ethical in nature and communal in its outworking.[18] For example, perfection is achieved when a person is able to control her speech (3.2); it is also at work in those who abide in, and act according to the perfect law of liberty. Perfection finds its expression in what James describes as religion that is pure and unblemished in the sight of God the Father: "caring for the widows and orphans in their affliction, and keeping oneself from being defiled by the world" (1.25-27).

The adjective *tēleios* is used in the LXX to translate the Hebrew *tāmîm*. It conveys and is connected to ideas of blamelessness, righteousness, purity, and complete devotion to God (e.g., Gen. 6.9; Exod. 12.5; Deut. 18.13; 2 Sam. 22:26).[19] The communal aspect of holiness is evident even when the individual is in focus. For example, Gen. 6.9 reads, "Noah was blameless [perfect], a righteous man *among* his generation." Noah's way of life is being contrasted with the rest of his contemporaries. Noah's ability to walk with God while living in a world where unrighteousness was prevalent is also important here. In 2 Samuel 22.26, David is singing praises to God for delivering him from his enemies. There the language of perfection is equated with righteousness, refraining from iniquity, being pure in God's sight. "I was perfect before him,[20] and I refrain from committing iniquity. Therefore, the Lord has rewarded me according to my cleanness in his sight" (2 Sam. 22.24-25). The same thought is expressed earlier in the song (vv. 21-22).[21] In other words, David's perfection, his righteousness, his purity in the sight of God have to do with the kind of response he displayed toward his enemies, which is an outworking of his obedience to the law of God.[22] In Deuteronomy 18.13, the community of Israel is addressed collectively and urged to be perfect; i.e., completely devoted to YHWH. Their devotion to God, a sign of obedience, is demonstrated through a lifestyle and set of practices that underscore their differences over against the other nations around them.

A similar understanding is conveyed in the exhortation to holiness found in 1 Peter. The author's treatment of this theme contains ethical and communal characteristics and is also firmly rooted in the OT. For example, like in

---

[17] Bauckham, *James*, pp. 177-85; Patrick J. Hartin, *James*, SP 14 (Collegeville, MN: Liturgical, 2003), pp.71-75.

[18] H. Hübner, "*tēleios*," EDNT 3:342-44.

[19] Hübner, "*tēleios*," EDNT 3:343.

[20] The MT uses the same word *tāmîm* here, which the LXX renders *āmomos*, unblemished, without defect.

[21] It is worthy to note also that in contrasting the blameless and the pure over against the crooked and the way God deals with them, David makes a statement that is conceptually identical to the wisdom saying recorded in Prov. 3.34 and appropriated by James and 1 Peter: "...You save those who are humble, but you bring down those who exalt themselves" (2 Sam. 22.28).

[22] The second half of the psalm focuses on the victory that God brought on his behalf. As a result of his righteousness, the Lord strengthens him and enables him to destroy his enemies.

Deut. 18.13, the epistle is replete with the language of non-conformity, obedience to God, purification, and devotion to God that need to be displayed by the elect living in diaspora (e.g., 1.17, 22-23; 2.11-17; 3.8-12; 4.1-6). Further, the author draws on Leviticus 19.2 and uses it as a basis for his call. "As obedient children no longer conforming to the passions you had during your time of ignorance, rather [conforming] after the image of the one who called you, you yourselves must become holy, because it is written: you will be holy for I am holy" (1.14-16). In its wider context, Lev. 19 contains the guidelines God has set forward for community life in Israel. In appropriating this text, the author is suggesting that as Israel was called to display God's character in everyday life, so the present community is required to display behavior that is characteristic of those who now are members of God's family. In addition, as Israel was set apart to show the nations the way to God, so the community is expected to witness God's grace and loving-kindness to the people around them, even their detractors.[23] This is attested also in 2.9-10, "But you are an elect race, a royal priesthood, a holy nation, a people acquired by God, so that you may proclaim the virtues of the one who called you out of darkness into his wonderful light; you who formerly were, now you are the people of God...." The image of the "living stones" built as a "spiritual house" and constituting a "holy priesthood" in 2.4-5 also contributes to this understanding. The "spiritual house" is reminiscent of the Temple where God dwells and fellowships with his people. This highlights the community's corporate identity, their relationship with God, and the role they play toward the world.

In sum, the exhortations to the audience are framed in communal terms. Though the commands are intended to be lived out by each individual, the focus is on the community. They are squarely rooted in the OT and come as a way of instructing those in *diaspora* on how to live within the family of God, on the one hand; and how members of the family of God should relate to the outside world, on the other hand. That James and 1 Peter exhibit a communal understanding of the concept of holiness can be further demonstrated through the familial language present in both letters.

B. The Family of Believers as a Socio-theological Boundary Marker

The "family of believers" as a socio-theological construct, permeates both epistles and serves as a boundary marker that helps identify who belongs, who does not belong, and the kinds of behaviors, attitudes, and actions that determine each group. This is attested through the use of "God as Father" and the language of "brotherhood" that pervade the epistles.

1. The Fatherhood of God

---

[23] See further, Joseph, *A Narratological Reading of 1 Peter*, pp. 84-85.

First, the fatherhood of God is one of the key concepts used in both epistles as a boundary marker. James and 1 Peter both seem to make a distinction between God as father/creator to whom all human beings and creation as a whole are accountable, on the one hand; and God as father/giver of new life from a soteriological perspective, on the other hand.[24] God as father/creator is attested in Jas. 3.9, where the "Lord and father" is used in relation to human beings (tous anthrōpous) who are made in the likeness of God. This distinction is evident in Jas. 1.17-18 where the author highlights the fatherhood of God in the context of God's acts of creation of inanimate objects, "the father of lights,"[25] and the entire cosmos, i.e., all God's creatures (ktismaton, 1.18)[26] over against giving new birth to members of the community he is writing to. The language of "new birth" paired with the concept of being a first-fruit from among his creatures has soteriological implications and links the community with Israel whom God calls "my firstborn son" in Exod. 4.22-23.[27]

Ng suggests that the fatherhood of God, i.e., God's universal creatorship, is in view in 1.27a while the redemptive dimension is present in 1.27b.[28] However, the evidence suggests that God as father of the believers, the soteriological dimension, is in view throughout. The focus is on proper worship, the kind that God the father accepts, in which social action and ethical behavior are intrinsically tied. Ng argues rightly that James is urging the audience to imitate God. The ability to imitate God is the socio-theological boundary marker parexcellence. It is what members of the family of believers aspire to. It is how one knows who belongs and who does not belong. Those who have experienced new birth constitute the family of believers who are in a more intimate relationship with God. As a result, they are required to live by God's standards, to

---

[24] See also, Esther Yue L. Ng, "Father-God Language and Old Testament Allusions in James," *TynBul* 54 (2003): 41-54.

[25] For a discussion of possible meaning of "father of lights," see Ralph Marin, *James*, WBC 48 (Waco, TX: Word Books, 1988), p. 37; McCartney, *James*, pp.108-113; McKnight, *The Letter of James*, pp. 126-28.

[26] See further, Martin, *James*, pp. 38-41; McKnight, *The Letter of James*, pp. 128-32.

[27] This relationship is also highlighted in Deut. 32.6 and Hos. 11.1. The language of "new birth" is not explicitly stated in the OT, but the concept is present. There is some affinity between the language of God's election of Israel in the OT and God giving new birth to the community. On this, see further, *A Narratological Reading of 1 Peter*, pp. 80-81.

[28] Ng, "Father-God Language," pp. 48-50. Ng's handling of the evidence is a bit puzzling at this point. Her conclusion seems to be based on the premise of a lack of emphasis on the presence of widows and orphans as Christians in James (p. 49). Though James does not use "wealth" and "poverty" exclusively in economic terms, it is evident that the economically poor is part of the community, therefore, may include those addressed here (e.g., 2.2, 15-17). Further, in the OT the fatherless, the widows, and even the strangers in question are part of the congregation of Israel. This does not negate the fact that God's people are to care for all (insiders and outsiders alike) as God the father cares for all.

represent God faithfully within the family of believers and in the world, to partake in God's holiness and to embody the love with which God loves the world, to protect the feeble and care for the destitute as he protects and cares for his own. It is primarily in this context that James evokes the fatherhood of God in 1.27.

In 1 Peter, the soteriological dimension is predominant. From the outset, the fatherhood of God is established in connection with the audience's election. The author addresses his audience as "the elect sojourners [living] in the diaspora of Pontus, Galatia, Cappadocia, Asia, and Bithynia, in accordance with the foreknowledge of God the Father..." (1.1-2). In the eulogy that follows, the fatherhood of God is described in terms of God's relationship to Jesus, the new birth God has wrought on behalf of the audience, the means through which he made it possible, and the implications: "Blessed be God, the father of our Lord Jesus Christ, who in accordance with his great lovingkindness has caused us to be born again into a living hope through the resurrection of Jesus from the dead..." (1.3). The fatherhood of God comes again in focus in 1.17-21, where the author uses it in conjunction with his call to holy living and as a basis to urge the audience to lead non-conformist lifestyle in diaspora. Further, the author uses the metaphor of the "household of God" to highlight the difference between those who bear God's name and suffer as a result, and those who live in disobedience (4.14-19). The audience's "new birth" by God, their status as "obedient children", and their alien status are used as the impetus for the way they should conduct themselves in dealing with those who are inside and outside the household of God (e.g., 1.22-23; 2.11-12).

The concept of God's universal creatorship is attested in 1 Peter. Here, the focus is on God's ability to hold everyone accountable, including those who oppress the elect, God's children. God the faithful creator is mentioned in a similar context as God "the impartial and just judge" (cf. 2.23 and 4.19). God's ability to vindicate God's children, as demonstrated in the case of Jesus Christ (1.18-21; 2.21-25; 3.18-22), and God's rule over human leaders are part of this picture (2.13-17). It is against this background that the audience is urged to submit to all human authority (literally *anthropinēi ktisei*[29], "human creature"), as part of the call to holy living in diaspora. It is done for the sake of the Lord (2.13), the "faithful Creator" (*pistōi ktistēi*, 4.19).

2. The fellowship of believers

The fellowship of believers is another element of the familial language that highlights the communal nature of holiness and serves as a socio-theological boundary marker in the epistles. James uses the endearment language of "brother and sister" throughout the epistle to establish rapport with the audience and to emphasize the relationship that exists between members of the community (e.g., "my brothers" [1.2; 2.1, 14; 3.1, 10, 12; 4.11; 5.10, 12, 19], 'my beloved brothers' [1.16, 19; 2.5], "an undistinguished brother" [1.9]; a brother or sister who is naked [2.15]). In addressing the audience as "brothers [and

---

[29] Cf. with James 1.18.

sisters]", the author implicitly locates the basis for the exhortations in the status and roles members of the community have assumed as a result of experiencing new birth. It emphasizes their collective identity and sets them over against the world. In a context of suffering and trials, this also creates solidarity between members of the community.[30] This language determines the standards required and serves as impetus for living them out.

In 1 Peter, the exhortation to the audience in the "haustafeln" section is structured around the author's instructions to everyone:[31]

1. 2.13-17 – Instructions to everyone
2. 2.18-20 – Instructions for slaves
3. 2.21-25 – The example of Christ
4. 3.1-7 – Instructions for wives and husbands
5. 3.8-12 – Instructions for everyone

The author uses "brotherhood" language in the opening and closing sections to speak of the love members of the community need to display to one another [tēn adelphonta agapate] on the one hand, and the respect that is due to everyone (else), including the emperor, on the other hand (2.17). A similar understanding is evident in the way he frames the following exhortation: "Finally, all of you, be of one mind, compassionate, loving one another [philadelphoi], tenderhearted, and humble-minded, not repaying evil for evil, or insult for insult, but blessing instead because to this you were called, so that you may inherit a blessing" (3.8-10). The way the members of God's household treat one another is an impetus for their interaction with the outside and often hostile world. The concept is reiterated at the end of the epistle to describe the solidarity in suffering that is experienced by "your (pl.) brotherhood that is in the world" (5.5-11).

While it is clear that James is aware of the Jesus tradition,[32] Peter goes a step further and inscribes the story of Jesus within the reality of his audience. God who gives the audience new birth is also "father of our Lord and savior Jesus Christ" (1.3). It follows that Jesus and the audience share a bond of brotherhood. The letter uses several devices to demonstrate how Jesus is at the center of the community. For example, He is the "corner stone" around and upon which the living stones join to form the "spiritual house" in which fellowship with God takes place (2.4-10). His chosen status in the sight of God and rejection by humans is paradigmatic to members of the household of God. More

---

[30] See David G. Horrell, "From *adelphoi* to *oikos theou*: Social Transformation in Pauline Christianity," *JBL* 120 (2001), pp. 293-311. Although this article focuses on the Pauline corpus, Horrell's discussion about how "fictive kinship" and "household of God" language works in constructing relationships within the church is helpful to this present conversation.

[31] Joel B. Green, *1 Peter*, THNTC (Grand Rapids: Eerdmans, 2007), p. 72.

[32] Many exhortations in James are reminiscent of Jesus' teachings as recorded in the Gospels. See, e.g., Hartin, "Called to Be Perfect," pp. 484-92.

importantly, He is the "obedient son" *par-excellence* whose suffering, death, resurrection, exaltation make possible the audience's new birth (1.2-4, 18-21). Therefore, his life of holiness and response to sufferings serve a perfect example for the audience to follow (2.21-25).

The exhortations to perfection in James and to holiness in 1 Peter are rooted in the audiences' relationship with God as father. Through giving new birth God creates a new household whose members are required to live by a set of standards that run counter to the ways of the world. Through the use of familial language the epistles highlight the communal character of the instructions. The familial language also serves as a boundary marker between the elect and their detractors. In what follows, I will discuss the holistic and practical nature of holiness as treated in James and 1 Peter.

IV. Holy Imagination, Holy Actions

Holiness is social in its outlook, but it is rooted in the imagination. Holiness in James and 1 Peter is holistic and practical: thinking is being, thinking is doing. It begins in the innermost part of person's thoughts and attitudes and ends in tangible expressions of appropriate behavior in interpersonal relationships. The following statement is true of James and 1 Peter: "You are what you think, you do what you think!"

According to James and 1 Peter controlling one's mind is a crucial step in the journey toward holiness. In James, double-mindedness characterizes the doubter who lacks wisdom, and whose requests may not be fulfilled as a result, while single-mindedness is a sign of integrity (1.5-7). The mind is also in focus in James' description of the process that leads from temptation to sin, which gives birth to death. The thoughts/desires that one nourishes are the seat of temptation and wrongdoing (1.13-15). Therefore, the warning issued in 1.16 "do not be led astray", though in the passive, seems to be directed toward the individual as a reminder to guard one's thoughts. Those who merely hear the word, do not think about it, forget it, and do not put it into practice are involved in self-deception (1.22-24). Similarly, those who think they are religious and are not able to control their speech are also engaged in self-deception (literally deceive one's heart, 1.26). The proximity with 1.27 suggests that James sees a very close connection between thoughts, speech, and actions. Indeed, perfection is attained when a person is able to control his or her speech (3.2). This is not merely the ability to refrain from speaking, but rather making sure that what a person thinks and says is in line with what one does. For example, speech is the vehicle for unholy action: anger (1.19-20), false religion (1.26-27), favoritism (2:3), disputes and conflicts (4.1-3), gossip and malicious talk (4.11-12), and boasting (4.13-16). However, controlled speech is tantamount to perfection because consistency in speech, namely, not speaking evil against one another (4.11), not grumbling, and integrity in words (5.7-11), is a sign of single-mindedness, a godly attribute (1.17).

In 1 Peter, the author initiates his call to holiness by using the image of 'readiness of the mind' as the starting point of journey to holiness. "Therefore, having girded the loins of your understanding by being self-controlled (literally sober-minded), set your hope fully on the grace that will be brought to you when Christ is revealed" (1.13). The language used here is reminiscent of when God instructed the Israelites to eat the Passover "with your loins girded" (cf. Exod. 12.11, LXX). Given the OT background of 1 Peter, it is possible that the author is describing the journey to holiness as a new exodus, a journey toward wholeness where one finds a rightful place in communion with God and fellowship with other members of the household of God ("...all of you be of one mind, be humble-minded", 3.8-11). It also takes a right frame of mind; i.e., sober-mindedness, casting one's anxiety on God, to offer an appropriate response to sufferings and trials. That response needs to be offered individually in interpersonal relationships and as a community in social interactions with an abusive world (5.6-9).

Controlled speech as an expression of holiness is also attested in 1 Peter. Controlled speech is a sign of righteousness (3.8-12). A holy imagination is required as a prerequisite to making a [verbal] defense regarding one's hope, as well as a clear conscience (3.13-17). Controlled speech is linked with pure and reverent behavior as silent witness (without words) to outsiders (3.1-2). This is all the more important as Jesus' example of appropriate response to suffering and his display of holiness is equated with his ability to control his speech when he was abused.

> Christ also suffered on your behalf, leaving you a pattern so that you may follow in his footsteps, [he] who committed no sin, nor was deceit found in his mouth, who while being insulted did not insult in return; while suffering did not threaten but handed over to the one who judges just (2.21-23).

Controlled speech is holy action and an appropriate response to suffering because it arises out of and expresses dependence on God.

V. Conclusion

Holiness is rooted in the imagination and finds its expression in social action and personal interaction. By virtue of the new birth, members of the household of God are brought within a special relationship with God the Father and with one another. This also creates tension with the outside world to such extent that those who have experienced new birth now find themselves in *diaspora*. Therefore, they need to learn to lead a lifestyle that honors God, testifies about God's love, and represents God faithfully. To this end the epistles of James and 1 Peter draw from the OT and use the image of God as father, and the fellowship of believers as basis to urge their audience to a life of non-conformity, righteousness, perfection, and holiness. While James draws on the teachings of Jesus, in 1 Peter, Jesus' life is used as an example that provides the impetus for living a holy life. This study of James and 1 Peter has shown that the pursuit of holiness is a communal mandate and should be a communal endeavor.

3

Reclaiming Holistic Salvation: A Continuing Wesleyan Agenda[1]

Randy L. Maddox

When the elderly Wesley paused to contemplate the mediocrity of moral character and the ineffectiveness in social impact of Christians in eighteenth-century England, he diagnosed the most basic cause to be an inadequate understanding of the nature of salvation.[2] While he had most in mind the simple lack of knowledge of Christian teachings among those claiming adherence to the faith on this specific occasion, other instances make clear that Wesley was equally concerned about the anemic understanding of salvation assumed so broadly in the church. In response, he focused his renewal efforts on reclaiming an understanding and embodiment of the *holistic salvation* that he found affirmed in Scripture and the broad Christian tradition. The characteristic doctrinal emphases and distinctive practices of early Methodism were central expressions of these focal efforts, and the resulting spiritual vitality of the movement is well-known.

This vitality is less evident today in the various Methodist communities descended from Wesley's ministry. Both insiders and observers are more likely to speak again of mediocrity and ineffectiveness. The only consolation offered is that few Christian traditions appear to be doing better. Rather than acquiescing in this comparative justification, Wesley's precedent would suggest that his present heirs should probe our assumptions about salvation: Have we settled for the anemic understanding that he was contesting? Does this help explain why we fail so often to embody the fullness of salvation in our lives and in our outreach to others? The best way to answer such questions is to gain a better sense of Wesley's mature understanding of the salvation that God offers in and

---

[1]This essay is adapted and updated from Randy L. Maddox, "Celebrating the Whole Wesley: A Legacy for Contemporary Wesleyans," *Methodist History* 43.2 (2005): 74-89.

[2]See Sermon 122, "Causes of the Inefficacy of Christianity," in *The Bicentennial Edition of the Works of John Wesley*, edited by Frank Baker, et al. (Nashville: Abingdon, 1984ff), 4:86-96; esp. §6, p. 89. This edition will be referred to hereafter simply as *Works*.

through Christ. The following survey highlights five emphases in this understanding, ordered as they became progressively more central to his concern. Attention is also paid within each emphasis to growth that might be evident in Wesley's pastoral insight concerning the dynamics of God's saving work.

Not just Rational Assent, Responsive Trust as Well!

Wesley's concern about an adequate understanding of salvation is evident already in letters from his student years. What most drew his early attention was the desire for assurance. He expressed this in a letter to his mother: "if we can never have any certainty of our being in a state of salvation, good reason it is that every moment should be spent, not in joy, but fear and trembling."[3] The question that this raised, of course, is the source of such certainty. Wesley knew the classic answer to this question, given particular emphasis in Protestant traditions, was that assurance of salvation comes by faith. But he was also aware of competing understandings of the nature and dynamics of faith. His mature conception of holistic salvation was framed in part by revising his initial stance within these alternatives.[4]

Wesley was influenced initially by thinkers who, reacting against superstitious credulity, defined faith primarily as *assent* to the truth of a proposition based on its rational credibility. Dialogue with his parents and broader reading soon led him to question the adequacy of this conception of faith, but it was his encounter with the Moravians in the events leading up to Aldersgate that most helped solidify an alternative conception. This alternative focused the nature of faith more on the will than on reason; it emphasized faith as *trust*, rather than mere assent. As Wesley put it shortly after Aldersgate:

> Christian faith is then not only an assent to the whole gospel of Christ, but also ... a trust in the merits of his life death, and resurrection. ... It is a sure confidence which a man hath in God, that through the merits of Christ *his* sins are forgiven, and *he* reconciled to the favour of God.[5]

By the mid-1740s another transition can be discerned in Wesley's emphases concerning faith. The focus of his discussion increasingly broadened from our act of trusting in God's pardoning love to include the *divine evidence* that awakens this trust—i.e., the witness of the Spirit that sheds the love of God abroad in our heart. More to the point, Wesley's mature conception of faith eventually placed *primary* emphasis on the divine evidence that calls forth this response. His comment in a letter to Samuel Walker is characteristic: "I hold a divine

---

[3] Letter to Susanna Wesley (18 June 1725), *Works*, 25:169–70.
[4] The transitions traced below were pointed out by Rex Matthews; for more details and documentation see Randy L. Maddox, *Responsible Grace: John Wesley's Practical Theology* (Nashville: Kingswood Books, 1994), 124–28.
[5] Sermon 1, "Salvation by Faith," §I.5, *Works*, 1:121.

evidence or conviction that Christ loved *me* and gave Himself for *me* is essential to if not the very essence of justifying faith."[6]

These transitions in Wesley's emphases concerning faith reflected growing appreciation for the role of the affections in human willing and action. In essence, he was working through a major shift in "moral psychology" (that is, his basic assumptions about what inclines and enables humans to act in appropriate ways).[7] Wesley imbibed with his upbringing a long-standing model that portrayed the main obstacle to Christian life as our emotions, and that placed hope for moral action in the assertion of rational control over these unruly forces. But he became convinced over time that 1) reason alone was unable to effect human action, our acts flow instead from more holistic affections; and 2) these affections are not self-initiating, they are enlivened and inclined toward specific actions in response to external stimuli. To put this in terms of Wesley's mature conception of faith: 1) faith involves more than rational assent, it is a holistic affection of trust; and 2) this trust is not generated by human initiative, it is made possible responsively when the Spirit addresses our affections assuring us of God's love.

As the last point suggests, Wesley viewed that the temporal priority of the witness of the Spirit to our response of loving trust as a practical corollary of the conviction that humans are saved by grace, not works. This helps explain why *experiencing* the Spirit became so central to the definition of early Methodism. As Wesley once put it:

> [We affirm] that inspiration of God's Holy Spirit whereby he fills us with righteousness, peace, and joy .... And we believe it cannot be, in the nature of things, that a [person] should be filled with this peace and joy and love ... without perceiving it. ... This is ... the main doctrine of the Methodists.[8]

While Wesley was aware of potential dangers in this emphasis on experiencing the Spirit, and issued occasional cautions against these dangers, he continued to affirm the importance of experiential encounter with the Spirit throughout his ministry. However, he did eventually nuance this affirmation in one crucial way, revealing hard-won wisdom from his pastoral oversight of the movement. This refinement is hinted at in a comment near the end of his life:

> When fifty years ago my brother Charles and I, in the simplicity of our hearts, told the good people of England that unless they *knew* their sins were forgiven,

---

[6]Letter to Samuel Walker (19 September 1757), in *The Letters of the Rev. John Wesley, A.M.*, edited by John Telford (London: Epworth, 1931), 3:222. Hereafter: *Letters* (Telford).

[7]For more definition of "affections" and a detailed discussion of this shift, see Randy L. Maddox, "A Change of Affections: The Development, Dynamics, and Dethronement of John Wesley's 'Heart Religion'," in *"Heart Religion" in the Methodist Tradition and Related Movements*, edited by Richard Steele (Metuchen, NJ: Scarecrow Press, 2001), 3–31.

[8]Letter to "John Smith" (30 December 1745), §13, *Works*, 26:181.

they were under the wrath and curse of God, I marvel ... that they did not stone us! The Methodists, I hope, know better now; we preach assurance as we always did, as a common privilege of real Christians; but we do not enforce it, under pain of damnation, denounced on all who enjoy it not.[9]

As this quote suggests, in the initial glow of their own experience of the Spirit's assuring witness, John and Charles both tended to expect a uniformity in the psychological dynamics of this witness. They assumed that the Spirit would work in other persons with the same temporal patterns and intensity as the Spirit had worked in their lives, and judged examples that did not meet this norm to be invalid. John's pastoral advice in later years was much different. A good example is his response to one who was questioning the validity of her experience because it was not as dramatic as that of a friend. Wesley assured her that

> There is an irreconcilable variability in the operations of the Holy Spirit on [human] souls, more especially as to the manner of justification. Many find him rushing in upon them like a torrent, while they experience "The o'erwhelming power of saving grace." ... But in others he works in a very different way: "He deigns his influence to infuse; Sweet, refreshing, as the silent dews." It has pleased him to work the latter way in you from the beginning; and it is not improbable he will continue (as he has begun) to work in a gentle and almost insensible manner. Let him take his own way: He is wiser than you; he will do all things well.[10]

The conviction of the importance of experiencing the empowering affect of the Spirit remains clear in this response, but it is framed with an appreciation of God's sensitivity gained through Wesley's lifetime of ministry.

Not just Forgiveness, Spiritual Transformation (healing) as Well!

If Wesley's encounter with the Moravians played a positive role in forming his mature convictions about the nature of saving faith, his second mature emphasis about truly holistic salvation was framed in resistance to certain tendencies in Moravianism. The issues at stake in this case were expressed most vividly in a quote from the mid-1740s:

> By salvation I mean, not barely (according to the vulgar notion) deliverance from hell, or going to heaven, but a present deliverance from sin, a restoration of the soul to its primitive health ... the renewal of our souls after the image of God in righteousness and true holiness, in justice, mercy, and truth.[11]

The "vulgar" notion that Wesley is rejecting here reduces salvation to God's forgiveness of our guilt as sinners, which frees us from future condemnation.

---

[9]A comment to Melville Horne in 1788, recorded in Robert Southey, *The Life of Wesley* (New York: W.B. Gilley, 1820), 1:258.
[10]Letter to Mary Cooke (30 October 1785), *Letters* (Telford), 7:298.
[11]*Farther Appeal to Men of Reason and Religion*, Pt. I, §3, *Works*, 11:106.

While this may pick up the theme of Romans 1-3, it omits an equally biblical theme that can be represented by Romans 7-8, where the deepest impact of sin is our spiritual debilitation ("What I want to do, I cannot!") and God's gracious gift is the Spirit that enables our spiritual healing.

In the events surrounding Aldersgate Wesley came to appreciate more deeply the truth that God's pardoning love is not contingent upon our prior recovery of righteousness. But he showed no tendency to allow emphasis on our gracious acceptance to displace the (equally biblical) concern for our present spiritual healing. Instead, Wesley stressed how assurance of this acceptance is what provides the impetus for spiritual healing. He made this connection by means of the emphasis in his revised moral psychology about the responsive nature of human action. Consider another of his seasoned definitions of salvation:

> What is *salvation*? ... It is not a blessing which lies on the other side of death ... it is a present thing .... There is a *real* as well as a *relative* change. We are inwardly renewed by the power of God. We feel the "love of God shed abroad in our heart by the Holy Ghost which is given unto us," producing love to all humankind.[12]

Note that it is our experience of God's pardoning love that enables and inclines us to love God and neighbor, reflecting the renewal of our nature.

While some strands of Moravianism were prone to emphasize the gratuity of justification in a way that undercut concern for holy living, this was not the case with the English Moravians who were so influential upon Wesley prior to Aldersgate. They connected justifying faith with holy living, but in a way that Wesley soon found to be equally problematic. They encouraged him to expect that when he experienced the assurance of God's love he would be immediately and completely renewed—all of his doubts and fears would be gone, and all sinful inclinations would be replaced by Christ-like inclinations.[13]

Wesley's experience after Aldersgate quickly cast doubt on these expectations. Assurance of God's love had awakened new strength to resist his sinful inclinations, but he recognized that the inclinations themselves were still present. As he noted in his *Journal*, "my wound was not fully healed."[14] But this realization did not lead Wesley to downplay the concern for full spiritual healing. Instead, reflecting on his own experience and his pastoral supervision of the early Methodist movement, Wesley eventually distinguished carefully between the initial renewing effect of the "new birth" and the further transformation of our inclinations that the Spirit makes possible in the ongoing journey of salvation. In the new birth the Spirit gives us power to resist our unholy inclinations (or, as Wesley called them, "unholy tempers") and evokes nascent

---

[12]Sermon 43, "The Scripture Way of Salvation," §I.1-4, *Works*, 2:156-58.

[13]The best study of these expectations, and Wesley's later revisions, is Richard P. Heitzenrater, "Great Expectations: Aldersgate and the Evidences of Genuine Christianity," in *Mirror and Memory: Reflections on Early Methodism* (Nashville: Kingswood, 1989), 106-49.

[14]*Journal* (6 June 1738), *Works*, 18:254.

holy tempers. In the subsequent process of sanctification, made possible by the Spirit's continuing empowerment, these holy tempers grow in strength, displacing the unholy tempers. The goal—which Wesley could call "Christian perfection," and which he insisted was available in this life—was the emergence of a stability of character with "the humble, gentle, patient love of God, and our neighbor, ruling our tempers, words, and actions."[15]

The deepest pastoral wisdom in Wesley's mature understanding of salvation is found not in his affirmation of this progressive "growth in grace" but in his appreciation for the means of grace in facilitating this growth. One of his most succinct accounts is in the sermon "On Zeal":

> In a Christian believer love sits upon the throne which is erected in the inmost soul; namely, love of God and [neighbor], which fills the whole heart, and reigns without a rival. In a circle near the throne are all holy tempers—longsuffering, gentleness, meekness, fidelity, temperance; and if any other were comprised in "the mind which was in Christ Jesus." In an exterior circle are all the works of mercy, whether to the souls or bodies of [others]. By these we exercise all holy tempers; by these we continually improve them, so that all these are real means of grace, although this is not commonly adverted to. Next to these are those that are usually termed works of piety—reading and hearing the word, public, family, private prayer, receiving the Lord's Supper, fasting or abstinence. Lastly, that his followers may the more effectually provoke one another to love, holy tempers, and good works, our blessed Lord has united them together in one body, the Church.[16]

Notice how this account relates the means of grace directly to forming holy tempers. It also reflects Wesley's hard-won conviction (against other one-sided perspectives in the Christian tradition) that the means of grace serve not only as avenues by which God conveys gracious empowerment, they are also formative disciplines by which we responsively shape our character into Christ-likeness. Wesley made the means of grace central to salvation because within the various means we are exposed to the ever-deeper empowering affect of the Spirit and we are enabled to exercise our affections, shaping them into holy tempers.

Concern for providing his followers with this twofold benefit is evident in the specific set of means of grace that Wesley developed as the framework of Methodist life. In addition to regular use of such valued traditional means as prayer, liturgy, and Eucharist, Wesley enjoined those serious about salvation to live within the rhythms of less common means like class meetings, love feasts, and works of mercy. Some of these other means were adopted primarily for their tendency to open us to God's empowering affect while others were incorporated more for their role in habituating (tempering) our affections. As a case in point, Wesley's stress on works of mercy in the preceding quote focuses particularly on the second benefit.

---

[15]"Brief Thoughts on Christian Perfection," in *The Works of John Wesley*, edited by Thomas Jackson (London: Wesleyan Methodist Book Room, 1872), 11:446. This collection of Wesley's *Works* will be cited hereafter as *Works* (Jackson).

[16]Sermon 92, "On Zeal," §II.5-6, *Works*, 3:313-14.

In his encouragement of his followers to weave experience of God's pardoning love into God's broader gracious concern for their spiritual transformation, and in the well-rounded and balanced set of means of grace that he discerned over the years best fostered this transformation, Wesley bequeathed his present descendants an admirably holistic model of salvation.

Not just for Individuals, for Society as Well!

The third emphasis in Wesley's mature teaching on holistic salvation is suggested by his well-know aphorism: "The gospel of Christ knows of no religion, but social; no holiness, but social holiness."[17]

This aphorism is well known because it has been invoked by so many Methodists since the late nineteenth century to warrant their focus on socioeconomic transformation as they embraced the emphases of the Social Gospel movement, Liberation Theology, and the like. In other words, this is one place where his heirs have been ready to claim Wesley's legacy. But few of those making this claim have seemed to recognize that Wesley's primary focus in the specific text cited is different from the implication they were suggesting.[18]

In the early years of the revival—the context of this quotation—the dimension of the *social* character of salvation on which Wesley focused most attention was the importance of corporate support and accountability for our ongoing growth in grace. He was championing small groups as a crucial means of grace. Thus, his preface to the aphorism on social holiness read: "'Holy solitaries' is a phrase no more consistent with the gospel than holy adulterers."[19] In a later sermon he elaborated:

> Christianity is essentially a social religion ... to turn it into a solitary religion, is indeed to destroy it. ... I mean not only that it cannot subsist so well, but that it cannot subsist at all, without society—without living and conversing with other [people]. ... Not that we can in anywise condemn the intermixing solitude or retirement with society. ... Yet such retirement must not swallow up all our time.[20]

Wesley inherited this appreciation for "religious society" from his father, who sponsored a small group in his parish at Epworth; and he shared it with his brother Charles, who described such corporate support as God's way to "nourish us with social grace."[21] The depth of John's appreciation is evident in the multi-layered structure of support groups that he progressively crafted for the benefit of his Methodist people.

While the dimension of corporate spiritual formation is always central in Wesley's affirmations of the social character of salvation, a second dimension can

---

[17]*Hymns and Sacred Poems* (1739), Preface, §5, *Works* (Jackson), 14:321.
[18]See on this point, Andrew C. Thompson, "From Societies to Society: The Shift from Holiness to Justice in the Wesleyan Tradition," *Methodist Review* 3 (2011): 141-72.
[19]Ibid.
[20]Sermon 24, "Sermon on the Mount, IV," §I.1-4, *Works*, 1:533-34.
[21]See his hymn written for love feasts, *Hymns*, #507, st. 1, *Works*, 7:698.

be discerned as well in nearly every case. He took it for granted that those who were being renewed in the Methodist societies would be expressing this change in society at large. Note how this comes through in his longest elaboration of the Methodist understanding of salvation:

> By *salvation* [the Methodist] means holiness of heart and life. ... a Methodist is one who has "the love of God shed abroad in his heart by the Holy Ghost given to him"; one who "loves the Lord his God with all his heart, and with all his soul, and with all his mind, and with all his strength." ... [and] this commandment is written in his heart, that "he who loveth God, loves his brother also." ... His obedience is in proportion to his love, the source from whence it flows. And therefore, loving God with all his heart, he serves him with all his strength. ... Lastly, as he has time, he "does good unto all men"—unto neighbours, and strangers, friends, and enemies. And that in every possible kind; not only to their bodies, by "feeding the hungry, clothing the naked, visiting those that are sick or in prison," but much more does he labour to do good to their souls.[22]

This "social service" dimension of holistic salvation found its most formal expression in the General Rules, which admonished Methodists 1) to do no harm to others and 2) to do as much good for the bodies and souls of others as they could.[23]

While more recent Methodists who have invoked the aphorism "no holiness but social holiness" would appreciate such acts of caring for the needy and suffering, their focal concern has typically been to transform political and economic structures that ignore the poor or cause human suffering. Is there evidence of concern for this third dimension in Wesley's affirmation of the social character of salvation? There is indeed, though it emerges only in his later years. The clearest expressions are two tracts: *Thoughts on the Present Scarcity of Provisions* (1773), which proposes several political and economic moves to increase production of basic foods;[24] and *Thoughts upon Slavery* (1774), which focuses on undercutting supposed humanitarian and theological justifications for slavery, but thereby lays the basis for his support of political moves to abolish slavery.[25]

What accounts for the rareness of emphasis on socioeconomic reform, particularly in Wesley's earlier years? Many have assigned it to conservative political commitments which they believe Wesley inherited, commitments that led him to distrust all revolutionary agendas.[26] One could also make a case that

---

[22] *Character of a Methodist*, §§4–16, *Works*, 9:35–41.

[23] *The Nature, Design, and General Rules of the United Societies*, *Works*, 9:69–73.

[24] See *Works* (Jackson), 11:53–59.

[25] Ibid, 59–79. Wesley's last known letter was an encouragement of William Wilberforce in his political fight against slavery; cf. *Letters* (Telford), 8:265. He had earlier included in the *Arminian Magazine* (11 [1788]: 263–64) a letter by Thomas Walker requesting petitions against the slave trade be sent to Parliament.

[26] A quick survey of alternative identifications of Wesley's political philosophy can be found in Theodore R. Weber, *Politics in the Order of Salvation: Transforming Wesleyan Political Ethics* (Nashville: Kingswood Books, 2001), 28–32.

Wesley rarely addressed the larger political arena, especially prior to the 1770s, because of how politically insignificant his movement was within the culture at large. But another major factor was the amillennial eschatology which Wesley imbibed with his Anglican training.[27] This long-dominant eschatology tended to postpone hopes for significant healing of societal ills until "heaven above," just as many had postponed such hopes for healing spiritual infirmities. While Wesley challenged the postponement of spiritual transformation from the beginning, his convictions about the parallel possibility of present transformation of socioeconomic reality coalesced only in his later years with his embrace of an emerging emphasis on the hope for "latter day glory" (what is now usually called "postmillennialism).[28]

While it is not without its problems, this new emphasis allowed the Wesley to broaden 1) his confidence in the present empowering affect of the Spirit and 2) his conviction that God values human co-operation, such that they applied not only to the personal realm but also to societal realities. But what is most significant is the way the mature Wesley wove personal and socioeconomic transformation together by continuing to highlight the role of small support groups in nurturing both the inclination and tenacity for serving others in need and for struggling to transform socioeconomic structures. Here again we have a heritage of truly holistic salvation.

Not just for Souls, for Bodies as well!

The fourth emphasis evident in Wesley's functional holistic model of salvation also ran counter to assumptions about eschatology that had reigned for some time in the church. Although Scripture speaks of our ultimate hope in terms of resurrection of our bodies and life in a future new "heavens and earth" (i.e., a transformed physical universe), a variety of influences had led most Christians by Wesley's day to assume that our final state is "heaven above."[29] The latter was seen as a timeless realm that our spirits enter the moment that we are set free from our mortal bodies, where we join all other spiritual beings in continuous worship of the Ultimate Spiritual Being. Those most concerned to honor biblical imagery allowed that our spirit would eventually be reunited with our body, but with a body transformed into an ethereal form that is fit to reside in the heavenly realm where we remain eternally.

---

[27]For elaboration of the following points see Randy L. Maddox, "Nurturing the New Creation: Reflections on a Wesleyan Trajectory," in *Wesleyan Perspectives on the New Creation*, edited by M. Douglas Meeks (Nashville: Kingswood Books, 2004), 21–52 (esp. 33–43).

[28]See Sermon 63 (1783), "The General Spread of the Gospel," §§13–27, *Works* 2:490–99; Sermon 66 (1787), "The Signs of the Times," *Works* 2:522–33; and Sermon 102 (1787), "Of Former Times," *Works* 3:442–53. The image of "latter-day glory" can been seen in §16 (493), §II.1 (525), and §23 (453) respectively.

[29]For a good history of the ascendency of this model, see Colleen McDannell & Bernhard Lang, *Heaven: A History* (New Haven: Yale University Press, 1988).

Wesley was raised within this spiritualized model of the afterlife, and through most of his ministry its assumptions were presented as obvious and unproblematic. They shine through, for example, in an often-cited portion of the preface to his first volume of *Sermons*:

> I am a spirit come from God and returning to God; just hovering over the great gulf, till a few moments hence I am no more seen—I drop into an unchangeable eternity! I want to know one thing, the way to heaven—how to land safe on that happy shore. God himself has condescended to teach the way: for this very end he came from heaven.[30]

However, in the last decade of his life Wesley began to take the scriptural imagery of bodily resurrection and of the new heavens and earth more at face value. In particular, drawing on a suggestion of Charles Bonnet, a prominent Swiss biologist, he described a model of the afterlife in which humans are embodied and reside in a physical universe, though we are higher on the "chain of being" than in our current setting.[31]

While late in date and speculative in nature, this emphasis on our bodies participating in ultimate salvation was consistent with Wesley's life-long conviction that God's saving intent in the *present* includes our bodies. The corollary that many drew from the spiritualized model of the afterlife was that physical health was incidental, if not antithetical, to spiritual welfare. Wesley's contrary conviction is evident is his advice to Alexander Knox: "It will be a double blessing if you give yourself up to the Great Physician, that He may heal soul and body together. And unquestionably this is His design. He wants to give you ... both inward and outward health."[32]

If this is God's design, then for Wesley it was obvious that we should cooperate by doing all that we can to restore and preserve our physical health.[33] How seriously he felt about this is evident in his instructions to his lay assistants about their ministry among the Methodist people. As they visited the various societies, Wesley charged them to leave behind books that could provide ongoing guidance, highlighting most often two works that should be in every house: 1) his excerpt of Thomas a Kempis's *The Imitation of Christ*, which Wesley valued as a guide to spiritual health; and 2) *Primitive Physick*, which he had prepared as a guide to physical health.[34]

Most Methodists today are unaware of the second volume, and scholars who come across it often dismiss it as a collection of "home remedies." This

---

[30] *Sermons* (1746), Preface, §5, *Works*, 1:105.

[31] The original suggestion was in Charles Bonnet, *La Palingénésie philosophique; or Idées sur l'état passé et sur l'état futur des etres vivans*, vol. 2 (2nd edition. Munster: Philip Henry Perrenon, 1770). Wesley republished a translation of the relevant last section as *Conjectures Concerning the Nature of Future Happiness* (Dublin: Dugdale, 1787).

[32] Letter to Alexander Knox (26 October 1778), *Letters* (Telford), 6:327.

[33] For more details on what follows, see Randy L. Maddox, "John Wesley on Holistic Health and Healing," *Methodist History* 46 (2007): 4–33.

[34] "Large Minutes," Q. 42, *Works*, 10:920.

seriously misjudges its nature and its centrality to Wesley's ministry. He read broadly on the topic of medicine throughout his life and gathered most of the remedies in *Primitive Physick* from prominent medical authors of his time. This was as much a use of his scholarly gifts to provide aids for his people as was his collection of theological writings in the *Christian Library*. Moreover, in the preface to this volume (and in other publications) Wesley added advice for preserving health to his suggestions for treating wounds and illnesses.[35] He was interested not simply in offering cures but in promoting wellness.

Wesley was also clearly interested that Methodist ministry to others address their needs for physical healing as well as for spiritual healing. This conjunction came naturally, because the Anglican model in which Wesley was trained expected priests to offer medical care as part of their overall ministry, at least in smaller villages. To be sure, he was aware of the efforts of the newly-founded Royal College of Physicians to professionalize the practice of medicine by restricting the ranks of those certified to offer treatment. But Wesley also recognized that there were simply not enough certified physicians available yet, and the poor were the ones most likely to be left without care. His deep concern about this led him to take the "desperate expedient" of opening free clinics in Bristol and London where he offered medical treatment for the poor.[36] It also led him to include basic medical texts in the readings assigned for his lay assistants, so that they could offer medical advice as they rode their circuits, and to create a lay office of the "visitor of the sick" within Methodist societies.

As all of this reflects, Wesley longed for his followers to see that participation in God's saving work involves nurturing not only our souls but our bodies, and addressing both of these dimensions in our outreach to others.

Not just for Humans, for the Whole of Creation!

The final emphasis that Wesley came defend about a truly adequate understanding of salvation is the one that most differed from the spiritualized model he had inherited. It is also likely the one that is least familiar to his present heirs.

We have noted that the spiritualized model of "heaven above" that became dominant in medieval Western Christianity found it difficult to admit our bodies to the afterlife, allowing them only in an ethereal form. It struggled all the more with notions of animals or the physical elements having a place in ultimate salvation. Even the early Protestant reformers, who worried most about conformity to scripture, and accordingly affirmed that God would recreate an earth populated with animals, denied that humans would reside on this recreated earth. Moreover, their heirs broadly reverted to the assumption that animals and the physical elements have no place in the afterlife, in part because of the dualism of contemporary thinkers like Descartes.[37]

---

[35] Cf. Preface of *Primitive Physick*, §16, *Works* (Jackson), 14:314–15.
[36] See *A Plain Account of the People Called Methodists*, §XII:1–2, *Works*, 9:275.
[37] Cf. McDannell & Lang, *Heaven*, esp. chapter 6.

We also noted above that in his later years Wesley became more explicit about the human body participating in ultimate salvation. This point can be made more broadly: as Wesley continued to probe the biblical witness to salvation in his sixties, he decisively shifted the focus of his ultimate hope from "heaven above" to the promised new creation. Indeed, the new creation became one of the most prominent themes of his late sermons. These sermons leave no doubt that this future creation will be a physical place, even as Wesley speculated about how each of its basic elements will be dramatically improved over present conditions.[38]

There is also no doubt that Wesley became convinced that the range of animals would be present in this renewed creation. He had actually shown sympathy for the minority view that animals have souls for some time, apparently devoting one of the required lectures in his Oxford degree program to this topic.[39] He offered a guarded reaffirmation of this point in 1775.[40] Then in 1781 he issued a bold affirmation of final salvation for animals in his sermon "The General Deliverance."[41] While not unprecedented, this sermon was unusual for its time and is often cited today as a pioneer effort at reaffirming the doctrine of animal salvation in the Western church.[42] Wesley reinforced the sermon two years later by placing in the *Arminian Magazine* an extended extract of John Hildrop's spirited defense of animal salvation, which contested the alternative comments of such notables as John Locke. In the preface to his extract Wesley noted that some might think that this issue was an ingenious trifle, but he considered it central to our confession of the wisdom and goodness of God. As Hildrop had argued, to allow that God did not redeem all that God created and called good would mean that God had not truly overcome the work of Satan.[43]

The connection of the issue of animal salvation to affirmation of God's goodness lies behind what is surely the most unusual element in the aged Wesley's reflections on the cosmic dimension of new creation. He had long doubted the adequacy of a theodicy that justified God's goodness in permitting the possibility of the fall by noting that God would eventually restore things to their pre-fallen condition. In Wesley's view, a truly loving God would only permit the present evil in the world if an *even better* outcome might be

---

[38] See in particular Sermon 64, "The New Creation," *Works*, 2:500–10.

[39] One of Wesley's "Wall lectures," delivered in February 1727, was titled *de anima brutou*. While we have no copy, it seems likely that it addressed the question of whether animals have souls, since his Oxford diary records discussing this topic several times in the prior year.

[40] See Sermon 55, "On the Trinity," §11, *Works*, 2:382.

[41] Sermon 60, "The General Deliverance," *Works*, 2:437–50.

[42] See the positive reference to this sermon in Andrew Linzey, *Christianity and the Rights of Animals* (London: SPCK, 1987), 36.

[43] The extract is scattered through *Arminian Magazine* 6 (1783), starting on page 33. Hildrop's reference to Satan is on p. 598. The preface is reprinted in *Works* (Jackson), 14:290.

achieved by allowing this possibility than without it. On these terms, he believed that God would not just restore of fallen creation to its original state, God would recreate it with greater capacities and blessings than it had at first.[44] What all might this entail? Drawing again on the work of Bonnet, Wesley proposed in "General Deliverance" that as compensation for the evil they experienced in this life God would move the various animals higher up the chain of being in the next life—granting them greater abilities, including perhaps even the ability to relate to God as humans do now![45]

Whatever we make of this speculation, the most significant aspect of Wesley's reflection on this cosmic dimension of ultimate salvation is his sense of its relevance for present Christian life. He recognized that convictions about God's ultimate purpose should serve as guides for what we value now. Thus, he defended his speculation about God's future blessings of animals on the grounds that it might provide further encouragement for us to imitate now the God whose "mercy is over all his works."[46] Lest this be left in generalities, he frequently exhorted against abusive treatment of animals.[47]

In other words, Wesley provided an impetus toward a truly holistic understanding of salvation that includes concern for animal welfare and broader ecological concerns.[48]

A Continuing Wesleyan Agenda

Such is the legacy that Wesley bequeathed to his ecclesial descendants and—through them—to the whole church. I wish that I could next recount how his descendants fully embraced this legacy and gladly shared it with others. Unfortunately, the historical reality was much more mixed than this, particularly in the North American setting where Methodism most flourished.

To begin with, in the interplay of Enlightenment culture and supercharged revivalism nineteenth-century Methodists found it difficult to retain Wesley's holistic assumptions about the affections. Many reverted to more polarized emphasis on reason or the emotions, and this helped drive the splits between the mainline church and the holiness movements, and then between the holiness churches and the Pentecostal movement.

In significant part because of losing touch with Wesley's mature moral psychology, his North American descendants found it increasingly hard to make

---

[44]Cf. Sermon 59, "God's Love to Fallen Man," *Works*, 2:423-35.

[45]See Sermon 60, "General Deliverance," §III.6-7, *Works*, 2:448. Bonnet presents the model of animals moving up the Chain of Being in the future life in *Palingénésie* 2:62-84.

[46]Ibid, §III.10, *Works*, 2:449.

[47]See Theodore Runyon, *The New Creation: John Wesley's Theology Today* (Nashville: Abingdon, 1998), 202-5 for a convenient collection of such exhortations.

[48]For more on this point, see Randy L. Maddox, "Anticipating the New Creation: Wesleyan Foundations for Holistic Mission," *Asbury Journal* 62 (2007): 49-66; and Howard A. Snyder, with Joel Scandrett, *Salvation Means Creation Healed* (Eugene, OR: Cascade Books, 2011).

sense of his affirmation of the possibility of Christian Perfection. Many sought to distance themselves from his perceived unrealistic claim about the goal of sanctification. In the process his emphasis on the centrality of spiritual transformation to salvation was muted. Add to this the impact of popular expositions of genetic determinism, psychological determinism, and the like, and it little wonder that Wesley's current descendants are as likely as anyone else to doubt that we can expect much transformation in our character.

While twentieth-century Methodists picked up and elaborated Wesley's emphasis on socioeconomic transformation, most of them did so in a context that had already abandoned the small groups that Wesley valued for nurturing the inclination and tenacity for consistent engagement in social service and advocacy.

The early circuit riders in North America followed Wesley's instructions to offer medical advice as part of their ministry, until increasing professionalization made this unacceptable. In the nineteenth century Wesley's commitment to this aspect of holistic salvation was honored more by building colleges across the continent that emphasized training physicians and nurses. At the turn of the century this was supplemented by establishment of several church-supported "charity" hospitals.[49] Then came the financial pressures of health care in recent decades, which have largely removed the church from direct involvement, and have again left the poor in danger of inadequate access. Methodists are only beginning to explore how to honor their Wesleyan legacy within this new reality.

Finally, it is clear that Wesley's support of animal welfare, and their ultimate salvation, continued in at least some strands of British Methodism into the nineteenth century.[50] But there is little evidence that this particular emphasis in the whole Wesley's understanding of holistic salvation ever carried across the Atlantic to the North American church, or that it was consciously echoed on either side of the Atlantic by the later nineteenth century.

In other words, we who stand today in the traditions tracing back to Wesley's ministry face much the same challenge as he did—the challenge of reclaiming an understanding and embodiment of the full scope of salvation that is affirmed in Scripture and in the broad Christian tradition.

---

[49]These transitions are traced well in Elmer Brooks Holifield, *Health and Medicine in the Methodist Tradition* (New York: Crossroad, 1986).

[50]Cf. E. S. Turner, *All Heaven in a Rage* (New York: St. Martins, 1965), 50, 72, 161; and Samuel Thompson (a Methodist minister), *Essays Tending to Prove Animal Restoration* (Newcastle: Edward Walker, 1830).

Chapter 4

Kenosis not Control: The Social Holiness of Chicago's Urban Missions

Jonathan Dodrill

The greatest expressions of social holiness theology are found in times of crisis and moments of strife. This is precisely why, as a movement, we laud the efforts of our radical abolitionist forefathers and foremothers. We extol the Holiness people who were in the minority when they promoted social and clerical egalitarianism. And we pride ourselves in knowing that so many of our denominations were founded in defense of the common (wo)man (e.g. B.T. Roberts and the Free Methodists' stand against pew renting).

A crisis is easily remembered as it has a definitive beginning and ending, and it has clearly marked protagonists (abolitionists, feminists, B.T. Roberts) and antagonists (slavery defenders, sexists, the hegemonic class). Steady streams of strife are not as easily remembered. The efforts of a community of laborers, replicating their work on a daily basis, becomes a mundane and forgotten narrative. Yet in the engagement with perpetual strife, one can find other great expressions of social holiness. Urban Holiness missionaries of the nineteenth and twentieth centuries encountered the strife of city life on a daily basis, as they chose to live among the poor in the most desperate neighborhoods. From the fatally-diseased to the homeless immigrant orphan, urban missionaries cared for the least. They combated systemic sin; targeting saloons, prisons of forced prostitution, and unjust incarceration. As they grew in their understanding of the needs of the neglected, they sought to widen the bounds of their community through intentionally bringing a message of personal and social holiness to a forgotten people. Letting go of a life of privilege, they adopted a kenosis form of ministry.[1] Their daily encounters with the poor and

---

[1] The idea of a *Kenosis* presence in the city is explored in Robert A. Orsi, ed., *Gods of the City: Religion and the American Urban Landscape* (Bloomington: Indiana University Press, 1999), 7-8. In it, he discusses Jane Addams' desire to become intimately engrained in the community in which she served. This idea is based on individuals'

outcast influenced their religious practices and ultimately their understanding and presentation of holiness as a means of both individual betterment and social liberation.

It has been previously established that Holiness people were not absent from urban contexts.[2] In the nineteenth century, Chicago saw an influx of both migrants and immigrants. Some of these migrants were Holiness people who came to the city, not for job opportunities, but for mission opportunities. Such groups are absent in many Holiness histories, including Timothy Smith's definitive work, *Revivalism and Social Reform*.[3] The Olive Branch Mission and the Rest Cottage Mission were both located in Chicago at the turn of the twentieth century. The missions were operated by rural migrants, most of whom were women. These missionaries adapted their holiness theology both to make sense of the world in which they lived and to solidify a practical theology capable of reaching and converting those among whom they lived.

The holiness presence in the city manifested very differently than that of mainline Protestantism as well as Reformed-evangelical Protestantism. The presence of the latter two has been categorized by many social historians as an exercise in "social control" of the lower class.[4] Holiness urban missionaries

---

and communities' understanding of Philippians 2:1-11, where Jesus "empties himself" in order take on the role of a servant.

[2] Timothy Smith's *Revivalism and Social Reform in Mid-Nineteenth Century America* (New York: Abington Press, 1957) has made the argument that the Holiness movement was birthed primarily out of east coast cities such as Boston, New York, and Philadelphia. His pioneer project seriously challenged the established "Frontier Thesis" which attempted to situate the sources of evangelicalism primarily in a rural context. Smith's important but contested thesis sought to give revivalists of the Holiness movement a central role in the growing trend to engage the social sphere in order to bring about moral change. His thesis is contested in that he attempts to make the Holiness movement a proto-social gospel. However, it is undeniable that the Holiness movement was heavily involved in and even pioneered particular social efforts. Yet, there are few examples in his work of specific Holiness urban missionary efforts. The most notable is his treatment of the Five Points Mission, which he labels as Phoebe Palmer's "crowning achievement," 169-173.

[3] Some works that do take seriously the migrant Holiness communities in urban contexts include, William Kostlevy, *Holy Jumpers: Evangelicals and Radicals in Progressive Era America* (New York: Oxford Press, 2010) and most recently is Benjamin L. Hartley, *Evangelicals at a Crossroads: Revivalism and Social Reform in Boston, 1860-1910* (Lebenon, NH:

University of New Hampshire Press).

[4] "Social control" is the attempts by upper and middle class persons with social influence to promote "Protestant ideals." A double edged sword, this necessitates both a class system as one of the "Protestant ideals" is economic democracy, and the amelioration of lower classes. The idea of social control is a prominent feature in urban religious studies. Yet it has become a metanarrative that can often dilute the histories of urban humanitarian efforts by religious communities, assuming that their sole purpose in engaging in such activities was to control the lower classes.

maintained a kenotic presence and unique engagement with the urban poor which was not a desire to engage in social control, but was rather an attempt to transform their lives and the slum itself into a sanctified state of being. In addition to exploring the social holiness of Olive Branch and Rest Cottage missionaries, the centralization of a social control motif will be challenged.

Challenging the Historiographical Assumptions of Urban Missions

The social control thesis that has dominated urban religious historiography is an inappropriate lens by which to view urban Holiness missionaries. William Kostlevy suggests that this has been an ongoing issue for scholars of the Holiness movement, starting with Timothy Smith's work.[5] The social control thesis maintains that certain individuals and groups used religious practices, authority, and idioms – specifically idioms of benevolence – to safeguard their influence and wealth by controlling the behavior of the lower class. Undoubtedly, there were people groups and individuals who sought to control the poor and immigrant as they feared losing influence in their communities and the nation. But the thesis should not be used universally to understand Protestant engagement with the poor and immigrant.

One of the more important works utilizing the social control thesis is Clifford S. Griffin's essay, "Benevolence as Social Control," which examines the various organizations of the Evangelical United Front in the early nineteenth century. This included the American Bible Society, the American Tract Society, the American Home Mission Society, and others. Much of motivation behind their ministries is correctly identified as social control. Their goal was to convert people to Protestantism, but more importantly to keep the poor and immigrant in their places. There are limits in Griffin's essay, however. All of Griffin's actors came from the same social-theological-ethnic culture. They were typically from the New England aristocracy. They were primarily Anglo-Saxon Presbyterians or Congregationalists and the theological descendants of Puritans. The men he studied were mainly Federalists who were seeing their political ideals melt away. The sample size of Griffin's actors is far too limited to

---

Carroll Smith-Rosenberg defines "social control" as the "policies intended to insure the continuity of a stable, graded society based upon universal acceptance of traditional patterns of deference and morality." *Religion and the Rise of the American City: The New York City Mission Movement, 1812-1870* (Ithaca: Cornell University Press, 1971), 7:fn. 1.

[5] William Kostlevy, *Holiness Manuscripts: a Guide to Sources Documenting the Wesleyan Holiness Movement in the United States and Canada* (Metuchen, NJ: Scarecrow Press, 1994), 9, 13-15.

assume that all in the Evangelical United Front were engaging in social control.[6]

Paul Boyer's work, *Urban Masses and Moral Order in America, 1820-1920*,[7] is another important work that centralized the social control thesis. His work contains portraits of various urban missionary efforts that sought to control the lower class. Like Griffin's actors, Boyer exemplifies men with pious, well-to-do backgrounds, who rise to the top of economic statues and seek to reform the land "for Christ." In his effort to reform the city, the protagonist creates social networks with other likeminded, well-to-do businessmen and politicians to develop a strategy to aid the poor. He establishes educational institutes, social clubs, and other organizations to help the poor gain the skills to obtain upward mobility, procure working class respectability, and to make a purposeful contribution to society.

Nine years after writing Urban Masses and the Moral Order utilizing the social control thesis, Boyer wrote Mission on Taylor Street: the Founding and Early Years of the Dayton Brethren in Christ Mission.[8] This work provides an alternative paradigm to the social control thesis in understanding urban missions. The mission on Taylor Street was run by William Boyer (Paul Boyer's grandfather) who was a poor German Holiness-Anabaptist seeking to aid fellow German immigrants who had given up a life of agriculture for urban employment. His ministry did not seek to convert prostitutes or fight for better conditions for factory workers. Rather, his aim was to provide the kind of spiritual and communal support for the new city dwellers that they once received in their farm communities.

Boyer alone has provided an alternative historiography of his earlier work. While this one example may not satisfy a complete paradigm shift of urban religious historiography, it still shows that the theme of maintaining/gaining social control is not the only, or even the most important, interpretive tool in understanding urban missions.

Carroll Smith-Rosenberg challenged the centrality of social control in the study of ante-bellum city missions, stating, "Historians examining the objectives and rhetoric of antebellum reformers have frequently concluded that their underlying purpose was indeed social control...But to discount the depth of their religious commitment and to interpret this commitment as a rationale for the imposition of social control is to distort the mid-Victorian mind."[9]

---

[6] Clifford S. Griffin, "Benevolence as Social Control, 1815-1860" *The Mississippi Valley Historical Review*, 44, no.3 (1957), 423-444.

[7] Paul Boyer, *Urban Masses and Moral Order in America, 1820-1920* (Cambridge: Harvard University Press, 1978).

[8] Paul Boyer, *Mission on Taylor Street: The Founding and Early Years of the Dayton Brethren in Christ Mission* (Grantham, PA: The Brethren in Christ Historical Society, 1987).

[9] Carroll Smith Rosenberg, *Religion and the Rise of the American City: The New York City Mission Movement, 1812-1870* (Ithaca: Cornell University Press, 1971), 7.

Smith-Rosenberg sees a negative shift in urban missionary work from the eighteenth to the nineteenth century. Eighteenth century Quakers and Calvinists attended to the needs of the urban poor and shared the Christian message with them due to their belief that Jesus made this central to the mission of Christianity. But by the mid-nineteenth century "respectable New Yorkers" began assuming the role of caring for the poor but did so with the rhetoric of "social problems," which assumed a particular attitude about traditional class dynamics.[10]

The respectable New Yorkers who engaged urban mission work were often middle-class women or professionally educated clergymen who saw the position as a stepping-stone to a better job. Those who were part of these missions were often seen as bi(or multi)-vocational; one who blended religious missions with public health and relief concerns. These "experts" of city problem solvers were often socially recognized men.[11]

While this historiographical sketch may be true for a large part of urban missionaries, it is certainly not true of all. By examining urban Holiness missions, a counter-argument can be made, and an alternative understanding to the Christian presence in the city can be nuanced. Very few in the Olive Branch and Rest Cottage missions were middle-class women (those who were, abdicated their position and finances for the benefit of the mission) or trained clergy. Yet they operated city missions within Chicago as a mission to aid the poor, not as an exercise in making society safer from the poor.

A problem arises when one does not take seriously the possibility of the religious poor aiding the urban poor/oppressed through urban missions. Many of Chicago's urban Holiness missionaries were not only women of modest means; they were rural women of *radical* Holiness sects. This fact alone creates problems for the idea of social control as Smith-Rosenberg gives credence to the thought by saying, "The *well-to-do* church-going sponsors of urban charities...clearly revered private property and found distasteful the violence, the filth, the latent anarchy of the poor and the immigrant."[12] The *"well-to-do* church-going sponsors" do not summarize the totality of urban missions supporters. It may be true that they were a large part, perhaps even a majority. Yet the Salvation Army alone stands as an incompatible example: the Booths were hardly *"well-to-do."* The fact that the *"well-to-do"* found the realities of the poor and immigrant to be "distasteful," "anarchist," and "filthy" points to their critique of a lower class, not a people in need of "salvation" or "conversion."

Smith-Rosenberg's provides a great understanding of what upper class church goers held as important: peace, cleanliness, and order. Yet what of the poor and the immigrant who were engaged in urban charities? Certainly they did not see themselves or their fellow poor and immigrant neighbors as "filthy." Rather, they understood the atmosphere in which they were forced to live as "filthy."

---

[10] Ibid., 2.
[11] Ibid., 4-6.
[12] Ibid., 7. Emphasis added.

Smith-Rosenberg's description of a city mission in antebellum America represents the institution generally as, "Organized effort to disseminate the truths of revealed religion and the hope of eternal salvation among the city's unchurched and deprived."[13] Her attempt to displace social control as the ultimate interpretive lens in the antebellum era is buttressed by her understanding of the optimistic Jacksonian belief in the perfectibility of human (and as a result, the perfectibility of society). Hence, the case could be made that the social control lens could also be displaced in the Progressive Era by understanding the theology and revivalistic impulses of Holiness urban missions who promoted a perfectibility of humanity.

One of the overall problems with the social control thesis is that it simplifies motivation as stemming from religion. Lois Banner states that to untangle the motivations of these people leads to skewed results. Their concerns were political and social, albeit stated through religious terminology. Further, it cannot be assumed that religious people are motivated by fear and a want for social place. Such a pessimistic view may be appropriate some times, but certainly not all of the time.[14] Additionally, the motivation for social control should not be seen as solely stemming from a religious sphere. At the very least, the idea of social control needs to be understood as part of a class dynamic along with religious understandings. Even within those religious groups that were largely middle to upper class, emphasizing the social control aspect "Creates an artificial distinction...by assuming a nonexistent distinction between the realms of the secular and the spiritual."[15] In case of urban Holiness missionaries, their understanding of class and poverty was uniquely shaped by their places of residence and outreach.

Holiness, Poverty, and Class

In exploring the efforts of Holiness people in an urban context, issues of class and poverty come to the forefront. The general attitude of urban Christians toward poverty has been explored above. Much of the desire to engage in urban mission is based on controlling the lower classes. Even those who did not originally intend to engage in social control tended to fall into similar practices and modes of ministry that employed a kind of social control method. Yet if engaging in social control demands a certain place in society, then it is very unlikely that lower class urban missionaries engaged in social control. The urban Holiness missionaries came from a tradition of theological critique of the

---

[13] Rosenberg, 2.

[14] Lois Banner, "Religious Benevolence as Social Control: A Critique of an Interpretation," *Journal of American History* 60 (June 1973), 23-41.

[15] Inherent in Rosenberg's discussion is the role of social and economic class dynamics. She does not explicitly state these dynamics, but explores the blending of spiritual values and economic values. She states that the ante-bellum "respectable New Yorker" assumed that spiritual change beget economic social stability through thriftiness, temperance and prudence, 8-9.

upper class. From John Wesley's publication, *Thoughts on the Present Scarcity of Provisions*[16] to Seth Cook Rees publicized lament concerning the waste of material goods on pets, the Wesleyan-Holiness movement has often challenged the comfort and luxury of the upper class. Challenging inequality brought about by the class system was a key and defining component of their social holiness theology.

There are three main components to class that Holiness people combated: the economic, the social, and the ecclesial. The first component is economic distinction. The Holiness movement was comprised of people from every economic class from Phoebe Palmer, a doctor's wife in downtown Manhattan, to Mary Everhart, a Pennsylvanian farm girl. However, what is often seen as a strict moral code (plainness in dress, forbidding jewelry, etc.) was actually a protest against the frivolous spending of the wealthy. The economic class distinction of the late nineteenth century was closely tied to social class distinctions. Few Holiness people were from the privileged classes or held an abundance of cultural capital. Finally, Holiness people were very much against the "formal" institutionalized mainline churches. These three forms of class distinction (economic, social, and ecclesial) are closely tied together. Those who were very wealthy often had social influence and cultural capital while attending the established mainline churches.

Chicago urban Holiness missionaries where steeped in a tradition that challenged the lifestyles of the upper class. These challenges were aimed both outside and within the Holiness movement (especially those within the Methodist Episcopal Church).[17] Additionally, they sought to continue in the tradition of prioritizing ministry toward the poor. It was in Chicago that Seth Cook

---

[16] John Wesley, "Thoughts on the Present Scarcity of Provisions," in *Readings in Christian Ethics: a Historical Sourcebook*, ed. J. Philip Wogaman and Douglas M. Strong (Louisville: Westminster John Knox Press, 1996), 181-184.

[17] A major contribution to the laxity of Methodists was their upward class mobility, or *embourgeoisment*. As Methodists became wealthy and moved to the city, they lost their 'old-time religion' ways. Their financial and material prosperity manifested in the formalization of their churches (in architecture and worship style) and the desire to take part in worldly amusements and comforts. Those who were not part of such embourgeoisment became self-segregated and sectarian as they launched a competition between cultural styles and economic differences. Such Holiness communities harkened back to Wesley's ideals of simplicity and sanctification. This caused a rift against the urban bourgeois Methodists who wanted to worship in "respectable" churches. Charles Edwin Jones, *Perfectionist Persuasion: the Holiness Movement and American Methodism, 1867-1936* (Lanham, MD: Scarecrow Press, 2002), xiv-xvii. For the original use of the term "embourgeoisment," see Donald W. Dayton, "'The Search for the Historical Evangelicalism': George Marsden's History of Fuller Seminary as a Case Study" reprinted in Christian T. Collins Winn, ed., *From the Margins: A Celebration of the Theological Work of Donald W. Dayton*, (Eugene, OR: Pickwick Publications, 2007), 264.

Rees of the Rest Cottage Mission and the women of the Olive Branch Mission continued this tradition of ministering to the poor.[18]

Seth Cook Rees and the Rest Cottage Mission

Seth Cook Rees was a minister and urban missionary during the Progressive Era. He opened numerous rescue homes for the destitute: prostitutes, runaways, drunks, and orphans. Rees is associated with International Apostolic Holiness Union, an antecedent of the Pilgrim Holiness Church and the founding organization of God's Bible School in Cincinnati. The modern reality that God's Bible School is extremely conservative socially and theologically skews the understanding of Rees' mission and theology. Rees published a collection of stories that represent the work of the urban missionaries of the Rest Cottage Mission.[19] This work was written for those in a rural context: his project was to raise awareness within Holiness communities as to the realities of slum life. He, as well as the Olive Branch Mission, sought to bridge the communities of rural Christians with the urban destitute.

The text is a prime example of how religion in practice shaped theological understandings. Rees offers numerous critiques of the class system and the validity of the notion of America as a "Christian Nation" while employing revivalist tactics to embody a theology based on his concept of social holiness.[20]

Rees is obviously drawn to the slums because of his understanding of Christ's admonishment to reach the poor and destitute. It is also obvious that he is disgusted with the evangelistic efforts of revival leaders who seek out nice country folks for conversion because he believed such people were too comfortable and often turned away from the Gospel. Rees writes, "Thank God, the poor outcast, the hungry, the people that are down and can not get up, God loves them, Jesus died for them and wants to save them...These are times when God seems to take great pleasure in saving people that nobody else would

---

[18] Kostlevy claims that ministering to the poor has always been essential in Methodism and that different groups were founded (such as the Free Methodists) as a protest against those Methodist bodies which had abandoned such practices. William C. Kostlevy "Benjamin Titus Roberts and the 'Preferential Option for the Poor' in the Early Free Methodist Church," in *Poverty and Ecclesiology: Nineteenth-Century Evangelicals in the Light of Liberation Theology* ed. Anthony L. Dunnavant (Collegeville, MN: The Liturgical Press, 1992), 52.

[19] Seth Cook Rees, *Miracles in the Slums or Thrilling Stories of Those Rescued from the Cesspools of Iniquity, and Touching Incidents in the Lives of the Unfortunate*, in *"The Higher Christian Life"* series, ed. Donald Dayton, (New York: Garland Publishing, 1905, 1985).

[20] When Rees talks about entire sanctification, he rarely uses a doctrinal rhetoric (such as "entire sanctification or "perfectionism"). Rather he discusses it as the "true gospel" and "real Christianity."

think is worth saving...*My heart goes out to the poor.*"[21] It was this population that Rees sought to convert, writing "I seek especially the neglected."[22]

Aside from the desire to bring salvation to those on the margins, Rees saw a quantitative advantage to holding revivals in the city. He shared statistics of both a high number of conversions and a high percentage of people responding to a call to salvation in his urban revivals. He asks his rural counterparts if they can boast of a revival where 24 out of 28 women were saved. Such a high percentage was not uncommon, according to Rees. He wondered how much money was spent on manufacturing a revivalistic atmosphere in the country and showed his disgust by those who only sought converts from "nice" rural contexts. "A great deal of time and money is spent" stated Rees, "on people who do not seem to want the Lord."[23] Instead, he advised that there was a need to push out of the rural context and into the place where "God is giving His special attention."[24]

Urban missionaries urged their rural counterparts to engage in the redistribution of goods. The urban missionaries were from the lower classes themselves thus their social networks did not have the kind of access to abundant wealth that their upper or middle class urban missionary counterparts had. Rather, they had to appeal to their theological communities in the country to send material goods. Pants, shirts, socks, coats, hats, linens, coal, and food were sent in barrels from the country to the city. Upon receiving one such barrel of goods, Rees commented that "There was more gospel in that barrel, and more real piety and devotion."[25]

Rees' preferential option for the poor was based on his pneumatology. He believed that the Spirit of God was giving "special attention to the neglected and *submerged classes.*"[26] Part of his concern for the lower class was his belief that the upper class had largely failed to bring about salvation to the slums. Specifically, he critiqued the ecclesial seminaries as having failed to create an urban revival but had opted to become places for respected academicians. He further condemned upper class society for lavishing clothes and food upon their "poodle dog[s]" instead of spending that money to care for exploited working girls. Likewise, he denounced the business practices of large company factories that paid their employees' unlivable wages.[27] The problem of poverty

---

[21] Rees, 191-192, 194. Emphasis added.
[22] Ibid., 193.
[23] Ibid.
[24] Ibid., 194.
[25] Ibid., 247.
[26] Ibid., 29. Emphasis added.
[27] Ibid., 29-31. The concept of unfair wages leading to a life of sin out of necessity is pervasive throughout Rees' account. This is but one example of how he understood the greed of the upper class manifesting in the individual sins of the lower class. He never excused the sins of the lower class, but rather saw those sins as evidence of oppression and stemming from the systemic societal sin based on upper class greed.

is then seen to come from the upper class which refuses to pay the working class a decent wage while buying luxuries for their "poodle dog[s]." Rees further critiqued the social class system by pointing out the differences between the needs of the poor and the extravagance of the rich. He twice gave the statistic of money spent by Chicagoans for Christmas presents ($14 million) and contrasting it with both the physical and spiritual malnutrition of the poorest in the city.[28]

Inherent in his critique of society was the unfair punishments handed out by police forces. He compared a man who stole two lumps of coal for his freezing wife and child to the political corruptness of municipal figures who stole thousands of dollars. The former was separated from his family and thrown into a filthy prison while the latter was celebrated by society. This double standard, he said, contributed to the poor "becoming poorer every day."[29]

Rees and his urban missionaries made it a point to go to the Harrison Street prison on a weekly basis. He provided his readers with a glimpse of the conditions: a dank, poorly ventilated and overcrowded basement cell. The only water supply was a stream "running through an open groove in the stone floor." The odor was "stifling" and the vermin abundant. The food consisted of only bread and water served with a rusted cup from a wooden pail from which the "great Norway rats" also drank.[30] He accused the police of beating the prisoners mercilessly, even during the religious services that Rees conducted. At one point, the police had thrown an entire family of four into the prison and was starving them. The urban missionaries were able to get them out, but not before the infant died of malnutrition.[31]

Rees also attacked the ecclesial classism of the 'established' churches.[32] He drew a distinction between those Christian communities that were "experiential" and those that were "religious."[33] Many tales tell of a child reared in such a home where there was religion, but "no salvation."[34] After falling into a "life of sin," Rees told of such a young man who attempted to come back to faith. The man went to a Presbyterian church in Chicago but found that the preacher was expounding on the political ideology of McKinley and thus, "his poor starving soul found no food." He then went to Trinity Methodist Episcopal Church in Cincinnati, found the "learned doctor" giving a lecture on his recent trip to Europe so the young man "turned away from all churches in despair."[35] He finally found salvation through Rees' urban mission. This is but one example of the dichotomy that Rees draws. Preachers of established churches

---

[28] Ibid., 180, 182, 206.
[29] Ibid., 206.
[30] Ibid., 61-62.
[31] Ibid., 103-4.
[32] This would include The Methodist Episcopal Church as well as the other mainline denominations, which were often composed of economic and social elites.
[33] Ibid., 194.
[34] Ibid., 79.
[35] Ibid., 81-82.

preached that which their upper class congregants related to: politics and world travels. The urban missionaries preached what their poor congregants related to: "gospel salvation" and redemption from a life of sin. Even after those from the lowest classes were "saved and sanctified," the "aristocratic churches" wanted nothing to do with them.[36] Rees' understanding of the ecclesial class system caused him great bitterness toward the established churches and a belief that urban Holiness missionaries were the only ones who could bring true Christianity to the slums.

Converting the masses in the slum could only be done by preaching the "real old-fashioned gospel." Rees critiqued the high society of preachers and scholars who sought to transform the city for God through other means. The ways of the upper class were to hold meetings, giving "flowery essays" on the state of the city. But this was not a mode Rees saw as pragmatic: if it did not accomplish the salvation of souls, it accomplished nothing. But he was not satisfied to simply preach for salvation. He promoted social reform, not through policies but through grass roots efforts. He exemplified the Cremorne Mission in New York, which had purposefully situated itself directly adjacent to the Cremorne Saloon. Because of the presence of the mission, the saloon was closed. Thus Rees believed the task of the urban Christians was both to preach for salvation and to live and work among the poor and sinful, converting individuals and disrupting sinful businesses.[37]

The one tactic that established churches had abandoned was revivalism. The Rest Cottage missionaries held revivals both inside the urban mission and outside in public spaces. One story tells of a "bum" wandering down State Street in Chicago and into a street revival where there was the singing of hymns and the preaching of the gospel. These revivals functioned as a means to spark interest and point people to the mission. At points there were responses and conversions in the street meetings themselves.[38] One recurrent theme in these narratives is that of the "bum" converting and returning to the street to be a preacher him/herself. Thus, the revivals self-perpetuated and spread from slum to slum and even from city to city.[39]

Rees not only saw the ecclesial upper class as irrelevant to the lower classes, but as exploiting the lower classes. There are numerous stories of sexual assault in his narrative. In every story, the victims were girls from the lower class and the assaulters were socially advantaged men. In the case of Hallie, the assailant was a *"church member."*[40] Myrtle was assaulted by an "honored member" of the YMCA.[41] And Christine was assaulted by the mayor's son and later shunned by the town.[42] Not only were these girls sexually abused, but many like Christine

---

[36] Ibid., 207.
[37] Ibid., 196-197.
[38] Ibid., 83
[39] For example, the "bum" on State Street was converted, moved and began street preaching in his new town. Ibid., 86.
[40] Ibid., 65-68.
[41] Ibid., 159-162.
[42] Ibid., 119-122.

were casted out by society and found no home except for Rest Cottage. Rees accused modern society (both secular and ecclesial) of creating a system where a girl sinned against was punished for a crime of which she was the victim.

The connection between urban missions and rural communities was one of mutual benefit. The rural communities sent material goods and the urban missionaries educated the rural communities on how the cities' vice was a threat to their homes. Rees shared that 46,000 girls in prostitution die each year. He warned his rural readers that in order to maintain the brothel business, new employees must be added, thus he asked, "where are the 46,000 girls to come from next year?"[43] He suggested that they would come primarily from the country and from country villages: many would be from Christian homes. He compared the "dark procession" of girls duped into prostitution to the cattle that "march down to death" in the stockyards of Chicago.

Many of the stories contained in Rees' work forewarn the rural communities of the sly man who takes advantage of country girls and of the promises of employment made in newspapers, both which led to forced prostitution. The story of Lucy is one of deceit and slavery. Lucy was born into a rural Christian home but upon moving to Chicago sought employment. On her search for employment, she met a man who promised all sorts of niceties. She was then assaulted and starved for days and finally sold to a brothel.[44] The Rest Cottage Mission fought against such vice through preventative modes (warning country girls of con artists) and by engaging in the ministry in the heart of the slum. But they were not alone. Another Holiness mission had taken up residence in Chicago's "skid row" three decades earlier.

The Olive Branch Mission

During a hot June day at the St. Charles camp meeting of the Free Methodist church, Rachel Bradley, described as a "tall, queenly looking" woman, sought the experience of entire sanctification. She was later seen at the Morgan Street Free Methodist Church in Chicago having set aside her "worldly garments" and sharing a desire to open a mission for the poor. Though many in the church discouraged her from such work, a prayer meeting took place and the "Spirit of God was poured out" on all who were in the room. Bradley was from a well to do rural family, but in opening her mission sold everything that she had, voluntarily becoming impoverished.[45]

In 1867, Rachel Bradley started a sewing class for prostitutes in her church basement, which would become the foundation of The Olive Branch Mission.[46]

---

[43] Ibid., 222.

[44] Ibid., 185-188.

[45] "Olive Branch Mission 125 years later," anniversary program, (Chicago: The Office for Corporate Publications – Olive Branch Mission., 1999), 2.

[46] There has been some debated about the true inception of the Olive Branch Mission. Many believed it was 1876, but other accounts have Rachel Bradley starting the mission in 1867.

She soon established a mission on Wells Street in a building that was previously a saloon.[47] There, she shared with the homeless: food, sleeping accommodations, and eventually tuberculosis from which she died. The purpose of the mission was to provide a Christian presence not only to the people of the slum, but to the slum environment itself. Thus, Everhart believed, "No one ever helped another out of the pit by reaching up in the air. If we would save the lost, we must go where they are."[48] Upon her deathbed, Bradley sold the mission to Sarah Everhart who moved the mission to Desplaines Street in Chicago's "Skid Row."[49]

The Olive Branch missionaries understood their role in the city. They did not speak of lofty ideas to completely transform the entire city, rather they wanted to be the "light of the gospel" and the "city upon a hill" within their immediate surroundings.[50] Their mission was described by John H. Corcoran as a "spiritual oasis" within the "Sodom of America."[51] Essentially, the space they provided was one of safety and refuge. In one way, they were a spiritual and physical escape from the realities of the slum. Yet they were not content to remain within their own spaces, for their mission constantly infringed in both the public spaces of the slums and in the private spaces of brothels and saloons. The missionaries did not have to walk too far to engage the vices of the slum. According to their records, "Saloons, cheap lodging-houses, brothels and pawnshops abound almost to the exclusion of everything else on the street where the mission is located, both north and south as far as we are acquainted with the street. Then the intersecting streets east and west are but repetitions of the same."[52]

Like Rees and his missionaries, the women of Olive Branch produced their newspaper to bridge the gap between the rural and urban communities. One missionary wrote of the impossibility to imagine what life was actually like in the slums of Chicago. She spoke directly to those who came from the "pure, uncontaminated social atmosphere of rural towns," stating that they had no understanding of the dire realities faced every day. The women of the Olive Branch were almost all country women who "suppressed" their "longings for

---

[47] "142 Years of Frontline Service to Chicago." The Olive Branch Mission. http://www.obmission.org/home/obm_documetation.pdf (accessed 12 August 2012). Assumedly this was by no accident. The hallmark battle for the women of the Olive Branch Mission was the brothel and the saloon. Their efforts saw numerous brothels and saloons close.

[48] Ibid., 1.

[49] "Olive Branch Mission 125 years later," 2-3, 27.

[50] "Olive Branch Mission," *The Olive Branch Newspaper*, (Chicago: The Olive Branch Mission, 1895) Volume 2, No. 9, pg. 4.

[51] "The Oasis," *The Olive Branch Newspaper*, 1895, Volume 5, No. 4, pg. 4.

[52] "The Mission" *The Olive Branch Newspaper*, 1894, Volume 4, No. 1, pgs. 2-3.

fresh air, green fields and congenial companionship." According to one author, they were taking part in "daily martyrdom."[53]

The country women not only suppressed their longings for a country surrounding, but also suppressed their desires for fine accommodations. Their accommodations were depreciating houses in need of mass renovations. They did have material goods, but some rooms remained unfurnished for lack of funds. The three-story building where some of them lived provided both living accommodations and spaces for missional work. Not only did they work for the mission, but like Rachel Bradley, shared their personal space with the mission.[54]

The missionaries' embrace of poverty was a central component to their social holiness theology. Following the example of Rachel Bradley, the urban missionaries were never guaranteed any form of payment, and oftentimes had to creatively make use of the goods they had.[55] This gave them a sympathetic understanding of the plight of their neighbors in the slum. Unlike the urban missionaries that worked in the slums then retreated to their fine accommodations in the gentrified neighborhoods, the Olive Branch missionaries never left the realities of the slum. Not only did the missionaries adopt a life of poverty, but demonized the want for materials and societal status. They believed that those who strive for wealth, political honor and material niceties were misguided in their understanding of what is important in the world.[56]

From the beginning, the Olive Branch adopted an understanding of a preferential option for the poor. According to their second constitutional point, "The object shall be to maintain a mission in the city of Chicago for the purpose of aiding the *destitute*, rescuing the *fallen* and *outcast*, and for maintaining Christian services in connection with this work."[57] The destitute they sought to rescue was the drunkard, but even more so the prostitute.

Their understanding of prostitution was much like Rees' understanding. The girls very rarely chose such a life, rather they were forced into such a life out of necessity. They attributed such circumstances to the low wages paid to girls from large factories and retail stores. Even worse, were those who were "snared, trapped, bought and sold" into sex slavery.[58] The pages of the *Olive Branch Newspaper* told of numerous stories of women forced into prostitution

---

[53] "Love Feast at the Mission," *The Olive Branch Newspaper*, 1898, Volume 4, No. 2, pgs. 1-2.

[54] V.E. Worthington, "A Visit," *The Olive Branch Newspaper*, 1903, Volume 9, No. 2, pg. 2. And J.D. Marsh, "Olive Branch Mission Home," *The Olive Branch Newspaper*, 1902, Volume 8, No. 7, pg. 2.

[55] J.A. Murray, "Brands from the Burning," *The Olive Branch Newspaper*, 1894, Volume 1, No. 1, pg. 4.

[56] "Editorial Notes," *The Olive Branch Newspaper*, 1894, Volume 1, No. 8, pg. 1.

[57] "Incorporation," *The Olive Branch Newspaper*, 1895, Volume 2, No. 6, pg. 3. Emphasis added.

[58] Mrs. Charlton Edholm, "Startling," *The Olive Branch Newspaper*, 1895, Volume 2, No. 11, pg. 4.

for such reasons. The girls were often portrayed as "inmates" within the "prison" of the brothel. They felt that it was their job, not only to bring salvation to their souls, but to bring salvation to their lives. Thus the missionaries often engaged in midnight rescue missions where they would physically remove girls out of brothels (sometimes with the agreement of the madam, sometimes without).[59] This was also the case with the Rest Cottage missionaries. Rees tells of the story of a band of women storming a saloon where girls were known to be locked in cages. After demanding that the girls be set free, the missionaries were brutally attacked by the madam. Yet they did manage to free a number of the enslaved girls.[60]

While the missionaries made implicit statements about the causes of prostitution from time to time, they also made bold and explicit statements about the cause of prostitution: the class system. The prostitutes of Chicago were made up mostly of factory girls, clerks, and servants, many of whom were "ruined" by men and cast out by society. The socially rejected girls were then forced to work as prostitutes for their livelihood.[61] They explicitly blame the "monopolies – the rich who are continually oppressing the poor and making it almost impossible for a poor man or woman to earn an honest living."[62] Furthermore, they did not believe the Protestant presence in Chicago was willing to do much about the plight of the prostitute as they stated that the 605 Protestant churches in the city were "grouped in the wealthier regions" leaving over a million poor unreached.[63]

A pivotal movement for the missionaries happened in the autumn of 1903. While holding a revival meeting on the street, they heard the shouts and protests of a band of men who were advocating for social reform through the changing of laws.   The men were calling for the passage of laws to abolish poverty, but how would this happen? The missionaries were very suspicious about the efficaciousness of the government in bringing about moral change, as it had failed to meet the needs of the poor. Furthermore, they had grown impatient with a legal system that saw the obvious cause of vice (alcohol) and refused to do anything about it.[64]

Their realization that the government would not abolish the saloon led the missionaries to critique the notion that America was a Christian nation. Hence, when admonishing their readers to vote the prohibition ticket, they state, "This Christian(?) nation, instead of legislating in favor of the poor, is licensing

---

[59] "Who is to Blame?" *The Olive Branch Newspaper*, 1895, Volume 2, No. 11, pg. 2. "For Mother's Sake," *The Olive Branch Newspaper*, 1900, Volume 6, No. 7, pg. 4.

[60] Rees, 165-166.

[61] "Who is to Blame?" *The Olive Branch Newspaper*, 1895, Volume 2, No. 11, pg. 2.

[62] "Who is Responsible?" *The Olive Branch Newspaper*, 1848, Volume 4, No. 8, pg. 2.

[63] "Startling Facts," *The Olive Branch Newspaper*, 1900, Volume 6, No. 11, pg. 1.

[64] "In Favor of the Poor," *The Olive Branch Newspaper*, 1903, Volume 9, No. 3, pgs. 2-3.

and protecting this most infamous cause of poverty and crime – the saloon."[65] The phrase "Christian(?) nation" appears throughout the publication for the entire nineteenth and early part of the twentieth century. These urban missionaries did not hold stock in the idea of a Christian nation for their immediate context looked like anything but a Christian society. The ideals of the Christian nation were based on the prosperity of its people, yet the Olive Branch missionaries rejected any sort of material and financial gain as evidence of true Christianity.[66]

The missionaries not only criticized particular notions, they, like the Rest Cottage missionaries, engaged in revivals both inside and outside of their mission. There was a strong emphasis put on entire sanctification as well as conversion. Their belief was that while conversion saved the soul of a person, entire sanctification enabled them to rise out of their lives of sin.[67] Their employment of revival work within the city was a direct result of their rural upbringing. Yet their revival services were, to one observer, more effective, "I have attended revival services for thirty-five years, but have never seen clearer witnesses to both experiences- justification and sanctification-that some who have been saved in this mission."[68]

The newspaper functioned as a bridge between the rural communities and the urban missionaries. There were numerous calls to partner in the task of reaching the poor. The call was not of condemnation for not taking part in the mission. But many implicitly stated that while people comfortably sat in their country homes, the Olive Branch Mission was functioning in the direst slums in the Midwest.[69] The calls for help were often unapologetic in that they were asking people to sacrifice their comfortable lifestyles for the sake of others, "*Throw open your coffers! Distribute your store!*"[70] cried one poem. Such a call for personal redistribution was not uncommon. Nor was it uncommon for the missionaries to ask for goods instead of money because they knew their readers were not rich financial, but could often spare crop and clothes. Mary Everhart made it a point to travel to the various summer camp meetings in order to raise awareness, funds, and material goods for the mission. She called for the people to be "self-sacrificing pilgrims" and to share their "earthly store" with the slum residents.[71]

---

[65] Ibid.

[66] Rees held very similar views. He believe that the alcohol export business was ruining other countries and questioned how a "so called Christian Nation" could endorse such business ventures, 26-27.

[67] *The Olive Branch Newspaper*, 1894, Volume 1, No. 3, pg. 1.

[68] *The Olive Branch Newspaper*, 1894, Volume 1, No. 1, pg. 4. And *The Olive Branch Newspaper*, 1894, Volume 1, No. 8, pg. 2.

[69] Phebe C. Proper, "My Visit to the Mission," *The Olive Branch Newspaper*, 1898, Volume 4, No. 4, pg. 2.

[70] N.B. Ghormley, "Down in the Slums," *The Olive Branch Newspaper*, 1900, Volume 6, No. 6, pg 1.

[71] Mary Everhart, "A Trip East," *The Olive Branch Newspaper*, 1898, Volume 4, No. 1, pg. 1.

The connection between city and country was reciprocal. Both the Olive Branch Mission and the Rest Cottage Mission expanded their missions outside of the city. The Olive Branch Mission opened up a homeless shelter in Flint, Michigan in the early twentieth century and expanded globally (to Africa) at the end of the twentieth century. The Rest Cottage Mission opened up homes in Ashville and Greensborough, North Carolina as well as Pilot Point, Texas around 1900.

Conclusion

The two sketches of Holiness urban missions provide a different understanding of urban Christian communities in the Progressive Era. Certainly there are similarities between the lower class Holiness missions and the missions of the middle and upper classes. Yet the role of social holiness theology is very strong in the ethos of the former. The critique of material wealth and prosperity were at the heart of the Olive Branch Mission and the Rest Cottage Mission. The ideals of a prosperous Christian nation were rejected and the ecclesial upper class was demonized for their ineffective ministries toward the poor. Instead of seeking to control the lower classes the missionaries fought against the established vices of society and upper class ecclesial structures, while preaching to the poor among whom they lived. The street revivals and the revivals within the missions provided a call to the masses for salvation and a call to seek that which could guard against personal and systemic sin, entire sanctification.

Chapter 5

The Evolution of Social Ministry in The Salvation Army

Roger J. Green

I. Introduction

The Salvation Army was founded in East London in 1865 by William Booth.[1] Booth, born in Nottingham, England on April 10, 1829 was baptized in the local Anglican Church, but his family did not have much to do with the institutional Church. Booth was taken to the local Methodist Church in his teen years, and there he had a conversion experience and dedicated his life to God. After the death of his father he was responsible for the household, which included his mother and his three sisters. He worked as a pawnbroker's assistant, and at the age of 19 he continued that work after moving to London. He also worked as a lay preacher within Methodism.

In London he met and married Catherine Mumford, a lifelong Methodist.[2] Booth was ordained as a New Connexion Methodist preacher in 1858, but resigned from New Connexion Methodism after three years of service in two Methodist parishes. He wanted to be a travelling evangelist but the leadership of the movement insisted that he should limit his work to local parish ministry. By the time of his resignation Catherine Booth had begun preaching. In 1861, the Booths launched into an independent revivalistic ministry that lasted four years, finally taking them to London so that Catherine could fulfill a preaching responsibility while living with her aging parents.

That move proved to be providential. Booth found himself preaching in East London, and on July 2, 1865 he founded what would become known as The Christian Mission. That mission evolved into The Salvation Army in 1878.

---

[1] There are several biographies of William Booth, and some of them will be referred to in this chapter. The most recent one is Roger J. Green, *The Life and Ministry of William Booth: Founder of The Salvation Army* (Nashville TN: Abingdon Press, 2005).

[2] See Roger J. Green, *Catherine Booth: A Biography of the Cofounder of The Salvation Army* (Grand Rapids, MI: Baker Books, 1996).

II. Social Ministry in the Christian Mission

The Christian Mission, and other newly opened Christian Mission stations, tried to meet human need as much as possible. But no organized, centrally controlled ministry to the poor was undertaken in those days except for one. In 1870 Booth began a Food-for-the-Millions program that was intended to operate in all Christian Mission stations. Bramwell Booth, the eldest of eight of Booth's children, was put in charge of the program. He was assisted by James Flawn, a convert in The Christian Mission, who had worked in the food business.[3]

That program was initiated by Booth to provide nourishing food to the poor at little expense to them, although to preserve the dignity of the poor he felt that they should pay what they were able. The Food-for-the-Millions program was closed by Booth in 1874 and turned over to the Charity Organization Society. Booth felt that he had neither the finances nor the personnel to continue the program.

What moved William and Catherine Booth as they surveyed Whitechapel Road in East London was that men and women were living in rebellion against God. They were sinners who needed to be saved, and the preaching of both Booths called sinners to repentance and raised up saints in the way intended by God. Once The Christian Mission was established, its mission stations were called preaching stations, and by this name the central mission of each station was underscored. This emphasis was continued after the founding of The Salvation Army in 1878. The Booths were not unsympathetic to the physical plight of people, but that aspect of ministry had to give way initially to the ministry of preaching.

III. The Christian Mission Evolves into The Salvation Army

In explaining the change from The Christian Mission to The Salvation Army, Booth affirmed this single mission,

> We are a Salvation people—this is our speciality [sic]—getting saved and keeping saved, and then getting somebody else saved, and then getting saved ourselves more and more, until full salvation on earth makes the heaven within, which is finally perfected by the full salvation without, on the other side of the river... My brethren, my comrades, soul saving is our avocation, the great purpose and

---

[3] See the first chapter of Jenty Fairbank, *Booth's Boots: The Beginnings of Salvation Army Social Work* (London, England: International Headquarters of The Salvation Army, 1983).

business of our lives. Let us seek first the kingdom of God, let us be SALVATIONISTS indeed.[4]

In defining the work of The Salvation Army to the Wesleyan Conference in August of 1880, Booth stated that, "We go on the three broad lines of Repentance, Faith, and Holiness of Heart."[5] One would search in vain in this entire address in which he set forth the principles of The Salvation Army, and many similar addresses during this period, to find any references to soup kitchens or lodging houses, let alone any biblical or theological justification for the extended ministry of social salvation. Booth and his Salvation Army were still involved in the single mission of converting sinners. That, it was thought, was the highest service that could be rendered to the poor. "This impulse was purely evangelical; it did not become what is called humanitarian or economic till ten years later. At its beginning, The Salvation Army was a society of men and women which existed only to preach the repentance of sins."[6]

However, others in the movement began to recognize the complexity of their ministry, and there dawned an awareness in some of Booth's officers and soldiers that it was not enough to preach the gospel to the poor, but that preaching had to be complemented by taking care of the physical needs of the poor. The organized social ministry of The Salvation Army did not begin at the initiation of Booth in East London, but with Salvationists in Melbourne, Australia with the establishment of a halfway home for released prisoners.[7] This center was opened on December 8, 1883 as a kind of loving Christian response to the brutal transportation of the "criminal class" from England to Australia to empty English prisons of all those unwanted citizens. "In their most sanguine moments, the authorities hoped that it would eventually swallow up a whole class—the 'criminal class,' whose existence was one of the prime sociological beliefs of late Georgian and early Victorian England. Australia was settled to defend English property not from the frog-eating invader across the Channel but from the marauder within. English lawmakers wished not only to get rid of the 'criminal class' but if possible to forget about it."[8]

There is little wonder that the compassion of these English Salvationists toward their countrymen was manifested in this practical way. "Within four

---

[4] William Booth, "Our New Name," *The Salvationist* (January 1879), 1.

[5] William Booth, "The General's Address at the Wesleyan Conference," *The War Cry* 1 (August 1880), p. 1.

[6] Harold Begbie, *The Life of General William Booth, the Founder of The Salvation Army* (New York: The Macmillan Company, 1920, 2 Vols.), 1:434.

[7] Previous to this, in May of that year, a rescue home for women was opened in Glasgow, Scotland, but that home was evidently closed by March of 1884. Therefore, it is Australia that holds the distinction of beginning the sustained organized social work of The Salvation Army.

[8] Robert Hughes, *The Fatal Shore: the Epic of Australia's Founding* (New York: Vintage books, 1988), 1.

years five such centres had been set up in the state capital, and Booth dispatched an officer from England to Australia to study how this development could be applied to the home base."⁹

It was not until 1884 that social work began in an organized fashion in Booth's backyard. A rescue home for prostitutes was opened on Hanbury Street, Whitechapel, at the instigation of Mrs. Cottrill, a soldier at the Army's Whitechapel corps (church). The Purity Crusade and the Criminal Law Amendment Act came in 1885 as a result of that ministry. In the meantime, various officers and soldiers continued to involve themselves in diverse aspects of social ministry. In Toronto, Canada in 1886 the Army opened the first institution to give attention to alcoholic women, and in 1887 there was the opening of a day care center in one of the "slum posts" of London so that working mothers could be relieved of the responsibility of their children.¹⁰

The crippling dock strike in 1889 "tested the faith of settlers and Salvationists who responded with sympathy, enthusiasm and practical aid."¹¹ A food and shelter center for the homeless was established in the West India Dock Road. In 1889 a women's shelter was opened on Hanbury Street, and on June 29, 1890 The Salvation Army opened the first "Elevator," a "sheltered workshop" for men.

However, until 1889 Booth was still making few public pronouncements about these social operations. He was pleased with the initiative that his people were showing in taking care of the needs of the people in response to the commandment of Jesus to love God and neighbor. But his theology still reflected only a single purpose for his Army: that of winning souls. A typical article of Booth's is found in *The War Cry* of January 1887. After a thirteen-week journey of 16,000 miles, he wrote, "I have come back with the impression that the need of the world is bigger than ever I thought it was, and I have also come back with the impression that The Salvation Army is equal to it, if The Salvation Army will only do its duty."¹² In the entire article Booth made no reference to a second mission, to social salvation or to social work. His references were only to the soul-saving mission of The Salvation Army and to spiritual redemption.

The magnitude of the social problems that The Salvation Army was addressing in Great Britain came to sharp focus during the middle 1880s. Booth's sensitivity to the poor, to whom he had been preaching for many years, was heightened through the experiences of his Army. A severe economic depression had taken its toll in England, and the effects of that depression manifested themselves in the places where Booth's Army was at work, "1873 being the date

---

⁹ Frederick Coutts, *Bread for my Neighbour: The Social Influence of William Booth* (London: Hodder and Stoughton, 1978), 38.

¹⁰ See Fairbank, *Booth's Boots*, 59.

¹¹ H. J. Dyos and Michael Wolff, eds. *The Victorian City*, 2 Vols. (London: Routledge and Kegan Paul, 1973), 2:595.

¹² William Booth, "The General's Address," *The War Cry* 8 (January 1887), 9.

normally given for the beginning of the 'great depression' and 1874 as the beginning of the nineteenth century disaster to British agriculture."[13]

A one-volume analysis of poverty, homelessness, unemployment and religion in East London originally entitled *Life and Labour of the People* was written by Charles Booth (no relation to William Booth) in 1889, and was eventually expanded into the seventeen-volume work entitled *Life and Labour of the People in London*.[14] But the first volume was published before Booth published his *In Darkest England and the Way Out*,[15] and so William made use of Charles Booth's work, and was disturbed by the plight of the people with whom the Army and he had been working and to whom the gospel had been preached. There is no question that "Booth wrote *In Darkest England* against a background of both social unrest and growing political concern."[16] Hattersley has written the following,

> In the previous year, the London dockers had struck for a standard wage of sixpence an hour and, after a month of picketing and protest, won. Public opinion—at least the increasingly educated and articulate working classes—was on their side. The dockers—casual labourers who reported for work each day, but worked at best for three, had once been the powerless poor. But, although they remained amongst the worst paid of British workers, by 1889 they were powerful enough to defeat the increasingly prosperous dock owners. Part of their success was due to the energy and ability of their leader, Ben Tillet. But Tom Mann and John Burns guaranteed the dockers' success by bringing out the engineers 'in sympathy.' Victory for organized labour was, in itself, frightening enough for the political establishment. But building on the experience of the dock strike Tillet, Burns and Mann began to organize unskilled workers. The result was the powerful force of New Unionism. And it was created by men who might—had their inclination not been for politics—have marched with the Salvation Army. Tillet was brought up a Methodist. Mann and Burns were campaigners for total abstinence from drink. Their great victory was won on the battlefield of London's East End where William Booth had first taken up arms against the devil. New Unionism and the Salvation Army were for the poor and of the poor.[17]

Finally it was decided that an office be created to coordinate the social reform operations of The Salvation Army. Therefore, by 1890 the tentative efforts of The Salvation Army at social reform were placed under the office of

---

[13] G. Kitson Clark, *The Making of Victorian England* (Cambridge, Massachusetts: Harvard University Press, 1962), 32.

[14] The best and most comprehensive introduction to Charles Booth's work is Albert Fried and Richard M. Elman, eds., *Charles Booth's London: A Portrait of the Poor at the Turn of the Century, Drawn from His "Life and Labour of the People in London"* (New York: Random House, Inc., 1968).

[15] William Booth, *In Darkest England and the Way Out* (London: Funk and Wagnalls, 1890).

[16] Roy Hattersley, *Blood and Fire: William and Catherine Booth and Their Salvation Army* (New York: Doubleday, 2000), 353.

[17] Ibid.

what became known as the Social Reform Wing of The Salvation Army, commanded by Commissioner Frank Smith.[18] Smith played a significant part in moving General Booth's sympathies in the direction of social ministry. And a "Darkest England" Trust Deed was executed on January 30, 1891 in a public meeting in St. James' Hall, London.[19] To answer critics of the Darkest England Scheme that the money was misused, a Committee of Inquiry was established and a report was issued on December 19, 1892, completely exonerating the Army and its General. Booth had always been very careful to give an accurate account of funds given to The Christian Mission and The Salvation Army.

IV. War on Two Fronts: The Salvation Army and Social Ministry

With the establishment of the Social Reform Wing, The Salvation Army entered into a new stage of its ministry under the direction of its General, which one biographer has characterized as "an immense change in the direction of the Army."[20] Booth and his Army finally recognized institutionally the importance of the second mission that had gradually gained acceptance. Between 1889 and 1890 the commitment to social salvation became fixed. The timing was significant in the history of The Salvation Army. Hitherto its chief concern had been for personal salvation from sin, and social concerns were secondary, but increasing in importance. Now, however, the movement was engaged in two works—personal salvation and social salvation. It now had, as has been mentioned, a dual mission. There is little evidence to substantiate John Kent's statement that "*Darkest England* appeared when the original religious basis of the Army was proving too weak to sustain the initial success."[21] In fact, the opposite is true, *Darkest England* was written precisely because of the success and strength of The Salvation Army in many places in the world and because

---

[18] I am indebted to Kenneth G. Hodder, now a commissioner in The Salvation Army, for sharing his research on Frank Smith with me, research that he conducted while he was a student at Harvard University. The title of his research paper is "Report and Catalogue for Materials Obtained During Research on Frank Smith, M.P. and the B. B. C. Recording Archives" (September 1, 1978). See also E.I. Champness, *Frank Smith, M.P.: Pioneer and Modern Mystic* (London: The Whitefriars Press, Ltd., 1943). Smith resigned from the Army and channeled his energies into politics and journalism.

[19] See *The Darkest England Social Scheme: A Brief Review of the First Year's Work* (London: International Headquarters, 1891), 158. When the deed was publicly executed it was stated that "A copy of the Trust Deed will be sent free to any person who may desire to obtain it," 158.

[20] St. John Ervine, *God's Soldier: General William Booth*, 2 Vols. (New York: The Macmillan Company, 1935), 2:628.

[21] John Kent, *Holding the Fort: Studies in Victorian Revivalism* (London: Epworth Press, 1978), 335.

Booth had developed a biblical and theological justification for his growing work.

The surest public expression of this mission came from Booth himself. In October of 1890 he published *In Darkest England*, in which he gave theological expression to the necessity of social salvation in which The Salvation Army had already been engaged. However, the question needs to be asked: why did the transition take place, and why was Booth ready to focus his enlarged vision of salvation as a double mission. Indeed, W.T. Stead himself, who used his journalistic skills to assist Booth in the writing of *In Darkest England*, stated the following in *The Star* on January 2, 1891: "Everyone knows perfectly well that two years ago, nay, even one year ago, General Booth did not see his way to the utilization of The Salvation Army as an instrument of social reform."[22] Stead had intimate knowledge of *In Darkest England* because Booth asked Stead "if I could get him a literary hack who could lick his material into shape, and get the book out in time. I said, 'I will do your hack-work myself,' and I did. I was very proud to do it."[23]

There are many possible answers to this question, and many factors, both personal and institutional, coalesced at this time and gave rise to an expanded ministry. The first has already been noted, but bears repeating. Booth, himself reared in poverty, demonstrated social sensitivity toward the poor and needy in Nottingham, in Whitechapel Road, and in the ministry of The Salvation Army. However, at one time these social concerns were fleeting compared with the concern for the personal conversion of men and women. Experience, both personal and institutional, had heightened his sensitivities about people's physical impoverishment. He wanted to help the poor.

This heightened sensitivity was shared by many who had joined Booth's Army, and culminated in the 1880s through their continual exposure to the stark realities of depressed urban life in London and in other parts of the world. The experience gained by Booth and his Social Reform Wing, especially in the context of a great depression in England in the 1880s, caused them to come to grips with the fact that people were not interested in an escapist gospel, but welcomed a gospel that sustained them physically as well as spiritually. Stead himself noted that the experience gained by the Social Wing of The Salvation Army "encouraged the General to take a decided step in advance."[24] As

---

[22] W.T. Stead, "Letter from W.T. Stead regarding authorship of 'In Darkest England,'" *The Star*, January 2, 1891.

[23] "'In Darkest England' Entirely the General's Own," *The War Cry* (January 10, 1891), p. 7. In his biography of Catherine Booth, Stead wrote that he helped Booth "as a kind of voluntary secretary and amanuensis in getting the MSS of 'Darkest England' into shape." W.T. Stead, *Mrs. Booth of The Salvation Army* (London: James Nisbet & Co., Limited, 1900), 211.

[24] Ibid. An essay in The *Victorian City* noted that during the 1889 London dock strike, "Support from institution representatives such as Canon Barnett, Stewart Headlam, William Booth, and Cardinal Manning served both to give a sense of direction to public feeling, and to consolidate the positions of the institutions on the

has been mentioned, this was especially true in 1889 during the London Dock Strike, a devastating strike to the dockers and their families. Thousands of people were out of work and seeking food and shelter for their families.[25]

Second, Booth certainly recognized that virtually hundreds of other people and organizations were engaged in social work. Much of the work in England was under the auspices of an agency known as the Charity Organization Society, founded in 1867. The Charity Organization Society consequently saw no need for the Army's social ministry, and often opposed it, probably because, in Bennett's words, "Booth had valued his independence too much to become part of it, so there existed a degree of tension between the two organizations."[26] The work, so claimed the Charity Organization Society, was already being done. However, if the reports of Charles Booth were accurate, the work was inadequate and certainly having no lasting results, especially in the area of serious unemployment and its attendant problems. "The General was never good in acknowledging the work of others."[27] The basic problem was not that there was no charity toward the poor taking place at that time, but that there was too much of sentimental charity with no lasting results. In speaking specifically about Catherine Booth in this regard, Barbara Robinson wrote,

> In 1884, Catherine Booth delivered the sermon, "Sham Compassion and the Dying Love of Christ," a succinct critique of trends in late nineteenth-century social policy and philanthropy. It must be acknowledged that the social context she addressed was very different from the one faced by John Wesley. While Wesley sought to overcome widespread indifference to the plight of the poor, Catherine believed that Victorian charitable intervention had run wild. She was reacting to the late-nineteenth century proliferation of charities—a flood of what she termed "schemes without a Savior" or "religions of bodily compassion" which ignored serious soul-need. She ardently believed that much of the Christian activism of the period would only result in "a more eternal weight of misery at the cost of little present relief.[28]

East End" (2:595). In his essay on William Booth in the *Dictionary of National Biography, 1912-1921,* Harold Begbie wrote the following: "Deeper acquaintance with the problem he was so compulsively attacking led him to become a social reformer" ("Booth, William [1829-1912]," 52).

[25] See "Mrs. Bramwell Booth with the Dockers' Wives and Children," *The War Cry* (September 11, 1889), 7; "The Salvation Army and the Strike," *The War Cry* (September 28, 1889), 2; "Ramblings in the East End," *The War Cry* (November 2, 1889), 2; and "'272' Becomes Food and Shelter Headquarters," *The War Cry* (November 9, 1889), 7.

[26] David Malcolm Bennett, *The General: William Booth*, 2 Vols. (Camarillo, CA: Xulon Press, 2003) 2:300.

[27] Ibid., 2:309.

[28] Barbara Robinson, "The Wesleyan Foundation of Salvation Army Social Work and Action," *Word & Deed: A Journal of Salvation Army Theology and Ministry* 7:1 (November 2004), 38-39.

Booth echoed Catherine's critique and, convinced that he was now ready to improve on the work being done, offered the following criticism,

> And yet all the way through my career I have keenly felt the remedial measures usually enunciated in Christian programmes and ordinarily employed by Christian philanthropy, to be lamentably inadequate for any effectual dealing with the despairing miseries of these outcast classes. The rescued are appallingly few—a ghastly minority compared with the multitudes who struggle and sink in the open-mouthed abyss. Alike, therefore, my humanity and my Christianity, if I may speak of them in any way as separate from one another, have cried out for some more comprehensive method of reaching and saving the perishing crowds.[29]

Third, Booth perceived that much of the Church was unwilling to enter into a second mission in spite of the glaring needs of the people. Booth was convinced, "and with good reason, that the respectable churches—both Anglican and Nonconformist—would not reach out to offer either spiritual or material comfort to the undeserving poor."[30] Andrew Mearns, a Congregational minister, had published his book entitled, *The Bitter Cry of Outcast London*[31] as recently as 1883. That book "stirred up the public conscience as no other work had. It was a devastating indictment of the failure of churches to respond to the needs of the poor in any way other than to build churches and chapels and offer limited aid."[32]

And so by 1890 Booth, convinced that it was theologically correct to address social redemption systematically, was willing to commit himself and his Army in a way that he wished for the Church. He was at times critical of the Church for not understanding either the necessity or the nature of social redemption. "Why all this apparatus of temples and meeting-houses to save men from perdition in a world which is to come, while never a helping hand is stretched out to save them from the inferno of their present life?"[33]

This theological foundation was based on the great commandment of Jesus to love one's neighbor, a theological text that Booth referred to often in his

---

[29] Booth, *In Darkest England*, 2.

[30] Hattersley, *Blood and Fire*, 377.

[31] Andrew Mearns, *The Bitter Cry of Outcast London: an Inquiry into the Condition of the Abject Poor* (London: James Clark & Co.).

[32] Tim Macquiban, "Soup and Salvation: Social Service as an Emerging Motif for the British Methodist Response to Poverty in the Late Nineteenth Century," *Methodist History* 39:1 (October 2000), 32.

[33] Booth, *In Darkest England*, 16.

later ministry.[34] However, this foundation was not only biblical but also Wesleyan.[35] The Wesleyan theological option for the poor found expression in Booth's social ministry.

> There exist many parallels in the Army to the radical side of Methodist preaching. Booth remarks in his book *In Darkest England and the Way Out* that 'The Scheme of Social Salvation is not worth discussing which is not as wide as the Scheme of Eternal Salvation set forth in the Gospel. The Glad Tidings must be to every creature, not merely to an elect few who are to be saved... It is now time to fling down the false idol, and proclaim a Temporal Salvation as full, free and universal, and with no other limitations than the 'Whosoever will' of the Gospel.' Here one finds many of the Wesleyan themes of a personal 'gospel egalitarianism' overflowing into a social vision for the poor, though perhaps not with the same theological sophistication but with the same anti-Calvinistic polemic.[36]

Fourth, the authoritarian structure of the Army was important to Booth in spite of the growing democratic impulses of the nineteenth century, and was well in place and functioning by 1889-1890. Booth maintained that the structure was important for the second mission, believing that his organization was best suited for redemption in two worlds. The dual redemptive mission of The Salvation Army would succeed through proper leadership and management where other less authoritarian enterprises had failed. He wrote that "so far from resenting the exercise of authority, The Salvation Army rejoices to recognize it as one great secret of its success, a pillar of strength upon which all its soldiers can rely, a principle which stamps it as being different from all other religious organizations founded in our day."[37]

A final reason why Booth was now ready to enter into this second mission revolved around the changing influential persons in his life and ministry. Two of the most significant persons in Booth's life up to this point were Catherine

---

[34] One of the best expressions of the Army's social ministry being a reflection of the command of Jesus is found in a letter from William Booth to Bramwell Booth written on January 10, 1903. However, even with this biblical justification William still raises the question, "As to whether we get as much real benefit out of the time and labor and ability bestowed upon feeding the poor as we should do if spent in purely spiritual work is a very difficult question to answer," 2. See The William Booth File, The Salvation Army International Heritage Centre, London, England. See also the letter from William Booth to Bramwell Booth, April 19, 1911 in the William Booth File, The Salvation Army International Heritage Centre, London, England.

[35] See Donald Burke, "The Wesleyan View of Salvation and Social Involvement," 11-32 in John D. Waldron, ed., *Creed and Deed: Toward a Christian Theology of Social Services in The Salvation Army* (Toronto: The Salvation Army, 1986).

[36] Donald W. Dayton, "'Good News to the Poor': The Methodist Experience After Wesley," in M. Douglas Meeks, editor, *The Portion of the Poor: Good News to the Poor in the Wesleyan Tradition* (Nashville, TN: Kingswood Books, 1995), 87-88.

[37] Ibid., 243.

Booth and George Scott Railton, a Wesleyan who joined The Christian Mission in 1872 and who helped shape the theology of the Mission and the early Army.[38] Both were adamant that the primary work of the ministry of The Christian Mission and The Salvation Army was the conversion of sinners and the raising up of saints. However, Catherine Booth died in 1890 and there was a diminishing influence of Railton due to his continuing lack of sympathy with the growing social emphasis of The Salvation Army, climaxing with his protestations in 1894 of the launching of a Salvation Army Assurance Society.[39] There is no doubt that Railton "feared that the new departure would detract from the Army's work in winning people to Christ. It proved to be another step in his increasing isolation from the rest of the Army hierarchy."[40] Railton at this time was a tireless evangelist, travelling the world for the Army. In that capacity, he was, however, far removed from Booth and the organizational and administrative development of the Army in London.

Catherine Booth had been ill for quite some time previous to 1890, and she died (was promoted to glory) on October 4, 1890. Her influence in the Army was chiefly in the realm of encouraging the officers and soldiers, and preaching and teaching such doctrines of holiness and the role of women in ministry. This is not to say that she did not have some sympathy with the second mission, as her involvement in the Purity Crusade in 1885 amply testifies. Booth consulted her on the writing of *In Darkest England*, and dedicated the book to her. However, it remains a moot question of precisely how critical Catherine Booth would have been of the new direction of redemption once she saw it fully inaugurated. In his biography of Catherine Booth, Stead, himself one who influenced Booth in this new direction, quoted from a letter that Catherine Booth had written to him: "Praise up humanitarianism as much as you like, but don't confound it with Christianity, nor suppose that it will ultimately

---

[38] See Bernard Watson, *Soldier Saint* (London: Hodder and Stoughton, 1970).

[39] See Ibid, especially chapter 17. In an undated letter from Bramwell Booth to Railton, Bramwell wrote, "When you say that you object to the 'placing of the Salvation work second to the Social' you only say what we all say" (p. 3). However, he then reprimands Railton for suggesting that even in the General's public meetings, the General makes the social more important than the spiritual. See the Bramwell Booth File, The Salvation Army International Heritage Centre, London, England. On July 9, 1894 ten senior officers in The Salvation Army addressed a letter to "My Dear General" disagreeing with Railton's actions, recommending that some disciplinary action be taken against Railton, but allowing for the fact that "we cannot but think that Commissioner Railton would never have so acted, but for the physical and mental strain from which he is evidently suffering," and suggested that "you should order the Commissioner upon a lengthened furlough before coming to any final decision as to the future." The George Scott Railton File, The Salvation Army International Heritage Centre, London, England. It was inconceivable to these leaders that any disagreement with the Booth hierarchy, even that made by so faithful a follower as George Scott Railton, could be made apart from physical and mental strain.

[40] Bennett, *The General: William Booth*, 2:306.

lead its followers to Christ."⁴¹ One author has rightly noted that Catherine's "Wesleyan creed rested on the doctrine of human depravity. Soup and soap were, at best, ancillary to soul saving. Had she lived longer, she might have shared others' concerns about the gap between the army's spiritual and its social work."⁴²

Those closest to Booth in the development of the Darkest England Scheme were Bramwell Booth, Stead, and Smith. Bramwell Booth, the eldest son and Chief of the Staff, had long been convinced of the necessity of social ministries, but was cautious about the relationship of that ministry to the more overtly religious work of the Army.⁴³ Stead was the journalist whose sympathies were for the betterment of society by any possible means, not the least of which was the work of the Army, and he assisted Booth with the writing of *In Darkest England*. He protested, however, that the book was primarily Booth's own work, but Booth needed an editor. Stead, who left *The Pall Mall Gazette* to begin the *Review of Reviews* was a natural choice, even though Booth did not always agree with Stead. "He tolerated the editor and used him, but he did not like him, and certainly would not have trusted him to have a free hand at writing a book that was always going to result in significant changes to The Salvation Army."⁴⁴

Finally there was Frank Smith. "More than anyone, Frank Smith got Booth to champion the lot of the poor after 1887. Under Smith's tutelage, Booth adopted ideas from Henry George, Arnold White, H. Rider Haggard, Sidney and Beatrice Webb and others. . . .Smith filled Booth's ears with social reform and used *War Cry* reports to represent his own social views as Booth's."⁴⁵

However, Smith had other loyalties, and his political involvement and socialistic sympathies eventually caused him to leave the Army, but not before his significant influence in the Darkest England Scheme. Apart from Bramwell Booth, Stead, and Smith, there were others who may have influenced Booth

---

⁴¹ Stead, *Mrs. Booth of The Salvation Army*, 208.

⁴² Norman H. Murdoch, *Origins of The Salvation Army* (Knoxville, TN: The University of Tennessee Press, 1994), 165.

⁴³ Bramwell Booth's most poignant remarks about the Darkest England Scheme came in a newspaper interview after he became General upon the death of his father. See the *Daily News and Leader* (October 1912), 1.

⁴⁴ Bennett, *The General: William Booth*, 2:316. Booth did thank Stead in the preface to *In Darkest England*, although even that acknowledgment was a bit backhanded in that he did not mention Stead by name, and made it clear to the reader that this man was "not in any way connected with The Salvation Army."

⁴⁵ Murdoch, *Origins of The Salvation Army*,152-153. For some examples of Smith's writing see Frank Smith, "Salvation Socialism," *The War Cry* (December 25, 1889), 17-24; Frank Smith, "The Battle-Cry of the Social Reform Wing," *All The World* (August, 1890), 355-358; Frank Smith, "A Look at the 'Wing,'" *All The World* (October 1890), 510-513; and Frank Smith, "Wanted, Samaritans!" *All The World* (December 1890), 620-623.

with the writing of *In Darkest England*, but these three were the most important shapers of this new direction in ministry.[46]

By 1890 The Salvation Army was well launched on a second mission. It was now a movement that was committed to both spiritual and social redemption, and Booth's theology from this time forward reflected this dual mission. His public pronouncements attempted to maintain the tension of the dual mission. This developed theology of redemption still included personal salvation from sin for the individual who believes by faith. However, now Booth embraced a theology of redemption that included social salvation from the evils that beset people in this life. And just as there was the possibility of universal spiritual redemption in Booth's theology, reflecting his Wesleyan theology, so there was the possibility of universal social redemption, reflecting his postmillennial vision for the salvation of the world before the return of Christ.

V. "Salvation for Both Worlds" and *In Darkest England and the Way Out*

Booth was nothing if not a military strategist for God. He knew that before launching this new ministry publicly, he had to bring his own people into line with his enlarged theological vision, and knew that it would not be possible to win the hearts and minds of all his soldiers and officers on this issue. Many like Railton and perhaps even Catherine would still hold that the salvation of the soul is the surest way to bring about social redemption. However, as part of his strategic plan Booth wrote one of his most important articles in 1889 appropriately entitled "Salvation for Both Worlds" published in *All the World* in January of 1889. In that article he explained that he had always been aware of the physical impoverishment of the people to whom he had preached, having experienced poverty himself. He nevertheless saw no remedy for such poverty and so was determined to save people's souls even if he could not help them in this world.

However, he noted that his own and his people's experience had taught him "that the miseries from which I sought to save man in the next world were substantially the same as those from which I everywhere found him suffering in this."[47] And Booth concluded that he now had two gospels to preach—a gospel

---

[46] In his *Origins of The Salvation Army* Murdoch mentioned that Susie Forrest Smith, an American and a Vassar graduate who became a Salvation Army officer in 1889,"claims to have assisted with the writing of *In Darkest England and the Way Out* in 1890" but her claim has proved impossible to support from other writings, 159. She did write an analysis of the Darkest England Scheme in 1891, which the British Library has erroneously attributed to her sister, Elizabeth Reeves Swift. See *The Darkest England Social Scheme: A Brief Review of the First Year's Work* (London: International Headquarters, 1891).

[47] William Booth, "Salvation for Both Worlds," *All the World* 5 (January 1889), 2. Several of the articles mentioned in this chapter may be found in full text in Andrew

of redemption from personal sin and a gospel of redemption from social evil. He broadened his theological language to take into account his developed theology. He added new meaning and a new dimension to the redemptive theological language that he had been expressing for years. Salvation now had social obligations and dimensions as well as spiritual ones.

Ten months after writing "Salvation for Both Worlds," designed obviously to prepare his own people for a personal and institutional allegiance and commitment to a double mission, Booth began writing *In Darkest England*. Booth's Army had already demonstrated in many parts of the world both a willingness and a capacity to enter into social ministries. Booth was convinced of the theological justification of both personal and social salvation, and with the writing of this book he was now ready to commit his Salvation Army to war on two fronts. He wrote *In Darkest England* to explain his developed theology and thereby explain the evolution that had taken place in his own thinking and in the mission of the Army, which was increasingly placing itself in the public eye. And the date of the publication, October of 1890, was a critical date in the theology of Booth because it most clearly represents not only his broadened theological vision of redemption, but also his desire and his willingness to act in a way that was consistent with his own theology.

In Darkest England was Booth's most extensive work and proved to be his most widely read work, read not only by Salvationists but also by the general public for whom it was intended. Booth and Stead were wise in capturing the public imagination that was already enthralled with Stanley's bestseller, *In Darkest Africa*. "Booth always had a good eye and ear for a catchy title or tune, particularly if it was popular, and he borrowed and adapted this one for his own purposes."[48] Once Booth's book was published it did not escape notice and certainly did not escape criticism. Booth had his critics, many of them caustic and some vitriolic. He also had his share of defenders. "As Canon Dwyer pointed out, all of England became divided into Boothites and Anti-Boothites. Among Booth's sympathizers were Cardinal Manning, Archdeacon Farrer, Sir E. Clark (the Solicitor-General), and the Marquis of Queensbury; among his critics, Thomas Huxley[49], C.S. Loch (Secretary of the Charity Organization Society), Bernard Bosanquet, and Canon Dwyer. But even a critic like Dwyer had

---

M. Eason and Roger J. Green, eds., *Boundless Salvation: The Shorter Writings of William Booth* (New York: Peter Lang, Publishing, Inc., 2012). This book was written in honor of the hundredth anniversary of William Booth's death (promotion to glory) in 1912.

[48] Bennett, *The General: William Booth*, 291-292.

[49] For an excellent analysis of T. H. Huxley's attack upon Booth and his Darkest England Scheme see R. G. Moyles', Essay Six, "*The Times* of London, T. H. Huxley, and Booth's Social Panacea," 117-136 in R. G. Moyles *The Salvation Army and the Public* (Edmonton: AGM Publications, 2000).

to admit Booth had the right objectives in mind, although he was going about the matter quite wrongly."[50]

---

[50] Philip D. Needham, "Redemption and Social Reformation: A Theological Study of William Booth and His Movement," Th.M. thesis, Princeton Theological Seminary, 1976, 80. Cardinal Manning, supporting Booth's plan, commended Booth for his analysis of the social plight of London in the last quarter of the nineteenth century, and for his encompassing social program that addressed itself to that plight. Manning's commendations were mixed with criticisms of some of the methods that Booth used to accomplish his goals. However, as early as 1882 in *The Contemporary Review* Manning wrote: "What, then, is the spiritual desolation of London? Let any man stand on the high northern ridge, which commands London from West to East, and ask himself: How many in this teeming, seething whirlpool of men have never been baptized? Have never been taught the Christian faith? Never set foot in a church? How many are living ignorantly in sin? How many with full knowledge are breaking the laws of God? What multitudes are blinded, or besotted, or maddened by drink? What sins of every kind and dye, and beyond all count, are committed day and night? It would surely be within the truth to say that half of the population of London are practically without Christ and without God in the world. If this be so, then at once we can see how and why The Salvation Army exists." (Henry Edward Manning, "The Salvation Army," *The Contemporary Review* 41 [August 1882]: 342). See also Francis Power Cobb, "The Last Revival," *The Contemporary Review* 41 (August 1882): 183.

For further historical information on *In Darkest England and the Way Out* see the following: Commissioner Smith, "The Battle-Cry of the Social Reform Wing," *All The World* (August 1890), 355-358; "A Look at the 'Wing'," *All The World* (October 1890), 510-513; Major Sowerby, "'In Darkest England' Reviewed," *All The World* (December 1890), 651-655; William Booth, "'Darkest England' and Other Affairs," *The War Cry* 16 (January 1891), 9; Frederick William Farrar, "Social Amelioration," *The War Cry* 56 (May 1911), 2, and Susie Forrest Swift, *The "Darkest England" Social Scheme: A Brief Review of the First Year's Work* (London: The Salvation Army, 1891).

For criticisms, both positive and negative, which were written by Booth's contemporaries see "An American View of 'Darkest England'," *Review of Reviews* 4 (1891), 390; Archdeacon Farrar, "A Panegyric on The Salvation Army," *Review of Reviews* 3 (May 1891), 467; Thomas H. Huxley, *Evolution and Ethics*, 9 Vols. (New York: D. Appleton and Company, 1884); "In Darkest England and the Way Out: A Report of Progress with Criticisms and Comments," *Review of Reviews* 3 (January 1891), 14-17; "In Darkest England: Progress Along the Way Out," *Review of Reviews* 3 (February 1891), 160-161; C. S. Loch, Bernard Bosanquet, and Philip Dwyer, *Criticisms on "General" Booth's Social Scheme* (London: Swan Sonnenschein and Son, 1891); Francis Peek, "In Darkest England and the Way Out," *The Contemporary Review* 58 (December 1890), 796-807; W.T. Stead, "The Book of the Year—In Darkest England," *Review of Reviews* 2 (July-December 1890), 651-656; W.T. Stead, "The Darkest England Scheme," *Review of Reviews* 3 (January-June 1891), 14-17; "The Darkest England Scheme: General Booth's Farm at Hadleigh," *Review of Reviews* 4 (November 1891), 594; and Arnold White, Francis Peek and Frederick William Farrar, *Truth About The Salvation Army* (London: Simpkin, Marshall, Hamilton, Kent & Co., 1892).

For twentieth century criticisms see Herman Ausubel, "General Booth's Scheme of Social Salvation," *American Historical Review* 56 (April 1951), 519-525. For two

The Darkest England Scheme incorporated many ideas envisioned primarily by Smith, but also embraced by Stead, especially championing the poor and putting programs in place that would aid and assist the poor with money from the wealthy. Booth would only go so far, however, because "he did not share Smith's socialism. He did want to repair capitalism's flaws, however. Booth's aim was to change the man when character was the reason for failure. For him, man's nature was grounded in the heart, not the environment. He was not a classic Christian Socialist; he believed that only conversion could rid the heart of sin and change outer maladies, although at times the cause of ruin was beyond one's control."[51]

The Scheme was intended as a crusade to assist the "submerged tenth" of Britain's population, those whose lives were enslaved by poverty, vice, prostitution, and any number of circumstances that kept these people from the security of work, income, home, family, or safety. Booth expected the scheme to help not only England but also the world by providing a model of social salvation. The first part of the book, labeled "Darkness" dealt with an analysis of the problems. The second part of the book, "Deliverance" proposed solutions to the problems, those solutions being divided among the city colony, the farm colony, and the colony overseas. Each colony was designed to bring light to specific aspects of England's darkness through various programs established for each colony. The city colony provided food and shelter for the poor as well as employment for the unemployed. The farm colony took people from the city and established them on farms to learn agricultural trades that would benefit them for the remainder of their lives. The best known of the farm colonies is still operated by The Salvation Army today, the colony at Hadleigh in Essex,

---

works that deal at length with various aspects of Booth's Scheme see the following: K. S. Inglis, *Churches and Working Classes in Victorian England* (Toronto: University of Toronto Press, 1963), and Norris Magnuson, *Salvation in the Slums: Evangelical Social Work, 1865-1920*, The American Theological Library Association Monograph Series, No. 10 (Metuchen, New Jersey: The Scarecrow Press, 1977). See also Coutts, *Bread for My Neighbour*, chapters 6-13; Fairbank, *Booth's Boots*, chapter 11; Roger J. Green, "An Historical Salvation Army Perspective," 43-81 in John D. Waldron, ed., *Creed and Deed: Toward a Christian Theology of Social Services in The Salvation Army* (Toronto: The Salvation Army, 1986); Edward H. McKinley, *Marching to Glory: The History of The Salvation Army in the United States* (San Francisco, CA: Harper and Row, Publishers, 1980), 70-72, 303; second edition Grand Rapids, MI: William B. Eerdmans Publishing Co., 1995; Murdoch, *Origins of The Salvation Army*, chapter seven; Needham, "Redemption and Social Reformation: A Theological Study of William Booth and His Movement," 165; and Christine Parkin, "The Salvation Army and Social Questions of the Day," 103-118 in Michael Hill, ed., *A Sociological Yearbook of Religion in Britain* 5 (London: SCM Press, 1972).

[51] Murdoch, *Origins of The Salvation Army*, 161.

originally established with 215 men.[52] Both Cecil Rhodes and Lord Loch (the High Commissioner for South Africa) visited the Hadleigh Farm in 1898. One of the most important governors of that colony was David C. Lamb, who entered the Army under the Booths and helped with the shaping of the social ministry of the Army.[53] The overseas colony helped the poor of the cities through the Army's emigration bureau to find work overseas, primarily in Canada, Australia, and New Zealand. Booth had hoped to establish such work also in Rhodesia, but that project failed. Farm colonies were also established in the United States for those needing employment from the cities of America.[54]

However, those who read and interpret this book only in the light of its social analysis and constructive programs will seriously miss an important intention of the book, and in doing so will misunderstand Booth at this critical time in his life and ministry. The book is also an expression of Booth's expanded view of redemption to include social redemption. He wanted to maintain the delicate balance between personal and social salvation. Doing so was important to Booth for at least two reasons. First, he feared that social salvation would break loose from its ties to spiritual salvation, thus rendering The Salvation Army merely an ineffectual social agency. Second, he wanted to respond to his critics on the one hand who denied the validity of his social work, and his critics on the other hand who denied the validity of his religious work.[55]

---

[52] I am indebted to Salvationists Graham Cook and Gordon Parkhill of Leigh-on-Sea for taking me on a tour of Hadleigh and explaining the work of The Salvation Army in that colony today. See Gordon Parkhill and Graham Cook, *Hadleigh Salvation Army Farm: A Vision Reborn* (London: The Salvation Army, 2008).

[53] See Norman H. Murdoch, *Soldiers of the Cross: Susie Swift and David Lamb: Pioneers of Social Change* (Alexandria, Virginia: Crest Books, 2006).

[54] For an analysis of the Army's social ministry in the United States, including the Farm Colonies in the United States, see Frederick Booth-Tucker, *The Salvation Army in America: Selected Reports, 1899-1903* (New York: Arno Press, 1972, Religion in America Series).

[55] See Roger J. Green, "Theological Roots of *In Darkest England and the Way Out*," *Wesleyan Theological Journal* 25:1 (Spring 1990), 83-105; and Norman H. Murdoch, "William Booth's *In Darkest England and the Way Out*: A Reappraisal," *Wesleyan Theological Journal* 25:1 (Spring 1990), 106-116. The failure to connect the social ministry to Booth's theology is apparent in Hattersley's recent biography of the Booths. Gertrude Himmelfard noted this in her review of Hattersley's book, "First Save the Body, Then the Soul," *The New York Times Book Review* (July 9, 2000), 14-15. Himmelfard noted the following: "What did distinguish the Booths from most of the others was their linking of social and religious salvation. Today, when faith-based institutions are being proposed as the alleviation, if not the solution, of some social problems, we might reasonably look to the Booths for guidance and counsel. Yet here 'Blood and Fire' is disappointing, for there is little attempt to establish the connection, let alone a casual relationship, between their social and religious agendas." In the epilogue Hattersley intimates that perhaps there was none: 'It is not necessary to believe in instant sanctification—or in sanctification in any form—to admire and applaud their work of social redemption.' He means this in praise of his

Booth was not equally clear, however, in spelling out those intentions. Nevertheless, it was important for Booth to explain that the social ministry of the Army was not an end in itself. The work of social redemption was preparatory, necessarily, to the work of spiritual or personal redemption. Experience had taught him that some people were so disastrously oppressed by their present physical circumstances that "these multitudes will not be saved in their present circumstances."[56] A similar theme is reiterated throughout his book. Booth was convinced that "If these people are to believe in Jesus Christ, become the servants of God, and escape the miseries of the wrath to come, they must be helped out of their present social miseries."[57] The clearest statement of Booth's intentions is found in his assertion that "at the risk of being misunderstood and misrepresented, I must assert in the most unqualified way that it is primarily and mainly for the sake of saving the soul that I seek the salvation of the body."[58] Years later that theological position is reiterated in a letter to his officers on the occasion of his eightieth birthday, "But while you strive to deliver them from their temporal distresses, and endeavour to rescue them from the causes that have led to their unfortunate condition, you must seek, above all, to turn their miseries to good account by making them help the Salvation of their souls and their deliverance from the wrath to come. It will be a very small reward for all your toils if, after bringing them into condition of well-being here, they perish hereafter."[59]

Only when Booth's social mission is placed within the framework of his entire theological vision can it be completely understood. His newly formulated theology of redemption was sustained and supported by other aspects of his theology that he had articulated previous to 1889-1890. He had already conceived of his Army as a part of the universal Church that was blessed by God and sanctified by the Holy Spirit. He had developed his imagery of Christ to include the conquering Christ who was the model for deliverance from the evils of this world as well as from the wrath of the next world. He believed that evil was not finally triumphant, but that universal redemption, both personal and social, was possible. He believed in an ultimate eschatological goal: a goal that would embrace both spiritual and social redemption. He held out that

---

heroes, but it may be the most damning thing that can be said of them, for it deprives them of what might have been their best claim to our attention and to a place in the pantheon of eminent Victorians," 15.

[56] Booth, *In Darkest England*, 257.

[57] Ibid. See also 35, 205, 264, 268.

[58] Ibid., 45. See also 104, 110, 218. Begbie claimed that "his social work was chiefly an excuse for getting at the souls of men" (Begbie, "Booth, William [1829-1912]," 51).

[59] William Booth, *To My Officers: A Letter from the General on His Eightieth Birthday* (St. Albans: Salvation Army Printing Works, 1909), 44. See also 19-20; Begbie, *The Life of General William Booth*, 2:113, 329, 331; Needham, "Redemption and Social Reformation: A Theological Study of William Booth and His Movement," 74-76, 80, 83-84.

goal as hope for ultimate redemptive victory for his Army of salvation. It is interesting and not inconsequential that his most important article dealing with this eschatological goal was written in August of 1890, the same time that he was completing the writing of *In Darkest England*.[60]

VI. The Salvation Army and Social Ministry into the Twentieth Century

Finally, however, the question needs to be raised, was Booth completely settled with the direction that The Salvation Army took, especially after 1890? At the very least, there appeared to be some lingering question in the mind of Booth as to whether the decision to enter into social ministries was a wise one. In his book entitled *The Salvationists*, John Coutts refers to the issue of the Army's opening up a full-fledged medical work in India in 1893. Bramwell Booth tried to persuade William Booth of this necessity, and Coutts wrote, "The old man took some persuading. Might not the care of sick bodies divert attention from the salvation of perishing souls? But at last he agreed."[61] Owen Chadwick raised the same question in *The Victorian Church*. He wrote, "The most revivalist of sects was now willing to allow that a Christian had other duties to his neighbor apart from his duty to convert him. Yet in Booth's lonely old age...he sometimes wondered whether he had been right to allow the Army to divert its energies from conversion."[62] Tim Macquiban wrote that there is evidence that Booth "drew back in trepidation from the diversion from what he still saw as the primary tasks and preoccupations of his ministry—sin and salvation, hell and heaven, the devil and the Lord, features of the older-style evangelism."[63]

Booth's official biographer, Begbie, raised this question. He wrote that "after many years of incredible labour in the social work of the Army he came to wonder...whether he ought ever to have diverted any of the energies of the Army from the strictly evangelical responsibilities of the preacher's vocation."[64] And Ervine, when writing about William Booth getting back to preaching after so much of his energy had been given to the Darkest England Scheme, wrote

---

[60] See William Booth, "The Millennium; or, the Ultimate Triumph of Salvation Army Principles," *All the World* 6 (August 1890), 337-343. See also William Booth, "My Idea of the Millennium," *The Review of Reviews* 2 (July-December, 1890), 130, and William Booth, "All things New: A New Year's Message from the New World," *All The World* 15:1 (January 1895), 3-7.

[61] John Coutts, *The Salvationists* (London: A. R. Mowbray and Company, Ltd., 1978), 142.

[62] Owen Chadwick, *The Victorian Church*, 2 Vols. (London: SCM Press, Ltd., 1987), 2:297.

[63] Macquiban, "Soup and Salvation: Social Service as an Emerging Motif for the British Methodist Response to Poverty in the Late 19th Century," 35-36. See also Inglis, *Churches and the Working Classes*, 211; and Magnuson, *Salvation in the Slums*, 173.

[64] Begbie, *The Life of General William Booth*, 2:84.

that "Schemes of social reform had no interest for him any more, and he sometimes doubted his wisdom in adopting any."[65]

This question obviously lingered even after William Booth's death. Upon his becoming the second General of The Salvation Army, Bramwell Booth had to face the question again. A newspaper reporter asked him about the Darkest England Scheme. Bramwell Booth's reply is important not only because he was one of the shapers of that Scheme, but because now as General he would be the leader of the Army to move the Scheme into the twentieth century. Therefore, his vision of the Scheme is critical in providing some comprehensive view of what evolved in the ministry of the Army several years earlier. Bramwell Booth said,

> My answer...is that I have always looked on the Darkest England scheme and what came out of it as a comparatively small, though essential, part of the work of The Salvation Army—as a link rather than the main body of the thing. I say essential because it was, and is, an expression of the passion at the heart of the organism itself, but as such it takes a subordinate place in my own conception of the history—and, shall I say the hopes?—of the Army.
>
> At the same time, there is no doubt that the scheme has done two good things for the Army, as well as a good thing for the world. It helped the Army into the eye of those who were compassionate for the poor, but under the influence of a generous humanitarianism which hitherto looked upon the Army as little more than a small religious sect struggling for its own existence. Secondly, it opened the way for the Army to use a vast weight of previously unemployed power in its own ranks, because it provided a platform for action other than the platform of talking and solo singing, of great religious functions, and the publication of religious literature. It provided work for another type of soldier—the man or woman who could act but not talk. So far as its reflex effect upon the Army is concerned the Darkest England scheme has fully justified itself.[66]

The social ministry of The Salvation Army had evolved into an enormous undertaking, but care constantly needed to be taken to insure that the biblical and theological foundations of the second mission were clear both to Salvationists and to the general public. The Army was a Wesleyan holiness Christian denomination, and because of that (rather than in spite of that) governed its institutional life by love of God and of neighbor.

As for Booth, he moved forward with his beloved Army into an unknown future, but without Catherine by his side. He had undertaken immense responsibilities with the development of the Darkest England Scheme, and as the General of a growing Army he would have to maintain a delicate balance of all ministries of the Army. His love for the Army and commitment to its cause became the dominant force in his life. For that he paid a price because at times the interests of the Army came above the interests of the family, and losing three of his children from the ranks of the Army as well as another daughter to a premature death was almost more than he could bear. William Booth would

---

[65] Ervine, *God's Soldier: General William Booth*, 2:784.
[66] "New General & His Plans," *Daily News and Leader* (October 1912), 1.

learn the lessons of the pain as well as the glory of leadership as he moved beyond the events of 1890.

Chapter 6

Peaceful Pentecost: The Pentecostal Pacifist Tradition for Contemporary Political Praxis and Theology

A.J. Swoboda

I. Introduction

Placed squarely in the heart of the twentieth century story of nonviolence and pacifism in both Europe and North America are the earliest Pentecostals.[1] More particularly, Pentecostalism(s) share a considerable amount of common ground with the Historic Peace Churches of Protestant Europe (Brethren, Friends, and Mennonite) who were vehemently persecuted for their radical views on discipleship and church life, especially pertaining to pacifism.[2] A

---

[1] To begin, I wish to thank Aaron Friesen and Jay Beaman for their close reading of this text in the editorial stages. I am indebted to both of your words of influence. For historical overviews of nonviolence and pacifism in twentieth century North America and Europe, see Peter Brock, *Pacifism in Europe to 1914* (Princeton, NJ: Princeton University Press, 1972); Staughton Lynd, ed. *Nonviolence in America: A Documentary History*, ed. Leonard Levy and Alfred Young (New York, NY: Bobbs-Merrill Company, 1966); Theron F. Schlaback and Richard T. Hughes, eds., *Proclaim Peace: Christian Pacifism from Unexpected Quarters* (Chicago, IL: University of Illinois Press, 1997).

[2] I use "Pentecostalism(s)" because of the diversity of the movements. Pentecostalism is not a monolithic movement or denomination; rather, it is a conglomeration of like-minded and like-experienced Christians whose theology is deeply rooted in the "pneumatological imagination". This is a theme throughout Amos Yong, *The Spirit Poured out on All Flesh: Pentecostalism and the Possibility of Global Theology* (Grand Rapids: Baker Academic, 2005). "Pacifism"—from the Latin *pax* and *facere*—means "to make peace" and has many different expressions. On this, see Paul Alexander, *Peace to War: Shifting Allegiances in the Assemblies of God* (Scottdale, PA: Herald Press, 2009), 31-33.

small and oft-unrecognized vignette of Pentecostal history reminds us that a vast majority of early North American Pentecostal movements were pacifist in both theology and practice before, during, and after the global bloodshed of World War I (hereafter WWI; 1914-18). One might, as did Paul Alexander, "accidentally" stumble across this reality.[3] In stark contrast to our contemporary context, however, little to no lingering of such historical phenomenon are identifiable within global Pentecostal or Charismatic spirituality, excepting a few antiquated pacifist policies and denominational policies that play no role in contemporary ecclesiological practice. Where has pacifist Pentecostalism gone? As did the Mennonite theologian John Howard Yoder, scholars, historians, and theologians have lamented its sudden disappearance at the entrance of America into World War II (hereafter WWII; 1939-45). In reflecting upon the disappearance of Pentecostal pacifism which he believed fell victim to cultural accommodation, Yoder argued that the Pentecostal literal biblicism of the time never fully "matured into a solid ethical hermeneutic" that could sustain the test of time.[4] Quite simply, Pentecostal pacifism was a flash in the pan that sparked quite the fire in the early years of the movement but would not survive after the Second World War in the broader Pentecostal movement. Why is this?

This is an especially important conversation for today. As Evangelicalism and Pentecostalism have broadly grown synonymous with political conservativism and the militarism that accompanies it, it is important that we re-engage the central issue of the church's role in society and politics. To accomplish that, this chapter seeks to, (1) examine the historical and theological underpinnings of pacifism in earliest 20th century North American Pentecostalism(s), (2) give special attention to pacifism within Pentecostal denominationalism in the years leading up to WWII, (3) identify possible culprits for the decline of pacifism in Pentecostalism, and (4) suggest ways in which its re-appropriation in contemporary practice might shape a renewed political, social, and ecclesiological theology within global Pentecostalism.

II. Pre-WWII Pacifist Rumblings in Early Pentecostal History

While an historical analysis of Pentecostal pacifism demands an entire volume, we will resort to an overview.[5] The theology of Pentecostal pacifism can be traced along a number of lines, although best through 19th and 20th century

---

[3] Ibid., 22.

[4] Jay Beaman, *Pentecostal Pacifism: The Origin, Development, and Rejection of Pacific Belief among the Pentecostals* (Hillsboro, KS: Center for Mennonite Brethren Studies, 1989), iii.

[5] For a tremendously helpful overview, see Alexander and Jay Beaman and Brian Pipkin, *Pentecostal and Holiness Statements on War and Peace* (Eugene, OR: Pickwick, 2013).

Wesleyan Holiness and Reformed-evangelical revivalism.[6] The story of Pentecostal pacifism begins between the mid-19th century and the years preceding WWI. During this time, the United States of America found itself sitting happily atop an unparalleled national optimism on both the religious and political fronts. On one hand, widespread nationalistic optimism remained the ethos of a young nation that envisioned a bright future for itself (and many riches to be made). Alongside this, particularly in the years leading up to the American Civil War (1861-65), a widespread postmillennial eschatological ethos ubiquitously pervaded the religious context in America. This postmillennialism unquestionably paired perfectly with the optimism that gave rise to the American *Manifest Destiny*. Eschatological and political optimism fed each other exactly what it needed to thrive in a mutually beneficial symbiotic relationship. In this context, a visceral sense of optimism can be observed within the Holiness tradition of the late 19th and early 20th century, which would eventually be the theological seedbed for American Pentecostalism.

This eschatological fervor and optimism brought about a desire for widespread purification. Religious revivalism in the Holiness communities perpetually sparked an increased, at times feverish, awareness and desire for personal sanctification and holiness. That said, this desire for purification was not limited to *personal* iniquity and repentance. Rather, a new eschatological vision of *societal* revitalization soon emerged, offering a utopist dream of how human civilization should exist in preparation for Christ's *parousia*. Undergirding this vision for personal and societal renewal was a foundation of premillennial eschatology and biblical literalism prominent during the time. We observe this most particularly amidst Holiness traditions whereby the call to purge not only the individual's sins but combat the world of sin, disease, and societal evil was quite evident. For instance, Holiness Christians denounced tobacco use previous to any government or medical intervention that occurred later in the mid-20th century.[7] Similarly, slavery was vehemently opposed, viewed by Holiness Christians as such an abomination that they would eventually support violence and militarism to end it.[8] Finally, many Holiness and Wesleyan preachers were pacifist. Figures such as Thomas Upham, Amos Dresser, Dwight Moody

---

[6] William Faupel has argued that there exist broadly three lines in Pentecostalism: (1) Denominations which hold a Keswickian view of sanctification, (2) denominations which hold a Holiness view of "entire sanctification", (3) and denominations which hold a "Jesus only" view of the Godhead (Oneness Pentecostalism)." D. William Faupel, *The American Pentecostal Movement: A Bibliographic Essay* (Wilmore, KY: Asbury Theological Seminary, 1972), 44-45. Beaman shows that each group had a pacifist core of denominations. Beaman, chp. 2.

[7] Mickey Crews, *The Church of God: A Social History* (Knoxville, TN: University of Tennessee Press, 1990), 54-55.

[8] Beaman, 2-3.

were opposed to combatant military service.⁹ Moody himself was a conscientious objector during the Civil War.¹⁰ These societal critiques were viewed as the church's task in preparing for the awaited return of Christ. Historian Timothy Smith is quick to point out that this social vision had a long-term effect on not only Pentecostalism but Western Christianity as a whole. Smith suggests that such socio-cultural critiques against slavery, disease, poverty, war, and greed "helped prepare the way both in theory and in practice for what later *became known as the social gospel.*"¹¹ This Holiness social theology and worldview would likewise become the backbone of Pentecostal pacifism.

Any optimism based upon naieve confidence growing out of the success of the American Revolution, was lost by the end of the Civil War. War had taken its toll on the optimism of a war-torn nation. However, Pentecostal spirituality of the early 20th century would soon import this optimism; although Pentecostalism would hold much stronger anti-nationalistic sentiments than did their Holiness predecessors. Between the conclusion of the Civil War (1865) and the dawn of WWI (1914), classic American Pentecostalism emerged borrowing almost entirely the theological/eschatological paradigm of Holiness and revivalist Christianity.¹² Walter Hollenweger believed Pentecostals borrowed much of its ethos from Holiness Christianity: women in leadership, inter-racial worship, connection to the poor, and pacifism.¹³ Furthermore, Paul Alexander asserts that various similarities between earliest Quakerism and Pentecostalism show why the latter became such a favorable environment for pacifism; both emphasized radical discipleship, restorationism, defense of the poor, evangelization, women in ministry, and loyalty to government.¹⁴

Jay Beaman has illuminated the dynamics of this period. In his seminal study, *Pentecostal Pacifism*, Beaman examines this deep-rooted historical pacifist tradition in pre-WWI Holiness and revivalist movements and how it would soon be transferred to Pentecostalism.¹⁵ During one particular period (1906-08), many Holiness leaders whose tradition soon shaped Pentecostalism were reciprocally being influenced by Pentecostalism with widespread speaking in

---

⁹ This includes many from the Disciples of Christ and Quaker traditions who influenced them but were not within the Holiness tradition.

¹⁰ Ibid., 13.

¹¹ Timothy L. Smith, *Revivalism and Social Reform: In Mid-Nineteenth-Century America* (New York, NY: Abingdon, 1957), 7-10. (Italics mine)

¹² Pentecostalism must not be understood as one movement but rather as a set of movements that centered on pneumatology. Without question, there remains significant debate as to who owns the beginnings of Pentecostalism.

¹³ Walter J. Hollenweger, "An Introduction to Pentecostalisms," *Journal of Beliefs and Values* 25, no. 2 (2004).

¹⁴ Alexander, 89-97.

¹⁵ The text is a revised version of Beaman's Ph.D. at North Baptist American Seminary and begins with a foreword from John Howard Yoder. Although Beaman's study is quite dated, it continues to offer valuable insights into the wax and wane of early Pentecostal pacifism and biblical peace readings. Beaman.

tongues, prophesy, and healings.[16] For a time, Pentecostals envisioned societal repentance as a part of preparation for Christ's return. Most notably, Beaman examines the pacifist movement within the Assemblies of God (hereafter AG). During this time, members of the AG formulated not only a pacifist theology, but encouraged peaceful living and discouraged participation in military service even when it was not required of its members. Because Pentecostals were eschatologically focused on the quick return of Christ, the war was often commonly perceived as the kind of birth pangs of soon apocalyptic end; thus, their participation in the war would be a kind of participation in the system of the soon-ending world.[17] Not participating in their war was a rejection of the world. Beaman suggests that up to 10% of all who were conscientious objectors during WWI were Pentecostal or holiness men who registered for the draft as religious objectors to the war.[18] Arthur Karl Piepkorn's text, *Profiles in Belief*, argues that 38 of the 117 Pentecostal denominations (32.5%) give some evidence of pacifism in their history. These pacifist practices were broadly connected primarily to a particular worldview that was grounded in both premillennial and pretribulation eschatology. Similarly, their anti-worldly sectarianism made them question what everyone else was doing. Furthermore, the Pentecostals expected the soon-coming *parousia*, a theology which "colored" every part of their practice.[19]

Pentecostal pacifism, as well, highlights the literalistic biblical/hermeneutic of early Pentecostalism. Quite simply, primitive Pentecostalism(s) were largely pacifist because they read and interpreted the Bible literally. Christ was *literally* coming back, we were *literally* filled with the Spirit, and miracles were *literally* a possibility. Alongside these literalist readings were the biblical commands to peaceful living and peacemaking found in the Ten Commandments and Matthew 5–7. Pentecostals practiced such pacifism because of their literalistic reading of the text that sought to incorporate and practice as much of the biblical narrative as possible. Beaman contends it was this literalism which would not only lead to the widespread practice of prophecy, speaking in tongues, and healing; it similarly became the hermeneutical cradle for observing the peaceful nonviolent teachings of the Sermon on the Mount. This hermeneutic was grounded in a desired return to early church practice. A renewal theology logically led, for these Pentecostals, to a renewal in nonresistant action in pre-WWI ecclesiology. Thus with the eschatological optimism, a vision for cultural and social critique, biblical literalism, and the historical/theological framework of Holiness spirituality, Pentecostalism was swept into history as a pacifist movement.

---

[16] This would eventually split the Holiness tradition.
[17] On this eschatological connection to Pentecostal pacifism, see Allan Anderson, *Spreading Fires: The Missionary Nature of Early Pentecostalism* (Maryknoll, NY: Orbis, 2007), 223-229.
[18] http://pentecostalpacifism.com/ (6/20/12)
[19] Beaman, vii.

III. The Distinctives of Pacifism in Pentecostal Denominationalism

Pacifist theology of the kind we have discussed influenced a great many Pentecostal personalities and denominations. For example, Agnes Ozman (1870-1937), a female student of Charles Parham's (1873-1929) at the Bethel Bible School (Topeka, KS), believed war entirely incongruent with Pentecostal Spirit-led practice and was a pacifist.[20] Ozman—by some accounts "the first Pentecostal"—eventually helped form the AG in Spokane, WA (1917). Parham himself had pacifist tendencies; although his were centered almost certainly on a millennial eschatology rather than for socio-ethical underpinnings. Parham believed war interfered with evangelism and worldwide mission that were, for him, integral to a millennial theology.[21] As well, Frank Bartleman, the chronicler of the Azusa Street revival (1906-1915) in Los Angeles, CA, had pacifist sensibilities influenced by his Quaker mother.[22] As early as 1914, Bartleman had traveled extensively throughout Europe proclaiming a theology and practice of non-violent Pentecostal practice, which would directly affect others. As a result of Bartleman's writings within *Pentecostal Evangel* alongside the text *Blood Against Blood* by post-Quaker pacifist Arthur Sidney Booth-Clibborn—whose family history had 250 years of Quaker practice—the British Assemblies of God would undergo a pacifist revival between the years of 1948 and 1966. Pentecostal Alpha Edward Humbard, the father of famed Rex Humbard, was a registered religious objector and pacifist.[23] Rex Humbard's influence upon the American televangelism culture as well as Kathryn Kuhlman's healing ministry left its identifiable mark for years to come. During this time, Donald Gee was the leader of the movement in the U.K.. Through dialogue with the works of Bartleman and Booth-Clibborn, Gee would come to hold a pacifist theology.[24]

Perhaps no better an example of this Pentecostal pacifism is found than in the character of Englishman Stanley Frodsham (1882-1969). Coming to Pentecostalism in 1908, Frodsham played an integral role in the formation of the AG as a denomination and eventually helped write the denominational creed in 1916. Frodsham was influenced by all those mentioned.[25] Frodsham was involved with the writing of the *Pentecostal Evangel* from 1916 to 1948, an early AG magazine. In one such article by Frodsham—"Our Heavenly Citizenship"—he calls upon Pentecostals to embrace their heavenly citizenship over and

---

[20] http://pentecostalpacifism.com/Kellogg1.html
[21] Beaman, 51-54.
[22] Ibid., 54-59. Quakerism had a larger effect on Pentecostal spirituality and its formation of a pacifist ethic as shown in Alexander, Ch. 3.
[23] Stanley M. Burgess and Eduard M. van der Maas, *The New International Dictionary of Pentecostal and Charismatic Movements*, Rev and expanded ed ed. (Grand Rapids, MI: Zondervan, 2002), 774.
[24] Beaman, 60-64.
[25] Ibid., 59-60.

against their patriotic identity. The Kingdom of God, for Frodsham, must transcend one's nationalistic or patriotic pride. Frodsham writes:

> National pride, like every other form of pride, is an abomination in the sight of God. And pride of race must be one of the all things that pass away when one becomes a new creature in Christ Jesus.[26]

In the same article, Frodsham says:

> When seen from the heavenly viewpoint, how the present conflict is illumined. The policy of our God is plainly declared in the Word, "Peace on earth, good will toward men." The nations who have drawn the sword to kill those of the same blood in other nations, for God "hath made of one blood all nations of men," are not merely fighting against one another, but with their policy of "War on Earth and ill towards men," they are without knowing it, again fulfilling the Scriptures, "the kinds of the earth set themselves and the rules take counsel together, against the Lord and against his anointed." Is any child of God going to side with these belligerent kings? Will he not rather side with the Prince of Peace under whose banner of love has chosen to serve?[27]

Yet, despite such a profound influence upon Pentecostal individuals, examinations of pacifism often go unattended to in their communal written or oral histories. Some of the most widely utilized texts—such as Robert Mapes Anderson's *Vision of the Disinherited*—entirely sidestep the issue of pacifism.[28] In fact, Beaman points out, regarding these omissions, that at the time of his writing (1989) only one of the three Pentecostal histories produced by the AG—William Menzies' *Anointed to Serve*—even mentions the topic of pacifism and only devotes three pages to the topic.[29] One might conclude that the topic has been systematically removed from the history books. However, the evidence suggests that the historical influence of pacifist thinking upon early Pentecostals in the AG is without question.

On April 28th, 1917, the United States was thrown into the depths of the bloody WWI with Germany. With the need for able-bodied serviceman at an all-time high, any male between the ages of 21-29 would be required to register on June 5th, 1917. This put Pentecostals in between what they perceived as faithfulness to the Kingdom of God and the pressing needs of the Kingdom of Earth.[30] Many of the newly formed Pentecostal denominations responded uniquely. One such example of this was the Church of God (COG), a largely

---

[26] Stanley H. Frodsham, "Our Heavenly Citizenship," *Word and Witness*, Oct. 1915, p. 3.
[27] Stanley H. Frodsham, "Our Heavenly Citizenship," *Word and Witness*, Oct. 1915, p. 3.
[28] Robert Mapes Anderson, *Vision of the Disinherited: The Making of American Pentecostalism* (Peabody, MA: Hendrickson, 1979).
[29] William W. Menzies, *Anointed to Serve: The Story of the Assemblies of God* (Springfield, MO: Gospel Publishing House, 1971), 326-28
[30] http://pentecostalpacifism.com/PentePacIntro.html

populist movement comprised of lower and rural classes, and staunchly pacifist. Alongside others, the COG critiqued the cultural normativity of early 20th century American politics. Because of their populist anti-war approach, the COG was largely the laughingstock of intellectual communities. Mickey Crews' social history of the movement points out various ways in which they rebelled against modern culture. Members were required to abstain from alcohol, tobacco, secret societies (e.g. Ku Klux Klan), labor unions, church bazaars, carnivals, dancing, movies, chewing gum, and kinds of dress; neglect of which was tantamount to heresy.[31] The COG came down hard on all forms of spectator sport and believed all film to be pornographic, entertaining the thought of banning televisions from pastors' homes at one point.[32] But this social critique had many arguable positives. For instance, they critically engaged the emerging modern industrial society with its emphasis upon purist capitalism that they believed overlooked the inherent value and well-being of individual people. Human beings, the movement argued, are not a means to wealth. What might be seen as the "health and wealth" gospel of today was viewed largely as heresy to the COG (Tennessee).[33] As well, the COG included women and blacks in their egalitarian fellowship. And, along with this, they challenged the patriotic assumptions of war.

Alongside these cultural critiques came a very natural and strong reaction against participation in WWI. Although many of the church's members were pro-war Republicans, they found themselves a part of an anti-war church.[34] Crews describes the COG's attitude towards war as being the powers of darkness and even shunned patriotism as an unhealthy turn towards earthly things. Evidence suggests that the church's evangelism efforts increased during the war because of the fear of people going to hell during these seemingly apocalyptic times. Although the draft was being created, they vehemently rejected conscription. By the council in Nov. 1917 in Harriman, TN, the church added its list of teachings "against members going to war."[35] They would come under scrutiny from the F.B.I. who would conclude that even some of their magazines, such as *Evangel*, were propaganda that couldn't be mailed out.[36] These teachings became inauspicious within the movement in 1921 most likely because of the widespread growth during WWI and the diversity of belief among the constituents. As the COG moved into mainline Evangelicalism, the belief subsided by the year 1921.

Even more amplified to that of the COG response was the pacifist response of the AG. When WWI began, the United States government refused to recognize the option of not registering. However, non-combat military service was a recognizable option of preference in certain cases. This gave Pentecostal de-

---

[31] Crews, 38.
[32] Ibid., 40-45.
[33] Ibid., 12-13.
[34] Ibid., 108-137.
[35] Ibid., 116.
[36] Ibid., 119.

nominations like the AG a viable middle ground of action: non-combat military service. In response, the military would grant certain permissions of freedom such as ordained ministers and made room for conscientious objectors to serve in special camps during the war. Since a denominational statement had yet to be crafted in 1914, conscription gave ample basis to write one. During a week and a half period (Apr. 1-10, 1914) in Hot Springs, Arkansas, the AG wrestled with the issue, the same year WWI began. The Executive and General Presbyteries formally adopted a written paper on pacifism that would officially be the position of the denomination.

The statement was entitled, "Resolution Concerning the Attitude of the General Council of the Assemblies of God Towards any Military Service which Involves the Actual Participation in the Destruction of Human Life."[37] The document articulates exclusively a pacifist non-combat military service perspective and denounces the "taking of human life". Furthermore, it argues for a biblicism that centers on "peace on earth, good will towards men" (Luke 2:14), the "Prince of Peace" who calls us to "live at peace with all men" (Heb. 12:14), the peace sayings of Jesus (Matt. 5:39, 44), and highlights the OT commandment against "killing" (Ex. 20:13).[38] It reads:

> THEREFORE we, as a body of Christians, while purposing to fulfil all the obligations of loyal citizenship, are nevertheless constrained to declare we cannot conscientiously participate in war and armed resistance which involves the actual destruction of human life, since this is contrary to our view of the clear teachings of the inspired Word of God, which is the sole basis of our faith.[39]

The intent of the text was twofold: to 1) protect the AG theology of loyal citizenship and 2) pacifist beliefs. Beaman points out that, "While the statement was absolute in tone, there was no attempt to enforce it upon every member for the congregation even where there was disagreement."[40] That is, it was not a binding letter; protecting the individual's right to choose. On April 28, 1917, the denominational document was forwarded to President Woodrow Wilson.[41] Soon, a number of denominations followed the precedent of the AG

---

[37] Published at Beaman, 24. Although the original text can be found in *Weekly Evangel*, Aug. 4th, 1917, pg. 6

[38] Jay Beaman, in personal correspondence, notes that following WWII, Pentecostal translations of Scripture no longer used "thou shalt not kill" and utilized "thou shalt not murder" clearly developing a new hermeneutical and theological trajectory. This trajectory is outlined in Wilma Ann Bailey, *You Shall Not Kill or You Shall Not Murder: The Assault on the Biblical Text* (Collegeville, MN: Liturgical Press, 2005).

[39] Beaman, 24.

[40] Ibid., 25.

[41] Menzies, 326-28. A copy of this letter can be found at *General Council Combined Minutes 1914-17*, Springfield, Gospel Publishing House, 1917, 11-12.

by writing documents including a number of Keswickian denominations.[42] In comparing the documents, one finds that many borrowed almost entirely from the AG model. Undertaking such a comparison, Beaman points out that the AG text gave a foundation for other documents based on: (1) affirmation of the legitimacy and loyalty towards government, (2) an absolute pacifist ethic based on scripture, and (3) a qualification of the absolute pacifism to allow noncombatant service in war.[43] Seven denominations followed with similar statements regarding loyalty toward government showing that the issue was "no mere appendage" to their theological system; this was a big issue.[44] Not surprisingly, denominational documents such as this put many Pentecostals at odds with much of the culture's positive attitude towards war. One document tells of many AG pastors imprisonment by U.S. Marshalls for opposing the war.[45] Another account tells of a COG Pentecostal by the name of Dave Allen being murdered by two policemen in Alabama for refusal to register for the draft.[46]

For some time following WWI, the pacifist position remained in place. Soon, the General Council would formally adopt this position in 1927 at the formation of its constitution. This positive attitude towards pacifism is seen in the Oct. 12, 1940 issue of *The* Pentecostal Evangel which reaffirmed unequivocally the 1917 decisions.[47] This would continue until the attacks on Pearl Harbor (Dec. 7th, 1941) when many leaders and pastors would quickly change their sentiment. In the history of the literature, by the fall of 1942, all had changed as articles in *The Pentecostal Evangel* began publishing pro-war articles, omitting pacifist pieces. In 1947, the General Council removed some of the biblical material for anti-war stances from the 1917 statement on military service and would eventually promote civil defense by 1957. By 1944, 50,000 AG men were serving in the armed services.[48] In fact, there are only 35 known AG conscientious objectors registered in WWII. The bylaws were drastically altered in August, 1967 in Long Beach, CA by the General Council, during the rage of the Vietnam War. The new resolution now read

> As a movement we affirm our loyalty to the government of the United States in war or peace. We shall continue to insist, as we have historically, on the right of each member to choose for himself whether to declare his position as a combatant, a non-combatant, or a conscientious objector.[49]

---

[42] Calvary Pentecostal Church, Church of God of the Union Assembly, Filipino Assembles of the First-Born, General Assembly and Church of the First Born, Olzabal Latin-American Council of Churches. List found at Beaman, 25.
[43] Ibid., 30-31.
[44] Ibid., 37.
[45] E.N. Bell, "Preachers Warned," *Weekly Evangel*, Jan. 5, 1918, pg. 4
[46] J.B. Ellis, "The Murder of Brother Dave Allen," *Evangel*, 27 Apr. 1918, p. 4
[47] *The Pentecostal Evangel*, Oct. 12th, 1940, p. 13
[48] *The Pentecostal Evangel*, Mar. 18, 1944, p. 12
[49] Quoted in Menzies, 328.

In 1967, a vote to remove the 1917 pacifist statement was done so with little to no challenge. So what happened? What changed? Murray Dempster called this a "death sentence" and even denied the 1967 resolution took place as it purports to have.[50] Dempster decried the lack of biblical foundation for their support of individual conscience regarding military service and called for a deeper theological undertaking. He writes, "The poverty of explicit biblical thinking in this rationale is an utter embarrassment to people who give first priority in a 'Statement of Faith' to affirming the authority of Scripture."[51] Finally, he reflects critically on this matter, writing "the Pentecostal believer's conscience on war no longer needed to be formed specifically by biblical teaching but was now to be informed by knowledge of certain political, theological and ethical propositions."[52]

IV. Where Did the Peace Go?

Through a quiet yet dramatic turn of events, the AG eventually shied away from pacifism and supported their country's militaristic response to the events of the attacks on Pearl Harbor. Few question the motives for war in 1941; a military response was unquestionably reasonable in light of the looming possibilities of Hitler's global reign. But once the bombs fell in Hawaii, the rubble of Pentecostal pacifism was effectively left on display for all to see. Soon, the general Pentecostal population would not only grow ignorant of their own history but would more and more cease to find any connection to conscientious objection or its viability for charismatic Christians. Extend this out to today and we find, not unlike many other conservative Pentecostal denominations, the AG is a pro-military, pro-American, and pro-patriotic denomination; few members of which are aware of their pacifist heritage.[53] But why such a dramatic change? Where did Pentecostal pacifism go? And how could the moderation of this socio-ethical practice within such movements take place both in North America and Europe so quickly? Forwarding definitive answers to these pressing questions will ultimately be challenging for one simple reason: the literature from the time is scant at best. But a number of discernable reasons may be suggested; three of which are mentionable here.

---

[50] Murray W. Dempster, "Peacetime Draft Registration and Pentecostal Moral Conscience," *Agora* 1, (1980): 2.

[51] Ibid., 3.

[52] A quotation attributed to Glen Stassen in Dempster, "Peacetime Draft Registration and Pentecostal Moral Conscience," 1.

[53] On the later developments of the end of co's from AG between the years of 1968 and today, see Alexander, Ch. 7.

First, the loss of Pentecostal pacifism unquestionably arose, in part, to what Jay Beaman has identified as "cultural accommodation."[54] *The Dictionary of Pentecostal and Charismatic Movements* critiques the loss of pacifism by stating that it "corresponded to the trends in public opinion in the population at large."[55] Ultimately, I believe both suggestions address the building sentiment within Pentecostalism at the time: a growing desire to be understood apart from its sectarian emergence just forty years earlier. Pentecostals desired, as Cheryl Bridges Johns has said, to be seen as "growing up."[56] One of the biggest signs that this process of "maturation" had begun came in 1942 when Pentecostals were formally welcomed into the National Association of Evangelicals (NAE). Quickly, the process of morphing into a more mainstream American Evangelicalism would solidify the Pentecostal identity for years to come. Keep in mind the AG acceptance into the National Association of Evangelicals came just one year following the bombing of Pearl Harbor in 1941. This one-two punch—unsolicited military attack and growing desire for cultural acceptance—left little to no room for any kind of seemingly sectarian theology such as pacifism. Even more so, these created a perfect entry-point for Pentecostals to find common ground with the general American public. Not to mention that war itself became a new kind of mission field where evangelism was a much needed ministry and Pentecostals would thrive. There was now a clear shift from ethical concerns *over* military force to ministry *to* those in the military during and just after WWII.[57] This cultural accommodation is described by Warren McPherson in a darkly prophetic tone. He writes, "The military ceased to be the place where a Christian could not go. To the contrary, it was considered a place to which a Christian *must go*, both as a loyal citizen of the United States and as a missionary for Jesus. The military had become 'the world's greatest mission field.'"[58]

Keep in mind, on that token, that Pentecostals were less and less identifying with the lower-class in American society; Pentecostals were becoming upwardly mobile.[59] Literature appears to indicate that the AG grew increasingly connected to American Evangelicalism which brought with it American exceptionalism.[60] This development brought Pentecostalism out of the social lowliness

---

[54] Beaman, viii.

[55] Dwight J. Wilson, "Pacifism," in *Dictionary of Pentecostal and Charismatic Movements*, ed. Stanley Burgess and Gary McGee (Grand Rapids, MI: Zondervan, 1988), 658.

[56] This desire for perceived maturation is rather emblematic of Pentecostal spirituality. See Cheryl Bridges Johns, "The Adolescence of Pentecostalism: In Search of a Legitimate Sectarian Identity," *Pneuma* 17, no. 1 (1995).

[57] Alexander, 200-01.

[58] Warren McPherson, "Missions and the Military," *The Pentecostal Evangel*, 7 July 1963, 8. (Italics mine)

[59] Murray W. Dempster, "Review of Jay Beaman, *Pentecostal Pacifism: The Origins, Development and Rejection of Pacifist Belief among the Pentecostals*," *Pneuma* 11, no. 1 (1989): 60.

[60] Alexander, 201.

and brought it into the status of civil religion and mainstream American Christianity. Them came the perks; upward mobility, money, power, and education were new realities for Pentecostals. In fact, we see a strong rise in Pentecostal chaplaincy during WWII that undoubtedly rose from both the education and cultural need for Pentecostals in the military. Robert Mapes Anderson asserts, "These Pentecostal groups, like the Assemblies of God, that first achieved a modicum of stability and realized some improvements in their social circumstances, were the first in which ecstasy began to subside."[61] That is, social upwardness instigated the demise of a once eschatologically-driven movement. With social improvement came patriotism. With patriotism came a tolerance then out-right acceptance of war. And soon, anti-war voices that were viewed as prophetic one generation earlier were viewed as enemies of a God-blessed nation. Their voices were soon quieted.

Secondly, alongside cultural accommodation, the diminishing of pacifist practice came about due to new Pentecostal hermeneutical stances. Two historical developments, in particular, had the strongest effects on Pentecostal hermeneutics and thus the loss of pacifist theology. First, following their joining the NAE, Pentecostals would continue reading Scripture with a primarily dispensationalist set of lenses.[62] With its newfound relationship with Evangelicalism, Pentecostalism will increasingly rub shoulders with dispensationalist theology which would find a warm and inviting home in many Pentecostal circles. Along with this comes a more potent Zionist theology with all of its eschatological apocalyptic undertones and militaristic imagery. America is, in dispensationalist theology, God's new Promised Land. Through the lens of dispensationalist Zionism, America is seen as the new "promised land" that is to help protect the old "promised land" of Israel. Patriotism, in such a framework, is part and parcel of protecting God's people (Israel) from God's enemies (anyone else). I find Joel Shuman's argument helpful. He suggests two reasons for the demise of pacifism: First, he notes the loss of self-identity as an eschatological community. But, secondly, he points to the uncritical acceptance of American nationalism and democratic liberalism. Shuman says these happened because, (a) the AG gained acceptance into the NAE, and (b) the AG succumbed to the notion that America was founded on Christian principles and is therefore under God's favor.[63] This patriotic pride, undergirded by dispensationalist nationalism, emerges in stark contrast to both the holiness social critique and the early Pentecostal critique of earlier years that saw patriotism as an unnecessary or secondary issue of full-gospel spirituality.

---

[61] Robert Mapes Anderson, 1979, 231. Thanks to Alexander for this quotation. Ibid., 299.

[62] I am thankful to Aaron Friesen for reminding me that this dispensationalist tendency was afoot long before Pentecostalism's connection to the NAE.

[63] Joel Shuman, "Pentecost and the End of Patriotism: A Call for the Restoration of Pacifism among Pentecostal Christians," *Journal of Pentecostal Theology* 9, nos. 70-96 (1996): 73, 85-86.

The second development in Pentecostal hermeneutics comes at a time when Pentecostals are now thrust into a whole new post-sectarian hermeneutic. We soon see Pentecostals begin to engage with the broader biblical and academic world over time. While Pentecostals largely continue to hold to a Biblicist and literalist approach to Scripture-reading, the effects of twentieth century biblical studies helped to mute certain readings such as pacifism. As Pentecostals began to establish Bible colleges and even start to attend seminaries, the sectarian hermeneutic to which they had long held began to shift dramatically. The benefits to such integration and conversation are unquestionable: new biblical insights, new theological ventures, openness to the broader ecumenical community. What I believe this does is effectively mute the prophetic elements of the Pentecostal voice. Now that Pentecostalism is growing into a mainstream movement that must increasingly read the text alongside the broader Christian community, prophetic hermeneutical stances (such as pacifist ones) are not welcomed as fully-accepted conversation partners.

Thirdly, and finally, I would suggest that the institutionalization of Pentecostalism made it more and more challenging to exist with such a scandalous social position. Because of its youth in the years preceding WWII, Pentecostalism largely went where its leaders took it. The seat of authority was (and in many ways still is) in a charismatic leader who could gather people. Thus the biblical description becomes a sociological maxim in Pentecostal history: "like priest, like people" (Hos. 4:9). David Harrell has described it well: every Pentecostal movement started with a founding prophet but is later managed by ruling priest.[64] Pacifism, in the earliest years, was the theology of the founding prophets and never fully translated into a theological development. Edith Blumhofer, the onetime official AG historian, notes that the 1917 resolution did not seek to answer theologically the challenges at hand regarding pacifism. Rather, it was to ensure exemptions. One of the greatest problems was that there was, as Blumhofer writes, not an AG "just war theory or theology."[65] That is, pacifism was more sociological than theological. A theology of pacifism, then and now, would be considered only when the leaders of Pentecostal denominations were considering it. Murray Dempster lays the gauntlet down claiming that because Pentecostals had not connected pacifism with their pneumatology, it ended.[66] Ultimately, this is one of the ongoing weaknesses of Pentecostal praxis; our charismatic theology is always at least one step behind our charismatic leaders.

---

[64] In the Introduction to Crews, xiii.

[65] *The Assemblies of God: A Chapter on the Story of American Pentecostalism*, vol. 1, *To 1941*, (Springfield, Gospel Publishing House, 1989), 352.

[66] Murray W. Dempster, "Reassessing the Moral Rhetoric of Early American Pentecostal Pacifism," *Crux* 26, no. 1 (1990): 32.

V. Rediscovering Peace Theology in Contemporary Pentecostalism

In our first section, we examined the historical and theological pacifist rumblings in early Pentecostal history. Then we undertook a brief examination of pacifism in denominational life in section three. Finally, we asked the broader question: why did pacifist theology go away after WWII? Moving ahead, our study will now forge some new ways forward. With all of this in mind, our final section will consider how and why we might further undertake a robust and thorough conversation with this undercurrent of historic Pentecostal pacifism and suggest how it might move forward the theological and practical conversation in contemporary Pentecostalism.

On one hand, Pentecostal pacifist history warrants a thorough revisit because it has much to offer about what it means to identify as a Pentecostal. In the earliest years Pentecostals were identified boldly as the "full gospel" people, implying their wide-scale attempt at taking the whole biblical story seriously in Christian practice. Paul Alexander comments that these "full gospel" Pentecostals "did not want to leave anything out."[67] This gets at the heartbeat of Pentecostal identity: to reconsider all the vignettes of the biblical tradition is perennially the assignment of a "full gospel" people. So in searching out, articulating, and embodying the gospel message in *all* of its particularities, one attempts "full gospel" Christianity. Examining Pentecostal pacifism is searching out how "full gospel" people have actually expressed their faith. On the other hand, by returning to whence they came, Pentecostals embody their "restorationist" character. I do not want to be sentimental here as some things in history we should never re-consider or attempt to re-live.[68] However, a Spirit-led people seeks out the Spirit's voice not only in the Scriptures, but also in the pages of today's newspaper and yesterday's history. As a restorationist movement, Pentecostals love to re-live the glory of the past. I might challenge, however, that Pentecostals must practice being *holistically* restorationist; by this I mean their aim must not simply be to re-kindle the passion of the early church but also the passion of early Pentecostalism! To do so is an act at holistic restorationism, kindling, in the words of Grant Wacker, a "determinination to return to the first things…however great or small".[69] Peace theology in Pentecostal history was a Spirit-led activity in the past. Might it be again? Let us consider some ways in which it would be helpful.

First, such a re-discovery would force a biblically literalist Pentecostalism to once again conceive a more well-rounded hermeneutic that takes the entire biblical text and its meaning into consideration in its contemporary mission.

---

[67] Alexander, 107.
[68] Such as racism.
[69] Wacker, Heaven Below, 12

Pentecostalism became "rather directly and simply pacifist in the first generation. The simplest reason is that they take the whole Bible straight."[70] Literalism of this kind is seen in many ways in early Pentecostal history: a rejection of wine at the Eucharist because of its omission in the gospel accounts, a literal reading of "by his stripes we are healed" (1 Pet. 2:24), and a literal reading of the Sermon on the Mount.[71] They understood the Sermon on the Mount to be by no means a suggestion—it was as central to the New Testament as "be being filled with the Spirit" was (Eph. 5:18). However, the challenge is that contemporary Pentecostal hermeneutics are not actually literal; they are, at most, *selectively* literal, ignoring almost entirely the peace sayings of Jesus. Pentecostalism has historically taken Acts as a *literal* pattern of the church today, the power of healing, the possibility of tongues, and even, in some cases, the handling of snakes. But why not the peace sayings of Christ? In the context of global violence, religious radicalism, and political polemics, a need for a re-reading of the peace sayings for Pentecostals is at an all-time high. How might this happen? Martin Mittlestadt suggests a fresh reading of Luke-Acts would invigorate and enlarge a novel approach towards peace theology in both contemporary Pentecostalism and Anabaptist ecclesiology.[72] Mittelstadt points out that Luke offers a theological foundation of the Spirit in light of suffering, persecution, and martyrdom. He contends that in light of a brutal Roman world marked by occupation, war, brutality, and persecution, a revised reading of Luke-Acts based on "peace" may offer new insights.[73] Clearly, every Christian tradition will follow a canon within a canon. As Mittelstadt has written, "no matter how much a movement desires to follow the Scriptures, it is impossible to embrace their message in totality."[74] The key is an openness to "theological exploration" and not getting bogged down in one's tradition or forgetting the need for new readings in new times.[75] The peace message of Luke calls a Pentecostal expres-

---

[70] John Howard Yoder in his introduction to Beaman.

[71] Alexander, 108-09.

[72] Martin Mittelstadt, "Spirit and Peace in Luke-Acts: Possibilities for Pentecostal/Anabaptist Dialogue," *Didaskalia* Fall, no. (2009). Mittelstadt points out that many Lukan studies do not have a category for peace. He points out Francois Bovon, *Luke the Theologian: Fifty Five Years of Research* (1950-2005), Waco, TX, Baylor, 2006 nor Willard Swartley, *Covenant of peace: The Missing Peace in the New Testament Theology and Ethics*, Eerdmans, 2006 as evidence of this. Swartley says that of 25 major studies in NT thoelogy or ethics, no piece has covered the Luke-Acts peace motif (x).

[73] Mittelstadt points out that Luke's gospel uses the term "peace" some 14 times and 7 times in the book of Acts. This is significant in contrast to the other gospels. He writes, "based on a simple word count, Luke appears to be more interested in associating the word and concept of peace with Jesus' story than other Gospel writers." Ibid., 21-22.

[74] Ibid., 35.

[75] Ibid.

sion to envision the ethical, political, and personal implications of peacemaking today. Luke's vision of peace is not merely one of individual peace but rather of an entire eschatological community marked by peace.

With that, secondly, a re-contextualized historic Pentecostal pacifism would usher in a fruitful dialogue stimulating a much needed theological imagination regarding Pentecostal and charismatic ecological stewardship and care, especially in the context of a robust pneumatology. Renewal of the Spirit's love and freedom provokes, in Yoder's words, a renew*ing* community that, in all forms, is "free from violence."[76] But can a community of the Spirit truly claim to be filled with the Spirit of freedom while simultaneously ignoring any of its participation in said oppression? Quite simply, the Spirit of peace seeks freedom for the oppressed *and* the oppressor.[77] War must be questioned not simply because of its effects upon the victims. The damage is much larger. War, likewise, must be challenged because of its endless psychological, emotional, and spiritual effects on the victors. Following WWII, in which the process of mass transportation, cars, suburbanization and more arise, Pentecostals grew more and more out of touch with creation. Pacifism and peacemaking theology remind us something; justice and peace are holistic realities that have bearings on everyone involved. We must not read pneumatology in a purely individualistic or anthropocentric light. In the words of the apostle, "where the Spirit of the Lord is, there is freedom." (2 Cor. 3:17) Any attempt at a peacemaking ethic must take into consideration the entire creation and would rightly include freedom from violence in farming practice, land degradation, species loss, and unjust working conditions. Peacemaking, in this way, refuses either anthropocentrism or nationalism as main framework; peacemaking must be cosmos-centric. Unjust violence done unto any of God's creatures hurts not only creation but God's Spirit. Violent oppression in *any* form where creation "groans" seeks freedom under mission of Jesus. Peaceful eating is the Spirit's business. For instance, peaceful eating might be seen in the following examples, among others:

- Bringing freedom through what we eat and buy every day.
- Eating foods that minimize the suffering and abuse of animals, trees, and peoples.
- Choosing products not simply on the basis of whether they get the job done but whether they bring about justice in an injust system.
- Considering economic choices through a pneumatological lens.
- Bearing freedom in choosing a simple lifestyle.
- Cage-free chickens and choices of sustainability are pneumatological issues because they are freedom issues.

---

[76] In the foreword to Beaman, iii.
[77] This is a general theme of Miroslav Volf, *Exclusion and Embrace: A Theological Exploration of Identity, Otherness, and Reconciliation* (Nashville, TN: Abingdon, 1996).

The lacuna of this theological-ethical work within Pentecostal scholarship is expansive. Isaiah prophesied that the coming Messiah (*Moshiach*) would come and bear peace; lion would lie with the lamb, child with the snake, enemies would be reconciled. Jesus, just following his Spirit-infilling moment at baptism, is sent into the desert to be with the wild animals thus signaling a sign of his Messiahship.

Thirdly, and finally, a re-examination of Pentecostal pacifism would help stimulate a renewed interest in the role of Pentecostalism in being a "community of resistance" which challenges the social norms of culture, technology, and politics in a serious and prophetic way. John writes that the Spirit will "convict the world of sin" (John 16:8). Thus, by extension, a community of the Spirit will question the status quo. Violence and polemics have become a cultural staple in Western culture. But, Joel Shuman points out, that a Pentecost theology can serve as the reversal of the division of Babel and ending of violence based on the coming of the Spirit upon the church.[78] This helps illustrate the recovery of the role of the prophetic witness in speaking against the harmful and dangerous aspects in human culture. This pacifist connection may further in-roads of learning between Pentecostals and the historic peace-churches such as the Anabaptists who have long understood their witness as being a sign against the world.[79] Peace-making is a powerful expression of that sign; one of which both Pentecostals and Anabaptists share a unique story.

---

[78] Shuman, 94-95.
[79] Argued by Mittelstadt.

Chapter 7

Speaking Truth to Power—with a Twist: Reenvisioning the Task of Theology and the Academy[1]

Joerg Rieger

This lecture will do two things: it will give a brief overview over a few key themes that I have developed in my work at Perkins and SMU over the past fifteen years, and it will offer a programmatic statement of the future direction of this work.

I. Don't Think as a Thinker, but as a Living Being: The Epistemological Task

"Don't think as a thinker, but as a living being." This directive was penned by the nineteenth-century German philosopher Ludwig Feuerbach. His book *Principles of the Philosophy of the Future*[2] was one of the first texts that I read as a graduate student at Duke University. This was 20 years ago, just after I had come to the United States from Germany. Feuerbach's encouragement to think as a living being sounds so common-sense and so heartwarming, that it probably would do very well on a Hallmark card. Nevertheless, it implies a fundamental challenge.

Let me describe this challenge in terms of my own biography. In the halls of the German academy, where I was brought up, we looked at things the other way around: There, you were considered to be a better thinker the more you were able to think unlike a living being. Our motto would have been something like: "Don't think as a living being, but think as a thinker." I quickly discovered that this expectation also existed in some parts of the U.S. academy, especially in my own field of systematic theology.

---

[1] Delivered as the Wendland-Cook Professorship Inaugural Lecture on October 8, 2009. Originally published by Perkins School of Theology, Southern Methodist University, Pp 1-16. It is republished here with permission.

[2] Ludwig Feuerbach, *Principles of the Philosophy of the Future*, trans. Manfred H. Vogel (Indianapolis, Ind.: Hackett Pub. Co, 1986).

The big question, of course, is whether it is ever really possible to think as a thinker, and not as a living being. To put it in very simple terms: is it possible to think with your brain alone, from the neck up so to speak, shutting out the rest of your body? And: what will the rest of your body do, if you shut it out? Since the days of Sigmund Freud, we understand that things that are repressed have a way of returning through the back door. But we are not just dealing with a question of how our minds and our bodies are connected. We are also dealing with the question of how our thinking is shaped by reality as a whole, including politics and economics.

Some eighty years ago, the Italian philosopher and politician Antonio Gramsci famously talked about thinkers in terms of "organic intellectuals," a term that has been picked up by various liberation theologians and that has since entered the mainline. Here, we might pause for another Hallmark moment, because today many of us seem to be agreed on the need to be organic intellectuals: who would want to be considered to be an "inorganic intellectual"?

But let's take another look at this matter. In order to understand Gramsci's notion of the organic intellectual we must understand the other alternative. The opposite of organic intellectuals, according to Gramsci, is what he calls traditional intellectuals. Traditional intellectuals, Gramsci says, "put themselves forward as autonomous and independent."[3] In other words, traditional intellectuals assume that they are free from outside influences and that they can do their work without taking into account their context.

The truth is, of course, that none of us are ever free from outside influences and from our context. The tragedy in the case of the so-called traditional intellectuals is this: because they are unaware that they are shaped by outside influences, their work ends up perpetuating precisely these influences. Almost invariably, such intellectuals end up supporting the status quo. To put it in the words of Feuerbach's statement: Even if we refuse to think as living beings, life still has a way of catching up with us.

In contrast to these traditional intellectuals, organic intellectuals are thinkers who take their context into account. Organic intellectuals own up to the fact that no one is ever free from outside influences. This enables them to take into account their biases. In other words, organic intellectuals understand that all thinking is contextual: "Don't think as a thinker, but as a living being." Those of you who have spent much time in the academy lately know that there is a lot of talk about context these days, in various academic fields. In theology, we talk about "contextual theology," which describes a form of theology that is intent on taking seriously people's contexts.

There is, however, one more problem that needs to be addressed here: I am going to argue that not just any talk about context will do. About a decade ago,

---

[3] Antonio Gramsci, *Selections from the Prison Notebooks*, ed. and trans. Quintin Hoare and Geoffrey Nowell Smith (New York: International Publishers, 1971), 7. See also the discussion in Joerg Rieger, *Remember the Poor: The Challenge to Theology in the Twenty-First Century* (Harrisburg, Pa.: Trinity Press International, 1998), 225-26.

I published a chapter in a book where I challenged contextual theology. I know this will surprise many of my colleagues and students, but contextual theology as we normally go about it has some deep flaws. The biggest problem with contextual theology and other forms of contextualized reflection in the academy, is that context is often taken at face value. Context appears to be whatever is closest to home. An almost comical example of this sort of contextual theology is the case of the white, male, middle-class and middle-aged theologian who once mused about doing theology in a warm bathtub.[4] The warm bathtub, it might mistakenly be assumed, is the perfect context for white, male, middle-class and middle-aged academics who have tenure and not much else to worry about—in the same way that patriarchy is the context of women, that racism is the context of racial and ethnic minorities, and that economic exploitation is the context of workers. When seen in this way, it is no wonder that contextual theologies are considered to be special interest theologies: everyone gets to explore their own niche in life, and afterwards we write for other people who are like us.

This sort of understanding of contextual theology is no longer helpful, however, and I doubt that it ever was. While I agree that it is better to discuss matters of context than not to discuss them, once we begin to take note of our context we are only half way there. We need to understand our context at a deeper level. The problem is that our context may not be what we think it is. For example, if I were to think that my context is primarily in a warm bathtub, or at my desk in the comfort of my own house, or here on the SMU campus where I teach, I would be forgetting the more important aspects that make up my context. At a deeper level, my context as a white middle-class male academic includes all those whom I usually fail to see: my context, for instance, includes those who have sewed the clothes that I am wearing, probably for low wages; my context includes those who clean our buildings but who don't live in our neighborhoods; and my context includes many others of whose existence I am not even aware but on whose back I tend to live my life, benefiting from a privileged position in terms of race, gender, and class.

In my challenge to contextual theology a little over ten years ago, I concluded that context is not what it appears to be on the surface; rather, I said then "context is that which hurts."[5] In other words, my context—and all of our contexts—deep down are linked to where the pain is in this world. While I have quoted Feuerbach, Freud, and Gramsci so far, this insight is much older and goes deeper, as it is also part of ancient Christian wisdom. The Apostle Paul knew in his own ways that context is that which hurts. Speaking of the church as the body of Christ, he concludes that "if one member suffers, all suffer together with it" (1 Cor. 12:26). In order to get to that point, Paul had to subvert

---

[4] See Tom Driver, *Patterns of Grace: Human Experience as Word of God* (San Francisco: Harper and Row, 1977), 1-28. Driver's reflections have a good deal of depth, to be sure, but they also lack the depth of context that I am exploring here.

[5] Joerg Rieger, "Developing a Common Interest Theology from the Underside," in: *Liberating the Future: God, Mammon, and Theology*, ed. Rieger (Minneapolis: Fortress Press, 1998), 129.

the image of the body as it was used by the contextual thinkers of his own time: the Romans, while musing about society as a body, would not have worried too much about the suffering of what was considered to be the inferior members of the body; neither do many people seem to worry much about such suffering today, as some of the nastier outbursts of the current healthcare debate show.

Paul, on the other hand, was concerned precisely about those members of the body who suffer; he even states that "the members of the body that seem to be weaker are indispensable" (1 Cor. 12:22). For Christian theologians, there is an even deeper point to be made here, for context as that which hurts is ultimately the context of the divine itself, found at the margins of this world, with a nation of slaves in Israel and with the proverbial widows, orphans, and strangers in the Hebrew Bible.

Context as that which hurts is also the context of Jesus Christ, whose solidarity with those pushed to the margins in his own time led to torture and death on a cross: a cross on which he was put by imperial politics and religion. Unfortunately, this ancient Christian wisdom is often missing in the churches today. We can see it, instead, in other places where theologians and other academics often fail to look. In the labor movement, for instance, I have encountered a saying that "an injury to one is an injury to all." When Gramsci talked about "organic intellectuals" he too had something like that in mind. To sum up my point here: talk about context in general will no longer do. The context that is most fruitful for academic study, including the study of theology, is the context of our common pain.

This turns on its head a widely accepted understanding of what is *special* interest and what is *common* interest. In the model that I am proposing, common interest is not defined at the top, by a small group of academics in the know, or by those who claim to be the guardians of universals. Instead, common interest is defined at the bottom. For example: When women experience oppression along the lines of gender this is not a matter of special interest but of common interest: the pain that is felt here affects us all, those who suffer from it as well as those who ultimately benefit from it. As a result, the insights of feminist theology are just as relevant for men as they are for women. Moreover, when ethnic minorities experience oppression along the lines of race, everyone is affected: as Martin Luther King, Jr. reminded us, racism distorts not only the humanity of those who suffer from it, but also the humanity of those who benefit from it. Finally, when workers experience the pressures of an economy that pushes ever leaner and meaner forms of production, it is not only the workers and their families who feel the pain: our whole society "suffers together with them," to use Paul's phrase, since life itself becomes leaner and meaner at all levels.

Now it should be clear why a theologian is talking about all of this. The Apostle Paul is only one of a long succession of Jewish and Christian figures who understood the importance of this common pain. The prophets of the Hebrew Bible knew this as well, as they pronounced judgment precisely on those who failed to understand the deeper bonds of community, which always include the oppressed. According to the Prophet Isaiah, all of the problems with religious worship could be summarized in one short sentence: "You serve your own interest on your fast day, and oppress all your workers" (Isaiah 58:3b). Apparently, the two things are connected: serving your own interest in church and religion—and oppressing your workers.

In the New Testament, Jesus keeps reminding us of similar issues, for instance when he reverses the order of the first and the last. At the end of a story that deals with support for the casually employed, more commonly known as "the laborers in the vineyard," he has this to say: "So the last will be first, and the first will be last." The position of those who are considered "the last" is important, not because they are to be recipients of charity, but because they present a fundamental challenge for everyone. The salvation of all is tied up with their salvation.[6] Recall Jesus' conclusion when he talks about actions of solidarity with the least of these: "Just as you did it to one of the least of these who are members of my family, you did it to me." So goes the famous quote from Matt. 25.[7]

When we think about context, therefore, we can no longer do without that which hurts. All of our contexts, even the context of the theologian in the warm bathtub, become clearer when viewed from the underside, where the common pain is. Here, special interest is most effectively challenged and common interest begins.

This is one of the great opportunities that is captured in the description of the Wendland-Cook Professorship, as envisioned by the donors. Let me quote to you the beginning of this description: "The successive holders of the professorship are to make substantial contributions to the academic study of systematic and constructive theology that address current church and social issues; to address issues of inequality of power and to show commitment to the liberation of all people, the promotion of justice, and the encouragement of nonviolence..."

My hope is that the Wendland-Cook Professorship will become one of the institutions that helps to connect us in terms of the context of our deepest common pain. It goes without saying that much of that common pain is tied up with the economy these days.

II. Speaking Truth to Power: A Matter of Life and Death

What we have done so far is what academics call "epistemology," the inquiry into how we know what we know. However, there is only so much epistemology

---

[6] See also Jon Sobrino, *No Salvation Outside the Poor: Prophetic-Utopian Essays* (Maryknoll, NY: Orbis Books, 2008).

[7] Matth. 25:40; conversely, see also Mark 9:42: "If any of you put a stumbling block before one of these little ones who believe in me, it would be better for you if a great millstone were hung around your neck and you were thrown into the sea."

that you can do before your head hurts. So let me talk about some of the practical challenges of this approach. How does it all relate to my title, "speaking truth to power"? And where is the promised "twist"?

The Perkins School of Theology Mission Statement identifies three contexts that are important to the work of our school: the university, the church, and the region (that is, our particular setting in the southwestern United States). Power is at work in each of these three contexts. This may sound self-evident, but this power gets very little attention. In most of our internal conversations about the university, the church, and even about the region, the question of power usually does not come up.

One reason why the question of power does not come up when we talk about the university is because it is often associated with the notion of the "ivory tower." Universities are often considered to be a little removed from the world, like secret societies that do whatever it is they do behind closed doors. As a result, the knowledge produced by universities is considered to be mostly for specialists, without direct relevance for the rest of society and the world. But look at the academy in light of what we said earlier, and the picture changes: If it is not possible to "think as a thinker," the ivory tower is really just an illusion. The reality is that even the most academic academy and the most universal university is deeply embedded in the world of the powers that be. Like all institutions, universities are shaped by powerful interests; these interests may operate just a little more behind the scenes in academia. To be sure, these interests will not go away if we ignore them, and, unless we address them, they will keep shaping us unconsciously. Even our most cherished notions of academic truth are affected by the powers that be.

Ask yourself how it was possible that academics—including ancient Greek philosophers and some Church fathers—could take for granted slavery for thousands of years? How could academics—theologians included—defend the full-blown institution of slavery in the United States? Or how was it possible that most German academics—theologians once again included—would accept the fascism of Nazi Germany? In these situations, speaking truth to power was not an option, because truth and power were too closely aligned. Similar dynamics are in place today, for instance when academics and theologians accept claims made by mainline economics that elevate capitalism to the place of ultimate truth. This is one of the key issues addressed in my latest book, *No Rising Tide: Theology, Economics, and the Future.*[8]

The term "ivory tower" is usually not applied to the other two contexts, the church and the region, but it might help us understand the problems there as well. On the surface of it, the church also tends to display the qualities of the proverbial ivory tower. To outsiders the church, like the university, for the most part appears to be a fairly closed society, as the bulk of what happens in church also seems to belong behind closed doors and tends to stay there for

---

[8] Joerg Rieger, *No Rising Tide: Theology, Economics, and the Future* (Minneapolis: Fortress Press, 2009).

the most part. Even insiders often see it that way, as church people are not always clear about the relevance of what is going on in church for their everyday lives. Add to that the phenomenon of "ecclesial narcissism" and you get an idea of what I am talking about.

But look at the church in light of what we found above, and the picture changes: Not even the church is as isolated as it appears. The church, too, is deeply shaped by the powers that be—too often without being aware of it. And this applies not just to the church: even our theologies are shaped by the powers that be. In my book *Christ and Empire*, I have shown how some of our most cherished images of Christ have been shaped by empires over the course of a 2000-year history. The good news in this case, let me hasten to add, is that none of these empires was ever able to take over theology and the church completely.

If, for some reason, you have trouble following my claim that the church is shaped by the powers that be, you might try a little experiment: try challenging powerful interests represented in your church and see what happens. One of my former students recently found out the hard way what happens when you do that: she preached a stellar sermon in which she made a strong theological argument that gently pointed towards universal health care. I don't think I need to explain to most of you that such a move, however gentle, can very quickly land you in hot water these days; never mind that the sermon made second place in a sermon contest.[9] Even in the context of the church, truth and power appear to be closely aligned.

Let me briefly address the third context, our region—our particular setting in the southwestern United States. Even here it can at times look as if things were taking on the shape of an ivory tower. On the surface, many of our communities appear to be just as isolated as the academy and the church. The concerns of different neighborhoods, for instance, seem to run on separate tracks: while some neighborhoods speak English, others speak mostly Spanish; while some neighborhoods have good schools, others have schools that are not doing so well, and so on. But the term isolation hardly captures what is going on: neighborhoods are related, for instance, through the labor of those who provide services, like lawn mowing, cleaning, and construction. As you all know, ethnicity is a factor here, but so is gender and—dare I say it?—class. As a result, power is a factor that must also be considered when we talk about our region and our communities. Such positions of power are reflected in real estate values, which in turn reflect the funding for schools and other public services. As any real estate agent will tell you, housing values are not primarily determined by bricks and mortar but by three other factors: location, location, and location; this is yet another way of talking about the alignment of power and truth.

If, therefore, power and truth are intimately connected in all three of our contexts, the university, the church, and the region, is it even possible to "speak truth to power"? Are those of us who use this phrase simply naïve? In order to make things work, we need the twist to which my title refers. The twist that I

---

[9] Sermon by the Rev. Mary Spradlin, St. Stephen United Methodist Church, Arlington, TX, http://www.youtube.com/view_play_list?p=B0D8EAEEED88B9C6.

am suggesting has to do with a move from critique—which is one of the staples of academic work—to *self*-critique. This move from critique to self-critique comprises one of the biggest differences between my work and the work of my predecessor Schubert Ogden, whom I succeeded some 15 years ago here at Perkins. Ogden's work consistently challenged us to think critically. Theology, as he once pointed out, needs to expose the rationalization of positions already taken.[10] While I affirm his point, I have argued for over a decade that we must take one more step: We need a self-critical approach in addition to the critical approach. Theology not only needs to deal with the rationalization of positions already taken but, as I like to say, with the rationalization of positions that we are not even aware we are holding.

In Ogden's case, when you are in the business of rationalizing positions that you have already taken, you know pretty well what you are doing, and you are able to stop it. What I am talking about is more complicated: When you rationalize positions that you are not even aware you are holding, you don't know what you are doing, and you are not able to stop without some help. In Ogden's approach, power is visible and you can speak truth to it; in my approach, power is less visible and it shapes truth to such an extent that "speaking truth to power" can appear to be almost impossible.

Those of us who benefit from the powers that be, theologians and academics included, have a hard time seeing power at work. This means that we need some help identifying power, and this help comes from unexpected places. While power is less visible from a position of privilege, power is more visible from the perspective of those who lack privilege and who get crushed by power: they cannot only see this power but they feel it in their own bodies, as it were. Please note that when I am talking about power here I am not talking about a sort of power play that merely swings back and forth, from one side to the other, where both sides hold roughly similar amounts of power. What I am talking about, by contrast, are differentials of power that are so great, that they are matters of life and death. Such differentials of power are most clearly seen by those whose lives are in danger, and here, another take on truth emerges.

Let me give you a few examples. Power differentials become visible, for instance, when workers get killed on the job, often due to a lack of safety equipment or to mounting pressure to produce. This is a matter of life and death, which is more prevalent in Texas than anywhere else in the United States. In Texas, more construction workers get killed than in any other state of the nation, including California, which has 12 million more residents than Texas. In 2007, 528 workers were killed on the job in Texas; in 2008 the number was 457.[11] What we are dealing with here is a matter of grave differentials of power: Texas is known for offering worse support and protection for workers than any

---

[10] See Schubert M. Ogden, *Faith and Freedom: Toward a Theology of Liberation* (Nshville: Abington Press, 1982), 31.

[11] See the news report on a Dallas area Worker Rights Board meeting, September 8, 2009, on the web: http://wrbdallas.blogspot.com/2009/09/kdfw-tv-coverage-of-sep-5-wrb-hearing_08.html.

other state in the nation, because workers have less power here. There are construction workers in Dallas—some are with us here tonight—who do not even receive sufficient drinking water on hot days on the job, and who are not provided with the necessary safety equipment. Note that the workers who work for this same company in Chicago do not have these particular problems. From the perspective of these workers, the power differentials of our society are seen with great clarity, and here another take on truth emerges that is not often recognized.

There is another matter of life and death that is closer to home than those of us who have some health-care coverage may realize: One American family goes bankrupt every 30 seconds, for reasons related to health care.[12] Worse yet, the full truth about this situation is hidden, as we have no clear idea how many people actually die from a lack of health care: these deaths commonly happen behind closed doors, out of the sight of the public or the media. Here, we are dealing with a genuine matter of life and death as well, which is directly related to the grave economic power differentials that mark our common context. Once again, power differentials are not hard to spot from this point of view.

Let me give you just one more example. When 50,000 people die every day around the globe from preventable causes, this is also a matter of how power differentials translate into matters of life and death. According to a United Nations Human Development Report, only four percent of the combined wealth of the world's 225 richest individuals would suffice to provide sufficient food, clean water, as well as basic health care and education for all of humanity. That the wealth of these 225 richest individuals matches the annual income of the poorest three billion people of the world's population (47 percent) is another indication of the grave power differentials about which I am talking.[13] Power is not hard to identify here, but it is in the interest of the powers that be that it goes unreported for the most part.

What does all this mean? It means that the truth—especially the truth about power—is best seen from the underside. You can best see the truth about what is going on from the perspective of those who are dying; and once this truth has given you pause, then you work yourself up from there. The truth about Nazi Germany, to use an extreme example, is best seen from the perspective of the victims of the Holocaust: these victims include six million Jews and six million others, including gays and lesbians, disabled people, socialists, communists, and labor leaders. Many ordinary German citizens never realized this truth, because they never had the nerve to encounter the victims. The truth about our current situation is best seen from the perspective of the victims as

---

[12] Dan Lothian, "Health Crisis: 'A Bankruptcy Every 30 Seconds,'" CNN Special Report (March 9, 2009), on the web: http://money.cnn.com/2009/03/05/news/healthcare_summit/

[13] United Nations Report on Human Development, referenced in Barbara Crossette, "Kofi Annan's Astonishing Facts!" *The New York Times* (September 27, 1998), on the web: http://www.nytimes.com/learning/general/featured_articles/980928monday.htm; 50,000 reported in See Kai Nielsen, *Globalization and Justice* (New York: Humanity Books, 2003), 33, and note 44.

well, whether they be workers, people without work, people without health care, people starving, minorities, or the many young people who are falling through the cracks of the system.

That truth is best seen from the underside can be affirmed from the perspective of various disciplines. We have a genuinely interdisciplinary project here: Psychoanalysts know this, for instance, and this is why they listen not to all the interesting details of your story that you tell when you lie on the couch; rather, they listen to what you have repressed. In my early work, I have demonstrated that the insights of psychoanalysis shed light not only on individuals but on theological, social, and political realities as well, using some of the tools developed by French psychoanalyst Jacques Lacan. There is a collective sort of repression going on in our society that is fueled by power differentials, and if we want to find out the truth, we need to study that which has been repressed.[14] Other disciplines have developed similar insights. From the perspective of literary criticism and cultural studies, Fredric Jameson has talked about the "political unconscious." Similar insights can be found in the approaches of subaltern studies and postcolonial theory.[15] Even in the field of economics there are now scholars who are pushing us to take a look at our economic unconscious.[16]

Elsewhere, I have talked about our "theological unconscious."[17] The study of theology needs to investigate the sort of things that we have repressed in order to understand the deeper truth about ourselves, and ultimately about God. In my book *God and the Excluded*, one of the main points was that we are only in a position to develop new respect for the divine if we start developing new respect for other people. The repression of others and the repression of the divine run parallel in many ways.

---

[14] In my book *Remember the Poor* I have shown what it means to study the truth that is located in the kinds of repressions that whole communities experience. Here lies the difference both to conservative and liberal approaches to poverty: both camps try to help integrate poor people back into society. I am aware that there are differences between the two camps, having to do with the means used to integrate people. What I am talking about is something else, however: the challenge of poverty and of the lives of people who experience repression is that they can hold up a mirror and show us the truth about ourselves that we have repressed.

[15] See, for instance, Fredric Jameson, *The Political Unconscious: Narrative as a Socially Symbolic Act* (Ithaca, N.Y.: Cornell University Press,1981); John Beverley, *Subalternity and Representation: Arguments in Cultural Theory* (Durham: Duke University Press, 1999); Homi Bhabha, *The Location of Culture* (London: Routledge, 1994); and Frantz Fanon, *The Wretched of the Earth* (New York: Grove Press, 1968). I have engaged these and other authors in various projects of mine.

[16] Steve Keen, *Debunking Economics: The Naked Emperor of the Social Sciences* (New York: Zed Books, 2002); Jim Stanford, *Economics for Everyone: A Short Guide to the Economics of Capitalism* (Ann Arbor, MI: Pluto Press, 2008); I have engaged alternative economics in *No Rising Tide*.

[17] Joerg Rieger, *Christ and Empire: From Paul to Postcolonial Times* (Minneapolis, MN: Fortress Press, 2007), 131 and *No Rising Tide*, 79.

Now it should be clearer how it might still be possible to speak "truth to power," and what this old Quaker truth might mean today. After all, the phrase "speaking truth to power" was not coined by the hippies of the 1960s but by the Quakers in the eighteenth century.[18] The common alignment of truth and power is best challenged from the bottom up, from the engagement with all that threatens life, in the midst of matters of life and death. Remember the Apostle Paul: "If one member suffers, all suffer together with it." And don't forget the example of Christ.

III. Constructive Theology: Constructed and Constructing

Some of you may have wondered about this new adjective that is part of my title: "Constructive Theology." Let me assure my colleagues and students that I have not left the time-honored field of systematic theology when I gave up my former title "Professor of Systematic Theology" on December 31, 2008. Talking about constructive theology is just another, and I would argue a more fitting, way of addressing the tasks of theology today.

While theology is still commonly defined as "critical reflection on Christian thought and action," I have argued so far that we need to define theology as the "*self*-critical reflection on Christian thought and action." We need a self-critical approach, rather than an approach that is merely critical, due to the fact that theology is located in a context of power and of power differentials. What needs to be analyzed self-critically is precisely this context of power in which we find ourselves—both because this context of power shapes theological thinking, and because this context of power needs to be challenged and transformed—at least as long as we live in a world of grave power differentials. Constructive theology, as I define it here, promotes this self-critical moment.

Another way of approaching constructive theology is to say that it acknowledges the constructed nature of *all* theology, both present and past. Once we recognize the constructed nature of all theology, it becomes all the more important to take seriously the constructive task of theology in our own time. For the record, constructive theology takes very seriously the thousands of years of Judeo-Christian theology on whose shoulders we stand: it is simply not true that we are only interested in what is going on in our own time and context. But it is precisely because we take this long history so seriously, that we need to reflect self-critically on what was said and done in the past in order to address the challenges of the contemporary world in constructive fashion.

Let me be very clear here: despite claims to the contrary, it is never an option for theology simply to repeat and to rehearse what was said in the past. Whenever theologians repeat and rehearse a statement made in the past, we must keep in mind that meaning is in flux. Language is a living thing, which cannot

---

[18] See, for instance, the following document http://www.quaker.org/sttp.html, which refers both to the background as well as to the contemporary challenges from a Quaker perspective.

be pinned down once and for all like hunting trophies. So, whenever we repeat and rehearse statements made in the past, we may be saying something completely different today from what that statement said in the past. The problem becomes even clearer in light of the problem of power: It is not only that meaning and language are in flux; they are in a kind of flux that is constantly shaped and fueled by the powers that be, just like our context is constantly shaped by the powers that be. Constructive theology seeks to help us resist this constant process of adaptation. I am concerned that rehearsing past statements without awareness of this constant process of adaptation, will result in contemporary statements that conform to the powers in our time.

This all may sound a bit abstract, so let me give you an example: Take, for instance, the traditional Christian confession that Jesus is Lord. This is one of the oldest Christian confessions, and it has become one of the most orthodox over time. Merely repeating that ancient formula in the present, however, will not guarantee that you capture its meaning: after all, we have different notions of what the title "lord" means. Without self-critical theological reflection the classical statement that "Jesus is Lord," is likely to be taken to mean today that "Jesus is like a typical person of power in our world, and a typical person of power in our world is like Jesus." Since the typical person of power these days is the CEO, the idea that Jesus is Lord might be taken to mean that "Jesus is like a CEO, and a CEO is like Jesus." This interpretation is more widespread today than you might think; and even if this had not occurred to *you*, such an idea appears to be almost second nature in our current cultural climate. There is even a book titled *Jesus CEO*, which appears to have done quite well for itself.[19]

These are just more examples of how the powers that be are able to modify and shape the truth. But if we remember how the ancient Christian confession that Jesus is Lord once challenged the powers in their own time, it cannot be domesticated so easily. If this ancient confession meant something like "Jesus is Lord, and the Roman Emperor is not," confessing Jesus as Lord was not a harmless religious statement; rather, confessing Jesus as Lord was a way of "speaking truth to power." What is rejected here is the sort of unilateral power that moves from the top down, as represented by the Roman Empire. Today, confessing Jesus as Lord in this sense might mean something like "Jesus is Lord, and CEOs are not," or, phrased even more provocatively, "Jesus is Lord, and the members of the ruling classes are not." To be sure, the problem is not with individual CEOs or individuals in positions of power—the problem is with a kind of unilateral power that moves from the top down and which writes the script for Emperors, CEOs and others in power.

When our churches confess that Jesus is Lord on Sunday mornings, I wonder how often this challenge is understood. Here, constructive theology could do us a huge service by helping us develop a whole new kind of respect for our traditions: if these traditions were to help us in speaking truth to power today as they did in the past, they would indeed command respect not only inside

---

[19] Laurie Beth Jones, *Jesus CEO : Using Ancient Wisdom for Visionary Leadership* (New York, NY: Hyperion, 1995).

the churches but outside the churches as well. To be sure, the problem with such an interpretation of Jesus as Lord is not whether or not it is going to be relevant today—the problem is that it will be all-too relevant and too challenging. Nevertheless, I would rather have this latter problem than the former.

Here is my challenge to the theological academy: Theology that does not acknowledge its beginnings in a struggle with the status quo where our ancestors spoke truth to power, and which therefore does not give thought to its ongoing constructive task of speaking truth to power, will not make much of a difference. This sort of theology is dangerous because it usually ends up justifying the respective status quos. Let us be honest about what is at stake here: too much theology, for too long, has ended up justifying the way things are. The same is true for the academy in general: too much academic thinking in too many academic fields for too many years has tended to justify the status quo.

That universities are often classified as "liberal institutions" makes little difference in this regard, because it does not matter whether you justify the status quo from a liberal or from a conservative perspective. Constructive theology, if it manages to promote a self-critical perspective, seeks to resist such justifications of the status quo, and it refuses to jump on the liberal or the conservative bandwagons. Put in positive terms, constructive theology is about identifying the difference that the divine makes in the world, a difference that finds expression as "speaking truth to power."

Allow me to mention one more thing in closing, and this may be well the most important point of my lecture. Speaking truth to power in a self-critical way pushes us beyond a mere analysis of power. Contrasting Jesus as Lord and the Roman Emperor as lord was not an academic exercise for early Christianity. It also enabled followers of Jesus to speak truth to power. Identifying an alternative truth also made it possible to become part of an alternative movement which embodied an alternative power. Jesus as Lord, in the minds of the early Christians, did not stand for powerlessness and defeat.[20] Jesus as Lord stood for an alternative power that moved counter to the power of the Roman Empire. That is the deeper reason why the Romans did not like Christianity: at stake was not a religious conflict—the Romans were religiously quite tolerant. At stake was a conflict about power: on the one side was Jesus' power, embodied in movements of the common people, and on the other side was the power of the Romans, embodied by their military, their globalizing culture, and their economic success stories.

This old story, as we all know, ended with a twist as well: while the Roman Empire commanded considerable power for centuries, it eventually faded and disappeared. The same is true for most subsequent empires, and none of the empires that exist today will last forever either. Jesus' alternative movement from below, on the other hand, continues despite all efforts to co-opt it for the

---

[20] This is a common misunderstanding. See, for instance, John Caputo, *The Weakness of God: A Theology of the Event* (Bloomington: Indiana University Press, 2006).

status quo. It will be interesting to observe how this story is going to continue in our own time. Constructive theologians will keep the watch, but we cannot do it without help. Many of those who might help us are here tonight—it is quite possible that Perkins School of Theology has never seen such a diverse crowd gathered for a single event[21]—and I am grateful for our continued journey together.

---

[21] The diversity of the approximately 150 people in attendance was not limited to the more commonly noted issues of race, ethnicity, and gender. Diversity here included different age groups, including a group of teenage theologians, a group of striking ironworkers, activists from labor and religion, and civil rights leaders. Some of the groups represented were the Progressive Christian Center of the South, the Dallas Area Christian Alliance, D.L. Dykes Foundation, the Teenage Theology Group, North Texas Jobs with Justice, the Workers' Rights Board, and the Progressive Reading Group.

Chapter 8

Understanding the Social Structure of Sin: *Han* and the Example of Racism

Nathan Crawford

In the Christian tradition, the question of salvation begs the question of sin: if we are being saved, from what are we being saved? Or, if we need salvation, from what is it we experience salvation? In Christianity, the answer to both is "sin." Taking this further, if we talk of experiencing salvation in a social sense, we then need to talk about how we experience sin in a social sense. And, following this, we also need to understand how we overcome sin in a social sense.

This essay aims to provide an entry point into discussions of the nature of holiness/ salvation[1] and sin as social entities. I am interested in exploring the social dimensions of sin and holiness in order to further our understanding of these two doctrines. I also do so because there has been a lack, especially in Wesleyan-Methodist-Holiness circles to deal with this topic. Thus, I am making an attempt to fill a blind spot in a tradition's thinking.

I begin to fill this lacuna in the Methodist-Holiness theological tradition by arguing for a social conception of sin. In order to do so, I turn to the ongoing discussion of race, especially as it is construed by thinkers coming from a minority position. These thinkers present a picture of racism as an ongoing construct in American society and, so, give a picture of the social nature of sin, even sin we are blind to. The second part of my argument is a more explicitly theological move by taking up the issue of social sin through the Korean concept of *han* in relation to sin. I do so in conversation with the thought of Methodist theologian Andrew Sung Park. In the end, we see the effects of the social sin of racism to keep the oppressed oppressed, creating a social structure that traps everyone.[2]

---

[1] While I understand there are certain differences, I use the terms "holiness" and "salvation" as synonymous. I do so because I understand both to be the interaction of God with people and the people's ongoing positive response as well as the furthering of such a response so that people continue to respond.

[2] I do not give a constructive "answer" or "solution" to the problem of race in this paper, even though I point to places where we can move forward. My goal in this paper is simply to describe the problem. For a more constructive contribution, see my "Race and Hospitality: Pursuing Racial Reconciliation through Derrida's

I. Racism: An Example of Social Sin[3]

Let me begin the discussion of the social sin of racism by following the genealogy of modern racism developed by Cornel West.[4] West shows that the problem of white supremacy exists in the very discourse used by people, black and white.[5] White supremacy has become engrained into the very way that people think: thus, to fight against racism is to fight against the very presuppositions and ways of viewing the world that people have embraced uncritically. West finds the very foundation of these ideas to be in the Greek heritage, with the Greek ideal being made so prevalent. This Greek ideal becomes especially prevalent when one looks at how the Greeks are copied, made an idyllic race, for much of the Renaissance and early modern period of the Western world. For West, this embrace of Greek metaphors and images produces a "normative gaze" in the Western world, where everything becomes compared to and measured against the Greeks.[6] Those things that fail to reach the specifically Greek ideal fail to be beautiful, good, and truthful, which poses an obvious problem for those who are not white.[7]

West continues his genealogy by noticing that at the same time as artists and thinkers were rediscovering the Greek ideal, the "hard" sciences were also beginning to develop—at times, it was the same artists involved in the development of these sciences (like Leonardo Da Vinci). He shows that racism becomes part of the Western consciousness with the emergence of sciences that seek to classify and compare. He shows, through an examination of natural history, how the intention of the sciences is "to observe, compare, measure, and order animals and human bodies...*based on visible, especially physical, characteristics.*"[8] The problem is that race becomes a major way of classifying, with those who are darker failing to live up to the Greek ocular ideal; the result is a "scientific," classificatory discounting of those people who fail to live up to the real ideal of being white. He also shows racism developing at this time through a discussion of the "sciences" of phrenology and physiognomy. Phrenology, the study of skulls, is used to develop a way of classifying people as beautiful, again with

---

Understanding of Hospitality," published simultaneously in *The Other Journal* 16 (Fall 2009) at theotherjournal.com and in Eric Severson, ed. *I More Than Others*, Cambridge: Cambridge Scholars Press, 2010.

[3] This section is partly derived from my "Race and Hospitality: Pursuing Racial Reconciliation through Derrida's Understanding of Hospitality."

[4] See Cornel West, *Prophecy Deliverance! An Afro-American Revolutionary Christianity* (Philadelphia: Westminster Press, 1982), 47-69.

[5] Ibid., 49.

[6] Ibid., 53-54.

[7] An example here would be the thoroughly Greek statue *David* by Michelangelo – the fact that Michelangelo feels the necessity to make the Semitic David into a Greek points to the problem West is articulating.

[8] Ibid., 55. Italics are original.

white being the standard.⁹ It is also used to show who is more intellectual, with white people being the standard because of the shape of their skull: the result was that those who were white had better brain activity and were smarter than those who were non-white.¹⁰ Physiognomy, the study of faces, uses the Greek ideal to measure the beauty of faces, producing a normative gaze, against which other people are measured. The result, again, is that those who do not look like the white Greek fail to meet the aesthetic ideal, making them ugly and less pleasing to the eye—usually the white eye of the "observer."¹¹

For West, the result of the rise of classificatory sciences is the development of a biological and ontological underpinning for a discussion of race, resulting in the lessening of non-white persons. From these sciences, no longer is black just different than white in color, but black is now fundamentally different than white. The white is expressed as the ideal, and the black is posited as less than the ideal, a genetic problem that keeps people from reaching what they were truly meant to be—white. The rise of natural history, phrenology, and physiognomy give a scientific basis to this idea, leading to the development of ideas and a language that is inherently racist, seeing the black person as less than the white and unable to reach the white pinnacle of human existence. The idea of what it is to be fundamentally human is to be white. As people then begin to think about how to organize society, the goal is to create a "white" society. The underpinning of the Enlightenment's progress on the nature of our world is that everything should look white. As the Enlightenment develops foundational concepts of our society, like democracy and capitalism, they build upon a racist ideology that is still prevalent today. We cannot escape the racism our understanding of the world is built upon, even though we must begin to work against it.

The normative gaze of white supremacy becomes systematized and is made part of Western discourse. West points to multiple examples, which actually give rise to this racism. West sees racism dripping from the writings of the following individuals – Kant, Montesquieu, Voltaire, Hume, and Jefferson. These thinkers are those who established the foundations of the liberal notions of democracy and equality, tolerance and peace, showing them to be built upon a racist foundation. For West, it was not that they were uncritically racist, but that their racism derived from the authority given to the sciences.¹² Racial differences become grounded in ontology and biology. Racism becomes a cultural attitude, predicated upon the sciences that give credence to racist attitudes.

---

[9] Ibid., 58.
[10] Ibid., 59.
[11] Ibid., 58-59. Lavater takes this further by making the nose the main feature of the face and using this to begin his discussion of ideal types; the problem of course, is that generally the African nose is quite different than the white nose, again causing the African to be considered less beautiful.
[12] Ibid., 61.

The subsequent development is a destructive discourse that has become in part of the Western world due to the normative gaze of the Greek ideal.[13]

Michael Eric Dyson points to an example of this normative gaze at work in his critique of Robert Sam Anson's *Best Intentions: The Education and Killing of Edmund Perry*.[14] Edmund Perry was a Harlem youth attending Phillips Exeter Academy, who had received a full scholarship to Stanford University, and was shot dead by a white off-duty police officer in Harlem after attempting to mug him.[15] Anson resorts to a "liberal" theory of race to explain why it is that a black youth who had gotten out of the ghetto and had "made something of himself" would still commit criminal activity. For Dyson, Anson's approach tries to show how the liberal theory has worked to overcome the problem of race, yet it fails. This failure is due to the inability of those subscribing to various liberal theories of race to adequately explain the "persistent forms of Afro-American oppression" at work in the lives of black people today.[16]

For Dyson, Anson's account fails to account for the frustration that existed in Perry while at Phillips Exeter. His theory of race does not deal with the different systemic problems that have led to the oppression of black people, especially when in white (oftentimes liberal) environments. Specifically, Anson cannot adequately deal with the problem of having "made it" by living the life of an upper middle-class youth at Phillips Exeter while also being the young black person who grew up and lived in Harlem. Anson does not understand, or even try to understand, what it is to juggle one's life between these two cultures, or the frustration that would ensue.[17] Thus, for Dyson, Anson's analysis shows why the very structures put into place to help Perry fail him, showing the continued racism in American society. The social critic Toure also points to this problem, saying that for many people, even black people, when they say the race has not made it or someone brings down the race, they mean that the race is being brought down in the light of "white eyes."[18] Both Toure and Dyson show that the usual explanations of a race's failures—the heart of which is still the latent Enlightenment racist attitudes—is the fact that a foreign, white society is forced upon those who are non-white. The result is either a capitulation to the white gaze or failure.

Dyson continues to critique Anson by arguing that he focuses on the issue of assimilation, rather than the experience of race itself. Dyson says that Anson's account is based more upon the European immigrant experience, which was more ethnic than racial. However, the problem for blacks is the experience

---

[13] Ibid., 64-5.
[14] Robert Sam Anson, *The Education and Killing of Edmund Perry* (New York: Random House, 1987).
[15] Michael Eric Dyson, "The Liberal Theory of Race," in *The Michael Eric Dyson Reader* (New York: Basic Civitas Books, 2004), 37.
[16] Ibid., 37.
[17] Ibid., 38-39.
[18] Toure, *Who's Afraid of Post-Blackness? What It Means to Be Black Now* (New York: Free Press, 2011), 28.

of being black.[19] The liberal theory sees race as part of one's broader ethnic identity, and then focuses on critiquing aspects of black culture for the failure to assimilate. Dyson argues, in contrast, that racism has been structurally engrained within the American psyche through not only racist structures, but also the history of the oppression of minorities within the United States.[20] Anson, and those like him, fail to take into account the structural problems that have kept blacks oppressed and continue to keep them oppressed, or at the very least make it incredibly difficult to overcome the oppression. Mostly, this inability to deal with racism stems from the fact that the many liberal thinkers continue to perpetuate the same structures and ways of thinking that have oppressed minorities, as ways to overcome racism.

The outcome of these failures is what Eduardo Bonilla-Silva calls "colorblind racism."[21] This is a response to the fact that most Americans do not see themselves as racist, nor have overt prejudices against other races that are similar to the Jim Crow era. However, when looking at society, Bonilla-Silva notices that there still exists racial inequality and a certain underlying prejudice on the part of white people against other races. This is manifested most often through the claim by whites that racial problems are the problems of other races, perpetuated by the minorities; that the only reason there is a race problem in the U.S. is because minority races keep bringing it up, "playing the race card."[22] Bonilla-Silva wants to counter this claim, which comes about through a liberal theory of race. This is due, mostly, to the fact that the racism perpetuated here seeks to have justice and equality as primary attributes, resorting to discourse of each individual being treated equally (an Enlightenment echo). However, as Bonilla-Silva will make clear, minority races are not treated equally, most often because they do not get a fair start.

Bonilla-Silva looks at race and racism as a structural issue, not an individual problem.[23] He argues that color-blind racism does not depend upon the overt racism of Jim Crow, but a "subtle, institutional, and apparently nonracial" problematizing of the other race.[24] This is done through an "otherizing"

---

[19] Ibid., 40. In my own thinking, it is much easier for an immigrant who is white to assimilate than a black person. This stems from the fact that a white immigrant can, for the most part, hide the fact that they are an immigrant through the learning of language and living among other whites in society. They can "blend in" because they meet the normative gaze and ideal. This is not true for the black person, as no matter how much one learns the language or tries to be neighborly, the person can always see that one is black (or brown or yellow or red or another race).

[20] Ibid., 41.

[21] For a full explanation of this, see Eduardo Bonilla-Silva, *Racism without Racists: Color-Blind Racism and the Persistence of Racial Inequality in the United States*, 2nd ed. (New York: Rowman and Littlefield Publishers, Inc., 2006).

[22] Ibid., 1.

[23] Ibid., 8-11.

[24] Ibid., 3.

of other races. So, he points to different arguments brought forward to discount the overcoming of the racial divide. One example is interracial marriage. He says that in color-blind racism, the argument is not that the other minority is evil or less than human, but that there are going to be more burdens in the marriage, like multi-racial children or the question of where does one live. So, he says that what occurs is the enunciation of positions by whites that "safeguard their racial interests without sounding 'racist.' Shielded by color blindness, whites can express resentment toward minorities; criticize their morality, values and work ethic and even claim to be victims of 'reverse racism.'"[25]

Apparent, then, is that racism is an institutional problem, a structure built into the fabric of being American. As a theologian, this comes across as inherently sinful but, really, by no one person in particular. Rather, the sin that exists comes in a social structure and perpetuation of those structures. The "color-blind" racism of our society is actually practiced by the oppressor (whites) and the oppressed (non-whites). Many non-whites strive to live in "white" neighborhoods, having the kind of lifestyle that whites have, gaining the middle-class status that comes from being white. However, the way that this comes is the perpetuation of structures that ultimately result in the oppression of minorities, keeping "them" in urban areas with high crime and unemployment. In the following, I want to develop a reason theologically that this sort of racism happens, as well as a way of beginning to open paths for the healing of the wounds of racism.

II. *Han* and Sin

In this section of the essay, let us explore what it means for the sin of racism to be structural. Mainly, I am interested in the way that sin affects people groups by placing them inside systems and structures that ultimately oppress and dehumanize. In this section, I turn to the work of Andrew Sung Park, a Methodist theologian originally from Korea, to analyze the way sin is not only a personal matter, but how it has social implications. I do so through Park's use of the concept of *han*. *Han* offers a way to view sin as a structural problem that ultimately enslaves entire populations of people. It is our goal to outline the problem so that in the future we may begin to solve it.

The first step that Park, and us, must take is to distinguish the notions of sin and *han*. While very similar, there are some differences that are important for what we want to accomplish in this essay. First, Park says that "our sin is not a simple human volitional act but is deeply entangled with the structure of *han*. It shows what we are, not necessarily what we were."[26] *Han* and sin are interconnected deeply, with sin often leading to the feelings and disposition associated with *han*. I would even say that sin is the action of creating *han* in

---

[25] Ibid., 3-4.
[26] Andrew Sung Park, *From Hurt to Healing: A Theology of the Wounded* (Nashville: Abingdon, 2004) 29.

other people; thus, sin comes before *han*, creating *han* in that it gives rise to the *han* of those who have been oppressed and dehumanized by various sinful structures. Park seems to allude to this when he says, "Sin is the volitional act of sinners (oppressors); *han* is the pain of the victim of sin."[27]

Defining *han* is very difficult. As Park notes, "*Han* is an Asian, particularly Korean, term used to describe the depths of human suffering…*Han* is the abysmal experience of pain."[28] The idea of deep-seated pain is central to the notion of *han*. The victim's anguish, experienced in emotional, rational, physical, mental suffering, is at the heart of *han*.[29] The result of *han* is a combination of anger, desolation, frustration, hopelessness, and helplessness.[30] Park says, "In other words, han is a physical, mental, and spiritual repercussion to a terrible injustice done to a person, eliciting a deep ache, a wrenching of all the organs, an intense internalized or externalized rage, a vengeful obsession, and the sense of helplessness and hopelessness."[31]

Ultimately, *han* results in a loss of self-control. One is no longer in control of one's own life, nor is a group in control of their own destiny. Instead, there is a foreign structure imposed upon people. From this loss of self-control comes a negative letting-go. *Han*'s negative letting-go results in the destruction of an individual or people because they have to resign themselves to the situation, renounce themselves in favor of the majority (think here of the white gaze), or participate in self-abnegation. The result is people who feel "desolate, barren, bitter, and meaningless."[32]

These feelings of *han* tend to not be relegated just to the individual, but to move throughout an entire group. An entire group of people feels *han* through their common experiences of oppression. This is when structural sin is a forerunner to *han*. Park argues that when the suppressed experiences of a people group, like African-Americans or *minjung* Koreans, come to the fore, then *han* appears within that group.[33] The group begins to experience a collective form of *han* where there is pressure on the group to be and exist in a certain way; or, the group must capitulate to the way that the majority is. Park says, "At the unconscious level, han is immersed in the ethos of group or racial mourning. Many years of social injustice, political oppression, economic exploitation, or

---

[27] Andrew Sung Park, *The Wounded Heart of God: The Asian Concept of Han and the Christian Doctrine of Sin* (Nashville: Abingdon, 1993), 12.

[28] Ibid., 15.

[29] Ibid., 17.

[30] Andrew Sung Park, "Holiness and Healing: An Asian American Voice Shaping the Methodist Tradition," in *Methodist and Radical: Rejuvenating a Tradition*, eds. Joerg Rieger and John J. Vincent (Nashville: Kingswood, 2003), 98.

[31] Park, "The Bible and Han," in *The Other Side of Sin: Woundedness from the Perspective of the Sinned-Against*, eds. Andrew Sung Park and Susan L. Nelson (Albany: SUNY Press, 2001), 47-48.

[32] Park, *Wounded Heart of God*, 18.

[33] Ibid., 19.

foreign invasions create collective unconscious han. The victims who experience unjust suffering over many generations develop collective unconscious han deep in the soul."[34] This reflects what Michael Eric Dyson and Toure said previously of blacks in the United States, where blacks try to live up to the "white ideal" found in the "white gaze." This is definitely an experience of collective *han* as black people feel the need to embrace the white ideal in order to "fit" in American society.

For Park, the idea of *han* asks us to change our views on the doctrines of sin and salvation. The fact that we now take into account the way the actions of the sinner make the sinned-against feel asks us to rethink the way that sin and salvation work. No longer is it acceptable to simply see sin as an action by an individual. Instead, sin is a structure that offends God but also causes hurt in people, resulting in injury that gives rise to bitterness, neglect, helplessness, hopelessness, etc. in the one(s) sinned-against. No longer can we simply focus on the way that the sinner is restored through salvation; we must also begin to focus on the way that the sinned-against are restored and made whole. This entails a broadening of salvation to move beyond the redemption of the sinner to the restoration of the sinned-against. As well, the restoration of the sinned-against is broader than just individuals. When the oppressed and the victims are entire groups, nations, and peoples, then their restoration is the purpose of salvation. God seeks to restore entire communities to places where they are fully human, overcoming their oppression.[35]

As we understand the *han* of the victims more fully, we realize that the only way to restore people to their place as human is through a mutual, collective rational understanding of the other. The overcoming of *han* can only come as people become aware of and comprehend other people's *han*. This is especially true for social aspects of *han*. The *han* of entire groups must be dealt with and solved through a collective, public undertaking. Park says, "To stop the vicious cycle of sin and han, both the problems of sin and the collective conscious and unconscious han of opposing communities must be dissolved. Collective conscious and unconscious han will be resolved only by the *understanding, envisagement,* and *compassionate confrontation* of involved communities."[36] It is only at the societal level that people groups can be made whole, and can only be done through the work of the entire collective to try to understand and then attempt restoration of the victims. Public cooperation towards restoration of the sinned-against eventually can alleviate the burden of *han* for entire groups.[37]

Andrew Sung Park believes that a way we can theologically begin to address the *han* of collective people groups by recognizing our interconnectedness. The realization of everyone's existence as interconnected can help resolve the *han* that exists in the sinned-against while helping the sinner(s) realize the harm

---

[34] Ibid., 38.
[35] Ibid., 13.
[36] Ibid., 74.
[37] Ibid., 142.

they are carrying out.[38] For Park, the interconnectedness of the world is found in the Christian rite of the Eucharist, which he views as a cosmic event. He makes this move to the Eucharist for two reasons. First, the Eucharist debunks any bifurcation of people or any dualisms. There is no separation between "we" and "they" in the Eucharist; instead, the Eucharist connects all to each other as well as to God. The divisions prevalent in class, socio-economic status, sexism, racism, etc. are shown to be an illusion.[39] The second reason for Park's turn to the Eucharist follows the first: it overcomes hierarchism. The dualism overcome in the Eucharist does not simply divide for the sake of division, but does so in order to make some people lower than other, to put others down, to keep people oppressed. Park says, "Hierarchism exploits human relations, including sexual and racial ones."[40] As the Eucharist points to the interconnected nature of all people with each other as well as with God, then this hierarchism is also shown to be an illusion. God restores people to their fully humanity by destroying this illusion in the practice of the Eucharist.

The Eucharist acts as a place where there can be healing of the sinned-against as well as the ongoing salvation of the sinner(s). Park believes this takes place through God's work of "synergistic healing." Park believes this occurs when the Holy Spirit frees the sinned-against from their oppression so that their wounds are healed. He says, "While sanctifying grace makes the justified holy by promoting fruition of the justified after being justified, healing grace touches the wounded to transcend their sorrows and affects them to keep broadening their healing circles. Graced by the Holy Spirit, the wounded can confront and transform the *han* of the world with their own wounds."[41] The wounds that the sinned-against have from their oppression can act as a means to helping the whole world heal. The Holy Spirit gives the energy and strength to confront oppression so as to set the captives free, to restore people to their full humanity.

The place for this healing to take place is in the ministry of the church empowered by the Holy Spirit. Following the work and thought of John Wesley, Park believes that the goal of the ministry is to "advocate for the wounded and to restore justice. Methodists need to focus on the ministry of justice in addition to the ministry of justification of the sinner by faith…This work of the restoration of justice is the expression of faith for both the sinned-against and sinners."[42] The church is a place to find justifying grace but also is a place where restoration takes place. The church does not allow the justified to simply be but asks all who participate to work for justice, to restore the sinned-against to a place of being human in our world. In this way, the church echoes the work

---

[38] Ibid., 151.
[39] Ibid.,150.
[40] Ibid., 151.
[41] Park, Holiness and Healing: An Asian American Voice Shaping the Methodist Tradition," 106.
[42] Ibid., 103.

of Jesus, as He "did not elevate private holiness first, but embodied God's justice and God's reign on earth."[43] This justice reverses dominant social orders and values so that "the first shall be last and the last shall be first" (Matthew 20:16).

The conclusion for Park is to follow Wesley in believing that all holiness is social holiness. This means that loving God is only understood and practiced rightly in the midst of a community. Park says, "An individual cannot fully grasp the meaning of faith apart from a community. [Wesley] elevated this doctrine of entire holiness to a social level, since a society is interwoven with the sins of individuals. God's power transforms social evil so that someday the world may grow into its full harmony and serenity of social holiness…a Christian world where we see justice, peace, and mercy prevailing."[44] When a community seeks holiness then the transformation of entire systems and structures can take place. God works through communities that seek to do God's will. Wesley believed this and practiced it in setting up his Methodist societies. Park draws from this tradition, saying that true restoration can only occur as the community pursues it.

IV. Conclusion

In order to conclude this essay, let me briefly make explicit the way that I see Andrew Sung Park's analysis helping us think through the nature of social/structural sin and how we may begin to pursue a path of restoration. I do so through a discussion of race and racism as a structural sin in the United States.

The structural sin of racism is difficult because we do not find many explicit "racists" today—we have less people associated with the Ku Klux Klan or Neo-Nazism or other racist organizations. However, the issues of racism still persist in our society. These issues include higher incarceration rates for minorities, lower income potential, higher poverty rates, etc. Minorities in the United States experience life as second-class citizens, even though our country seemingly gives the opportunity for "them" to get out of their situation. Why is this the case? Why are minorities not able to lift themselves up out of their oppression?

Park's analysis of *han*, sin, and salvation allows us to see why this occurs. They point to the fact that minorities are tied up in a system that is actually foreign to them and keeps them outsiders. The "white gaze" says that minorities must live up to a standard that is not placed upon them by themselves, but by the majority race. Also, due to this, there is a collective frustration among minority people that rises up in resentment, helplessness, and hopelessness, stemming from the fact that they are part of a system that is stacked against them. They have been told continuously that they are the minority, that black and brown is less than white, that black kids cannot make it, etc. They live in a

---

[43] Andrew Sung Park, *Triune Atonement: Christ's Healing for Sinners, Victims, and the Whole Creation* (Louisville: WJK Press, 2009), 79.

[44] Park, *From Hurt to Healing*, 161.

collective system that continues to oppress them and Park's analysis allows us to see the feelings, frustrations, and attitudes that come from this continued oppression.

As well, Park's thought gives way for a theological way out of such oppression. By stressing the interconnectedness of all people, not only in the church but in the moment of the Eucharist, Park pursues a line of thinking and being that empowers the minority. Minorities are now encouraged to see the white person as equal, brother and sister; as well, they are given the ability to choose their own future and to set up the means by which they "make it." The standards now become the minority's. Park believes that God does this, as well as the ministry of the church. By seeking justice for people, the church gives the credence for people to actually live as human.

Chapter 9

Zionism and the Subversion of Justice: A Lesson in Social Holiness

Barry E. Bryant

At its meeting in Durban, South Africa on August 8, 2011, the World Methodist Council passed a resolution concerning Israel and Palestine supporting both Israel's right to exist and the Palestinian right to have a viable state. It continued to declare:

> Therefore, the World Methodist Council resolves to:
> 1. Distance itself from any theology that justifies the illegal and sinful occupation of Palestine.
> 2. Recommend the Kairos Palestine document for study in the congregations of our member churches...
> 3. Urge member churches through their respective congregations to observe the annual World Council of Churches Week of Prayer for Palestine, and pray for the peace of Jerusalem.
> 4. Send warm solidarity greetings to members of the Christian Churches in Palestine.
> 5. Work and pray for a just and sustainable peace in Israel and Palestine.
> 6. Urge groups in our respective congregations to work with Kairos Palestine and Kairos Southern Africa in planning pilgrimages to the Holy Land that seek justice and connect the World Methodist Council Churches with persons of all faiths in the region.[1]

It should be noted that the World Methodist Council (WMC) consists of 77 Wesleyan and Methodist groups including, among others, the Church of the Nazarene, the Free Methodist Church, the Wesleyan Church, the African Methodist Episcopal Church, the African Methodist Episcopal Church Zion, and The United Methodist Church.[2] The WMC represents the rich diversity of

---

[1] The World Methodist Council, *Resolution from the Social and International Affairs Committee*, 8 August 2011, http://worldmethodistcouncil.org/wp-content/uploads/2012/03/RESOLUTION-ON-ISRAEL-PALESTINE.pdf (accessed September 9, 2013).

[2] See, http://worldmethodistcouncil.org/about/member-churches/ (accessed September 9, 2013).

the Wesleyan/Methodist tradition and naturally a wide variety of responses were given to the resolution. Some thought it did not go far enough, saying that if the occupation is "illegal and sinful" there should be a call for boycotts, divestments, and sanctions. Some were outraged at calling the Israeli occupation of Palestine "illegal and sinful" in the first place. Most probably just ignored the resolution and its encouragement to read the Kairos document.

For many in the Wesleyan/Methodist tradition it is a severe challenge to have any Palestinian sympathies. Many may even wonder if the Wesleyan/Methodist idea of "social holiness" can even be applied to the Palestine/Israel conflict. I want to argue that it can, but Christian Zionism is one the primary reasons for objections to the resolution and a serious obstruction to its application. I would further argue that the resolution with its support of the *Kairos* document is an opportunity for Wesleyan/Methodists to seriously engage Palestinian support through the Wesleyan/Methodist theological construct of "social holiness." But first, I will need to discuss how I will be using the idea of "social holiness" in this context. Secondly, the idea of Christian Zionism will be briefly discussed. Next, consideration will be given to the document referred to in the WMC resolution, *Kairos Palestine*, using "social holiness" as an interpretive lens. Finally, ways Wesleyans/Methodists might respond will be suggested.

The "Algorithm" of "Social Holiness"

In the introduction to a collection of hymns written during the throes of the "quietist" controversy with the Fetter Lane society John Wesley introduced the phrase "social holiness," making its debut into the lexicon of Wesleyan theology. Originally, Wesley used the phrase as a refutation of mysticism's emphasis on "solitary religion."

> "Holy solitaries" is a phrase no more consistent with the gospel than holy adulterers. The gospel of Christ knows of no religion, but social; no holiness but social holiness. "Faith working by love" is the length and breadth and depth and height of Christian perfection. "This commandment have we from Christ, that he who loves God, love his brother also;" and that we manifest our love "by doing good unto all men; especially to them that are of the household of faith."[3]

Here is the Wesleyan etymology of "social holiness." This paragraph alone provides enough of a mandate to hear what Palestinian Christians have to say about their status and situation and to "do good unto" them as members of the "household of faith." Wesleyans/Methodists now use a more evolved and nuanced meaning of social holiness to refute notions more complicated than that of a "solitary Christian." It does not mean that one should only use the phrase with its original meaning, or that the evolved meaning is inconsistent with the original. The evolved meaning of social holiness includes the sociality of holiness and other Wesleyan concepts.

---

[3] John Wesley and Charles Wesley, *Hymns and Sacred Poems* (London: 1739), viii. This is the only place that I know of where the phrase occurs in Wesley's works.

It could be thought of in this way. Just as mathematicians use mathematical formulas to construct algorithms to find solutions to complex mathematical problems we may use several theological principles from Wesley's own theology to construct a theological "algorithm" and label it "social holiness." It is the algorithm of social holiness that we use to apply to a wide variety of social justice issues and in this case it will be used to provide a response to the conflict between Palestine and Israel. The "algorithm" used here will consist of at least five theological principals constitutive to Wesley's theology and will be used to mean "social holiness."

First, social holiness begins with the sociality of holiness, which is how Wesley used the term with profound implications. The sociality of holiness means that human beings generally, and Christians more radically, have the essence of their being in communion.[4] To turn Christianity, or Wesleyan/Methodism itself, into a solitary religion is to indeed kill it.[5] Early Methodist societies themselves depended on the sociality of holiness. More significantly, Wesley's idea of the sociality of holiness implicitly becomes an ontological category relevant to personhood and finds expression through the idea of the "relational-being." The idea of "relational-being" is used here instead of the idea of the "social self" in that "relational-being" is extended beyond self and even community.[6] As relational-beings the parables of Jesus challenge us to expand our relationships to include our neighbor, the "other," even our enemies and persecutors or anyone else with whom reconciliation is needed. This need for sociality is grounded in Wesley's own understanding of the natural, moral, and political aspects of the image of God and represents the sum of human relationships between one's self and God, neighbor, and even creation. The idea the image of God as relational-being should be expanded beyond the limitation of emotion and propinquity. The relational and social nature of the image of God serves as the lynchpin to the sociality of holiness and any idea of "social holiness."

Secondly, the sociality of holiness and humans as relational-beings also provide significant insights as to what it means to exist as the church and is constitutive to any ecclesiology that aspires to compatibility with social holiness. This cannot be done without a robust doctrine of the perichoretic work of the Holy Spirit. It is the Spirit who works to make the body of Christ one. The social and communal nature of ecclesiology, as a result of the work of the Holy Spirit, means it must rise to meet the increasing demands of globalism with its complicated matrix of social, political, and economic relations, and conflicts such as the one between Palestine and Israel.

---

[4] For a fuller treatment of this see John Zizioulas, *Being as Communion: Studies in Personhood and the Church* (Crestwood, NY: St. Vladimir's Seminary Press, 1993).

[5] John Wesley, Sermon 24, "Upon our Lord's Sermon on the Mount" § I.1, in Sermons I, ed. Albert C. Outler, vol. 1 of *The Bicentennial Edition of the Works of John Wesley* (Nashville: Abingdon Press, 1976-), 533.

[6] Kenneth Gergen, *Relational Being: Beyond Self and Community* (Oxford: Oxford University Press, 2009), 352.

Thirdly, the sociality of holiness also suggests that one of the consequences of living in relationship to others is that one is obligated to open one's self empathically to the narratives and experiences of suffering by others. Hearing about such suffering means it is incumbent upon us to also see first hand such sufferings, and then bear witness against the sufferings by doing what we can about the injustices that create the situation. The sociality of holiness leaves us little option but to hear for ourselves the narratives of suffering and then to do all we can to end the suffering. The sociality of holiness requires empathy, and empathy involves compassion, and compassion necessitates justice. It is one thing to give water to the thirsty and food to the hungry. This is an act of compassion. It is all together different to do something about why people are thirsty and hungry in the first place. This is an act of justice. Compassion and justice together are constitutive to social holiness. To hear, see, and engage Palestinian suffering through acts of compassion and acts of justice is no exception.

Fourthly, the sociality of holiness must also include the willingness to hear Scripture being read to us. Wesley repeatedly suggested that "searching the Scripture" was a means of grace and its method included reading, meditating, and hearing. Reading and meditating may be seen as an abused spiritual exercise of a "solitary Christian." But, the sociality of holiness means that Scripture must also be heard, which in turn means there is one who reads and one who hears. This gathering for the reading and the hearing of Scripture, and the act of gathering itself, is constitutive to the meaning and nature of the church. This reminds us once again of the importance of the sociality of holiness and the relational-self to ecclesiology. Furthermore, by *hearing* Scripture one also experiences an exposure to hermeneutical principles discovered by another's reading and meditation. The challenge of any ecclesiology, particularly one in a global setting, is the challenge of reconciling contextual theology and the hermeneutic it inevitably creates with any social or connectional understanding of the church. Contextual theology will strain a connectional ecclesiology. Nowhere is this more manifested in those branches of Methodism with a connectional polity. The sociality of holiness and the role that it plays in the hearing of Scripture means we must engage in the always difficult and sometimes painful experience of hearing Scripture being read to us by suffering and oppressed brothers and sisters in Christ through a liberative hermeneutical lens. To do otherwise is neo-colonialism. Palestinians should not be an exclusionary exception to searching the Scriptures as a means of grace, and in hearing them read the Bible to us means learning about the hermeneutics of Palestinian liberation theology created through their own reading and meditation on Scripture.

Fifthly, because of robust relational attributes of the image of God, Wesley made connections between the image of God and its ethical implications. This demands action. As Wesley also repeatedly reminded Methodists, one must not be a hearer of the word only, but a doer also. The two most prominent examples of making connections between ethical implications and doing something from Wesley's ministry were his defense of the poor and his attacks on slavery.

He referred to the wealthy and their attacks on the poor and the existence of slavery as examples of "execrable villainy."[7] The ethical implications are informed by all of the above and become the hermeneutic of social holiness. It could be argued that even Wesley knew the implications of his own description of "social holiness" and its hermeneutical application regarding the reality of slavery. "Christian solitaries" may be able to choose to isolate themselves from being engaged in justice and reconciliation, but not those who realize the sociality of holiness and the work of social holiness.

These theological principles in essence construct a hermeneutic and have helped to create the algorithm of "social holiness." Indeed, there are ethical implications and moral consequences that arise from the sociality of holiness and our own ideas of social holiness. As both human and ecclesial relationships have become more global and hence more complicated, this relational complexity is a challenge to "social holiness." When seen from this perspective any system of oppression that seeks to dominate and subjugate anyone, in any place, at any time is, to borrow Wesley's phrase, an "execrable villainy." Each and every manifestation of "execrable villainy" must be challenged by social holiness.

Now that I have established what will be meant by social holiness it is time to identify what seeks to suppress the Palestinian narrative, namely Christian Zionism. In this context it is the immediate obstacle to social holiness.

The Nature of Christian Zionism

By Zionism it is meant, an ideology whose fundamental belief is that the best response to anti-Semitism is the creation of a Jewish state so that all Jewish people comprise a single nation, and that this goal can be attained by allowing as many Jews as possible to immigrate to Palestine and Israel for the continued establishment of a Jewish state. The originator of Jewish Zionism is traceable to Theodor Herzl (1860-1904) and the First Zionist Congress of 1897. The original vision was to begin a secular socialist state in either South America or Africa. However, the fall of the Ottoman Empire created the opportunity for the creation of a Jewish homeland in Palestine.

Christian Zionism is primarily associated with Dispensationalism, the modern origins of which can be traced to J.N. Darby (1800-1882) and predates Jewish Zionism. Dispensationalists are premillennialists by definition, believing that the second coming of Christ must occur before beginning the one thousand year rule of Christ on earth in an age of peace and prosperity. After

---

[7] See, John Wesley, *The Bicentennial Edition of the Works of John Wesley*, Vol. 21 Journal and Diaries IV (1755-1765), W. Reginald Ward and Richard P. Heitzenrater, editors (Nashville: Abingdon Press, 1992), 333; John Wesley, *The Bicentennial Edition of the Works of John Wesley*, Vol. 22 Journal and Diaries V (1765-1775), W. Reginald Ward and Richard P. Heitzenrater, editors (Nashville: Abingdon Press, 1993), 307; John Wesley, *The Works of John Wesley*, third edition, Thomas Jackson, editor, 14 vols. 12:507; John Wesley, *The Letters of John Wesley*, John Telford, editor (London: Epworth Press, 1931), 8:264.

that comes the final judgment. Several events must precede the return of Christ, such as the rapture, the revelation of the Anti-Christ, the giving of the "mark of the beast," the seven year tribulation, and the battle of Armageddon (the final and ultimate war near Tel Meggido, Israel). However, the most significant series of events for our purposes is the return of the Jewish people to create the nation of Israel.

From 1947, and the founding of Israel until the present day the return of the Jewish people to Palestine and Israel is for Dispensationalists the definitive indication that the last days are upon us and it is the church's task to provide unconditional support to Israel in order to fulfill all Biblical prophecy and hasten the return of Christ. At this point Dispensationalism becomes Christian Zionism. This means Palestinians must be removed from the land and any attempts to participate in a Middle East peace process, or to offer support to the Palestinian cause is to take part in the work of the "Anti-Christ." Before the return of the Prince of Peace there must be the mother of all wars, prior to which all the Jews will either convert to Christianity or die by the hands of the Anti-Christ. On one hand Dispensationalism is profoundly anti-Semitic. On the other hand it results in the subversion of justice for the Palestinian people. On either hand there is unconditional support for Israel and unconditional condemnation for any Palestinian plea for justice.

Not all Zionists are Dispensationalists. Among even the more progressive Wesleyan/Methodists, Zionism emerges through what some Jewish scholars have described as "Holocaust guilt," the result of remorse over Christian complicity where the Holocaust was concerned, and the Christian need to atone for it. Mark Braverman has described this as a "fatal embrace" between Christians ridden with Holocaust guilt and Jewish Zionists. Out of this fatal embrace Braverman pleads for Christians to do something else with their guilt, but they often fail to do so out of the fear of being labeled anti-Semitic.[8]

Indeed, Christian Zionism has Palestinians a "fatal embrace" between the guilt over the past and a superciliousness regarding the future. Whether through a bad atonement theory or through bad eschatology there is a subversion of justice for Palestinians. Both collaborate in assuming that Israel is exempt from international law and standards of human rights. Many Jewish theologians have argued that it is a more insidious form of anti-Semitism to think that Israel is incapable of either complying with law or practicing human rights in relationship to the Palestinians.

The "fatal embrace" of Zionism has succeeded for many years in suppressing the Palestinian story and finding a just resolution to the conflict. The labeling of Palestinian sympathies as "anti-Christ" or "anti-Semitic" are attempts to suppress the Palestinian narrative and make any rapprochement with Israel impossible. The prominence of Christian Zionism among Wesleyan/Methodists has muted the pleas of *Kairos Palestine*, a document that attempts to raise global awareness of the Palestinian narrative and their plight.

---

[8] Mark Braverman, *Fatal Embrace: Christians, Jews, and the Search for Peace in the Holy Land* (Coeurmanchante, 2011), 21.

The first task of social holiness is a willingness to hear the Palestinian story, told in their own voices, and from their own perspective. To better understand *KP* it must be put within a historical context from the Palestinian perspective, as an act of social holiness is to hear their story.

Kairos Palestine: The Context

Kairos Palestine: A moment of truth- a word of faith, hope, and love from the heart of Palestinian suffering (2009) is an ecumenical document written by 15 Christian leaders of the Church in Palestine.[9] From the start, *Kairos Palestine* invites the global Christian community to join Palestinians in a "stand against injustice and apartheid." The word "apartheid" is used advisedly and accurately as a description of the situation, based on the 1973 meaning ratified by the United Nations General Council, which defined it as "inhuman acts committed for the purpose of establishing and maintaining domination by one racial group of persons over any other racial group of persons and systematically oppressing them."[10] The Rome Statute of the International Criminal Court reaffirmed the definition in 1998.[11] The meaning of apartheid evolved in response to conditions in South Africa and has been used to describe reality on the ground in Palestine. In 1989, Uri Davis became among the first to write extensively about Israel as an apartheid state.[12] More recently, former president Jimmy Carter has used the term.[13] More significantly, Desmond Tutu used "apartheid" to describe the situation and the "security wall" in Palestine.[14] Literally joining her voice in call it apartheid, Alice Walker narrated the film, *Roadmap to Apartheid* (2012).[15] A growing number of Israelis and American Jews are refusing to call the situation and the wall anything other than apartheid. To those who may

---

[9] Kairos Palestine, *A Moment of Truth: A Word of Faith, Hope, and Love from the Heart of Palestinian Suffering*, 8th edition (Bethlehem, Palestine: Kairos Palestine, 2011). It may be downloaded at http://www.kairospalestine.ps [hereafter cited as *KP*, paragraph and page numbers will be used].

[10] For the document see, *The Legal Consequences of the Construction of a Wall in the Occupied Palestinian Territory*, http://web.archive.org/web/20061001200717/http://www.unhchr.ch/html/menu3/b/11.htm (accessed July 29, 2013).

[11] See the following for the UN's adoption of this treaty, http://treaties.un.org/Pages/ViewDetails.aspx?src=TREATY&mtdsg_no=XVIII-10&chapter=18&lang=en (accessed June 21, 2013).

[12] Uri Davis, *Israel: An Apartheid State* (London: Zed Books, 1989); *Apartheid Israel: Possibilities for the Struggle Within* (London: Zed Books, 2004).

[13] Jimmy Carter, *Palestine: Peace not Apartheid* (New York: Simon and Schuster, 2007).

[14] Desmond Tutu, "Apartheid in the Holy Land" *The Guardian*, 28 April 2002, http://www.theguardian.com/world/2002/apr/29/comment (accessed July 31, 2013).

[15] Ana Nogueira and Eron Davidson, directors/producers, *Roadmap to Apartheid* (2012), DVD. It may be viewed online at http://www.youtube.com/movie/roadmap-to-apartheid (accessed July 29, 2013).

still disbelieve, *KP* gives an invitation to "come and see" first hand what conditions are like there.[16] To better understand the development of apartheid in Palestine it will be necessary to become familiar with two Arabic terms, *nakba* and *naksa*.

The Palestinian *Nakba*

One of the twentieth century's most heinous evils was the Holocaust and the result of Christian Europe's anti-Semitism.[17] One of that century's most atrocious injustices was the Palestinians being deprived their land as a result of the manipulative European colonial powers of England and France, with continuous American complicity.[18] While it may have been conceived in the minds of Darby and Herzl, Zionism was birthed by the two hands of anti-Semitism and colonialism. This is the geo-political starting point in the historical setting of *KP* and fundamentally arises out of the *shoah* (holocaust) and the creation of a political state with a Biblical name, beginning with the British Mandate of 1922 and culminating in the United Nation Partition Plan for Palestine in 1947.[19] Many Palestinians today still think, "The main responsibility for our catastrophe lies with the British Mandate."[20]

It was also the beginning of what Palestinians refer to as the *nakba* ("catastrophe") and signifies the flight of over 700,000 Palestinians (approximately 80% of Palestinian inhabitants living in the newly created nation of Israel) who either left or were expelled from Palestine; the internal displacement of approximately 156,000 others who either remained in Israel or were resettled to refugee camps in Gaza and the West Bank; and, the hundreds of Palestinian villages

---

[16] *KP*, 2.

[17] See, Steve Hochstadt, ed., *Sources of the Holocaust*, (*Sources in History*) (Basingstoke: Palgrave McMillan, 2004); Robert Michael, *Holy Hatred: Christianity, Antisemitism and the Holocaust* (Basingstoke: Palgrave McMillan, 2006).

[18] See John W. Mulhall, *America and the Founding of Israel: An Investigation of the Morality of America's Role*, Los Angeles: Deshon Press, 1995. To explore the US part in the conflict, see, Rashid Khalidi, *Brokers of Deceit: How the U.S. has Undermined Peace in the Middle East* (Boston: Beacon Press, 2013); John J. Mearsheimer and Stephen M. Walt, *The Israel Lobby and U.S. Foreign Policy* (New York: Farrar, Straus and Giroux, 2008).

[19] Known as UN resolution 181. See Mitri Raheb, "Displacement Theopolitics: A Century between Theology and Politics in Palestine," *The Invention of History: A Century of Interplay between Theology and Politics in Palestine*, Mitri Raheb, editor (Bethlehem, Palestine: Diyar Publisher, 2011), 18.

[20] Jamal Khaddura in front of the Joint Parliamentary Middle East Councils, Commission of Enquiry – Palestinian Refugees (London: Labour Middle East Council, 2001), in Ilan Pappe, *The Ethnic Cleansing of Palestine* (Oxford: One Word, 2006), 125.

that were depopulated and destroyed.[21] Palestinian displacement has been documented by the "United Nations Relief and Works Agency for Palestine Refugees in the Near East" (UNRWA) since 1949, and continues to do so to this day.[22]

The depopulation of the Palestinians from the land was intended to achieve two crucial objectives: (1) to clear the land for Jewish settlers and immigrants, and (2) to establish a homogenous Jewish state, which could not be accomplished if the "indigenous inhabitants were allowed to remain."[23] Israeli historian, Ilan Pappe has argued that the Palestinian depopulation of Israel fits the definition of ethnic cleansing, which is the "expulsion by force in order to homogenise the ethnically mixed population of a particular region or territory," a definition held by both the US State Department and the United Nations. Ethnic cleansing is designated a crime against humanity and subject to adjudication by the International Criminal Court (ICC).[24] Palestinians have always been seen as obstructions to a more homogenous Israel, as the effort to control the demographics became a political and military objective, a policy still explicitly and unapologetically being carried out today.[25]

To be clear, both catastrophes, the Shoah and the Nakba, were the results of European colonialism and anti-Semitism. Michael Lerner has likened the Holocaust unto the Jewish people jumping out of a burning building in Europe and landing on the backs of the Palestinians.[26] The Shoah created the Nakba, leaving Palestinians to suffer from European and colonial sins. Ottmar Fuchs writes, "The Palestinian Arabs, who had nothing to do with the Holocaust would... function as scapegoats for what the Germans had done."[27] *KP* notes, "The West sought to make amends for what Jews had endured in the

---

[21] Walid Khalidi, *All That Remains: The Palestinian Villages Occupied and Depopulated by Israel in 1948* (Washington, D.C.: Institute for Palestine Studies, 1992); Nihad Bokae'e, *Palestinian Internally Displaced Persons Inside Israel: Changing the Solid Structures* (Bethlehem, Palestine: Badil Resource Center for Palestinian Residency and Refugee Rights, 2003).

[22] See, http://www.unrwa.org/index.php (accessed July 30, 2013); Helena Lindholm Schulz, *The Palestinian diaspora: formation of identities and politics of homeland* (New York: Routledge, 2003). To admit there is a diaspora there must first been a recognition of the cause for it and there is the rub for many. Schultz handily deals with problem and goes on to connect diaspora with national identity and land in a convincing manner.

[23] Nur Masalha, *Politics of Denial: Israel and the Palestinian Refugee Problem* (London, GBR: Pluto Press, 2003), 7.

[24] Ilan Pappe, *The Ethnic Cleansing of Palestine*, Oxford: One Word, 2006, 2-5.

[25] See Yakov Faitelson, "The Politics of Palestinian Demography," *Middle East Quarterly*, 16(2009)2:51-59.

[26] Michael Lerner, "A Jewish Renewal Understanding of the State of Israel," Barry E. Bryant, editor, *Quarterly Review* 25, no. 1 (2005): 73-74.

[27] Ottmar Fuchs, "The Invention of History: A German Perspective," *The Invention of History: A Century of Interplay between Theology and Politics in Palestine*, Mitri Raheb, editor (Bethlehem, Palestine: Diyar Publisher, 2011), 132.

countries of Europe, but it made amends on our account and in our land. They tried to correct an injustice and the result was new injustice."[28] The most pointed comment comes from Mark Braverman who writes, "Christians attempting to atone for the crimes committed against the Jews, are by this very fact blocked from confronting the crimes by the Jews."[29]

Zvi Bar'el, an Israeli journalist for *Haaretz*, writes, "The nakba terrifies Israel."[30] With its specter of depopulation and ethnic cleansing, the Nakba raises questions about the morality and nobility of the Zionist narrative that has dominated Israeli history since 1947. The Zionist narrative of Shoah has intentionally sought to suppress, even deny, the Palestinian narrative of Nakba. "Nakba" denial results in what Noam Chomsky calls "the erased chapters of evil."[31] Without these erased chapters what results is an invented history. This fear was manifested when an Israeli law was passed that expressly forbade the mention of *nakba* in history texts to be used by Arab school children in Israel.[32] Public remembrances of Nakba are often met with violent resistance.[33] In spite of attempts to eradicate its memory or suppress its public acknowledgement, Nakba still survives and is commemorated on May 15 accompanied by a growing number of Israelis, on the same day Israel celebrates its founding as a nation.[34] The remembrance of Nakba is important to Palestinian identity and liberation, explaining why *KP* sees Nakba remembrance as a sign of hope.[35]

Since the 1980's "post-Zionist" scholarship has emerged and has attempted to de-idealize Zionist history. Meyrav Wurmser has described the nature of post-Zionism.

> Israel is today in the midst of a cultural civil war in which one side would like to see their country continue to exist as a Jewish state and the other believes that

---

[28] *KP*, 2.3.2.

[29] Mark Braverman, *Fatal Embrace: Christians, Jews, and the Search for Peace in the Holy Land* (Courmanchante, 2011), 25.

[30] Zvi Bar'el, "Nakba denial and its consequences" *Jews for Justice for Palestinians*, accessed July 22, 2013, http://jfjfp.com/?p=42177, also, "Apartheid of the consciousness" *Haaretz*, 17 April 2013.

[31] Noam Chomsky and Ilan Pappe, *Gaza in Crisis: Reflections on Israel's War against the Palestinians* (Chicago: Haymarket Books, 2010), 59.

[32] Ian Black, "1948 no catastrophe says Israel, as term nakba banned from Arab children's textbooks," *The Guardian*, July 22, 2009, http://www.theguardian.com/world/2009/jul/22/israel-remove-nakba-from-textbooks (accessed July 27, 2013).

[33] See, Jack Khoury, Gili Cohen and Nir Hasson, "Palestinians clash with IDF forces in Jerusalem, West Bank on Nakba Day" *Haaretz*, May 15, 2013, http://www.haaretz.com/news/diplomacy-defense/palestinians-clash-with-idf-forces-in-jerusalem-west-bank-on-nakba-day-1.524117 (accessed July 27, 2013).

[34] *Zochrat* ("remembering") is an Israeli activist group collaborating with Palestinians in organizing Nakba remembrance events and educational activities.

[35] Masalha, Nur. "Remembering the Palestinian Nakba: Commemoration, Oral History and Narratives of Memory." *Holy Land Studies: A Multidisciplinary Journal (Edinburgh University Press)* 7, no. 2 (November 2008): 123-156. *Academic Search Premier*, EBSCO*host* (accessed June 28, 2013).

Zionism, the founding idea of the state, has reached its end. For the latter group, the time has come for Israel to enter its post-Zionist stage; for this reason, it describes itself as "post-Zionist." By their own definition, post-Zionists are anti-Zionist, meaning they believe that the Zionist enterprise has lacked moral validity since its conception and, therefore, must be undermined. Further, post-Zionists also question the moral bases of their religion.[36]

What has resulted is the inclusion of the Nakba by post-Zionist Israeli historians with the Shoah. Any attempt to deny either the Shoah or the Nakba is an attempt to erase the "chapters of evil" and the voices of suffering they represent. Social holiness must indeed listen to the story of the Shoah, but that does not seem to be the problem. The problem is convincing Wesleyan/Methodists that it is just as important for social holiness to hear the narrative of the Nakba.

The Palestinian *Naksa*

It was during the "Six Day War" of 1967, that Israel invaded and has since occupied Gaza and the West Bank, marking the start of the *naksa* ("setback"), commemorated on June 5. On March 22, 1979, in a decision largely based on Article 49 of the *Fourth Geneva Convention* of 1949, the United Nations passed resolution 446, declaring the occupation illegal.[37] Whereas depopulation and ethnic cleansing characterized the Nakba, the Naksa is characterized by Israel's illegal occupation of Palestine, the building of illegal settlements, and the beginning of the apartheid infrastructure as an attempt to sustain the occupation and to continue the work of the Nakba.[38]

To be clear, the Naksa did not replace the Nakba. Displacement continues to the present day, making the Nakba an ongoing reality and not just a past event. In 1967 alone over 350,000 Palestinians were displaced from homes in

---

[36] Meyrav Wurmser, "Can Israel Survive Post-Zionism?" *Middle East Quarterly.* March 6(1999)1, p. 3. Also see, Ilan Pappe, "Critique and Agenda: The Post-Zionist Scholars in Israel," *History and Memory*, Vol. 7, No. 1, Israeli Historiography Revisited (Spring - Summer, 1995), p. 85; also, Herbert C. Kelman, "Israel in Transition from Zionism to Post-Zionism," *Annals of the American Academy of Political and Social Science*, Vol. 555, Israel in Transition (Jan., 1998), pp. 46-61; Nur Masalha, "New History, Post-Zionism and Neo-Colonialism: A Critique of the Israeli 'New Historians'" *Holy Land Studies* 10.1 (2011): 1–53.

[37] For the full texts see, http://www.icrc.org/applic/ihl/ihl.nsf/1a1304 4f3bbb5b8ec12563fb0066f226/523ba38706c71588c12563cd0042c407 (accessed May 14, 2014); and, http://domino. un.org/UNISPAL.NSF/0/ba123cded3ea84 a5852560e50077c2dc (accessed May 13, 2014)

[38] For documentation regarding the international laws and United Nations resolutions that are being violated see, http://www.israellawresourcecenter. org/internationallaw/studyguides/sgil3f.htm (accessed 24 July 2013); and, the International Red Cross at http://www.icrc.org/eng/resources/documents/misc/ 634kfc.htm (accessed July 24, 2013).

Gaza and the West Bank.[39] According to the US State Department, the primary cause of the exodus was airstrikes that "hit many civilian targets on the West Bank where there are absolutely no military emplacements."[40] While military strikes are still used mainly in Gaza, the most common method of Palestinian displacement on the West Bank being used today is home demolition. Jeff Halper, founder and director of the *Israel Committee Against Home Demolition* (ICAHD) has reported that since 1967, over 28,000 Palestinian homes, businesses, and livestock structures have been demolished.[41] In the summer of 2013, Israel announced the "Prawer Plan" to remove over 70,000 Arab bedouins from their domiciles and destroy another 35 villages that are not "recognized" by Israel.[42]

Just as the occupation is illegal, so are the settlements, or colonies, that continue to be built. Appealing once again to Article 47 of the *Fourth Geneva Convention*, on March 1, 1980, the United Nations passed resolution 465 declaring the settlements illegal.[43] The Israeli group, Peace Now, has argued that 40% of all the settlements have been built in violation of Israel's own laws.[44] As Palestinian homes continue to be demolished, Israeli settlements have escalated in construction.

The Naksa is also characterized by what is often called the "separation barrier." Its construction was started in 2002, in response to suicide bombers under the guise of security. On July 9, 2004, the *International Court of Justice* rejected the security argument and ruled the wall illegal.[45] The path of the wall gives away its true intent. It has been characterized as a "land grab" since much of the wall's route does not follow the "green line" that established the de facto

---

[39] John Quigley, "Displaced Palestinians and the Right of Return," *The Palestine Question in International Law*, Victor Kattan, editor (London: The British Institute of International and Comparative Law, 2008), 41-99.

[40] John Quigley, "Displace Palestinians and the Right of Return," *The Palestine Question in International Law*, Victor Kattan, editor (London: The British Institute of International and Comparative Law, 2008), 51.

[41] See, http://www.icahd.org/node/458 (accessed July 27, 2013). As of March 16, 2003 it comes to about 2 structures a day being demolished for the last 47 years.

[42] "Protest in al-Naqab against the Prawer plan displacement of Bedouins" *International Middle East Media Center*, August 2, 2013 (http://www.imemc.org/article/65899 (accessed August 3, 2013).

[43] For the full text of the resolution see, http://domino.un.org/unispal.nsf/3822b5e39951876a85256b6e0058a478/5aa254a1c8f8b1cb852560e50075d7d5 (accessed May 14, 2014).

[44] Nir Shalev and Michael Sfard, *Breaking the Law in the West Bank* (Jerusalem: Peace Now, 2006).

[45] For a copy of the ruling in its entirety see, The International Court of Justice, http://www.icj-cij.org/docket/files/131/1671.pdf; for commentary see Roger O'Keeke, "Legal Consequences of the Construction of a Wall in the Occupied Palestinian Territory: A Commentary," *The Palestine Question in International Law*, Victor Kattan, editor (London: The British Institute of International and Comparative Law, 2008), 753-815.

borders between Israel and Palestine before the Six Day War.[46] Water sources, farmable land, and illegal settlements typically determine where the wall is placed, and by separating Palestinians from their farmland and other property, along with water aquifers it becomes another tool in the strategy of displacement.[47]

The occupation is accomplished through more than demolition and the building of a wall. In his thoughtful analysis of the occupation through the study of architecture, Weizman has argued, whether it is communication towers, checkpoints, settlements, water pumps, or military encampments, "The mundane elements of planning and architecture have become tactical tools and the means of dispossession" manifesting itself material as the "politics of verticality."[48] The architecture of apartheid has resulted in what Jeff Halper has described as a "matrix of control."[49] By which Halper means,

> ...a maze of laws, military orders, planning procedures, limitations on movement, kafkaesque bureaucracy, settlements and infrastructure – augmented by prolonged and ceaseless low-intensity warfare – that serves to perpetuate the Occupation, to administer it with a minimum of military presence and, ultimately, to conceal it behind massive Israeli "facts on the ground" and a bland façade of "proper administration."[50]

KP is set against the background of the Nakba with its displacement and ethnic cleansing, and the Naksa with its illegal occupation, illegal settlements, the illegal separation wall, the policy of apartheid, and daily human rights violations.[51] *KP* describes "reality on the ground" in more existential terms of

---

[46] See, Yehezkel Lein and Eyal Weizman, *Land Grab: Israel's Settlement Policy in the West Bank* (Jerusalem: B'tselem, 2002).

[47] See, "The Right to Water in Palestine: A Background" at http://www.cesr.org/downloads/Palestine.RighttoWater.Factsheet.pdf (accessed July 15, 2013); and Jamal L. El-Hindi, "The West Bank Aquifer and Conventions regarding Laws of Belligerent Occupation" (1989-1990), *The Palestine Question in International Law*, Victor Kattan, editor (London: The British Institute of International and Comparative Law, 2008), 391-404.

[48] Eyal Weizman, *Hollow Land: Israel's Architecture of Occupation* (London: Verso, 2012), 5-11.

[49] Samira Shah, "On the Road to Apartheid: The Bypass Road Network in the West Bank," *The Palestine Question in International Law*, Victor Kattan, editor (London: The British Institute of International and Comparative Law, 2008) 405-428.

[50] Jeff Halper, "The 94 Percent Solution: A Matrix of Control" *Middle East Report*, 30:216 (Summer 2000), 14-19.

[51] In 1975 the UN established the "UN Committee on the Exercise of the Inalienable Rights of the Palestinian People." See, http://domino.un.org/unispal.nsf/com.htm?OpenForm (accessed July 25, 2013). Also, see "The United Nations Office for the Coordination of Humanitarian Affairs" (OCHA), http://www.unocha.org/where-we-work/occupied-palestinian-territory (accessed July 25, 2013) the Israeli group documenting human rights violations is B'tselem, (see, http://www.btselem.org/); and, the Arab counterpart is "The Arab Association for Human

checkpoints, displacement, the curtailment of religious liberty, the denial of freedom of movement, the denial of civil rights to Palestinian citizens of Israel, political prisoners, the flaunting of international law by Israel, and the hemorrhage of emigration.[52]

Once the context and "reality on the ground" are better understood it should come as no surprise when the appeal in KP begins with both a sense of frustration and urgency as it,

> ...requests the international community to stand by the Palestinian people who have faced oppression, displacement, suffering and clear apartheid for more than six decades...[W]e Palestinian Christians declare that the military occupation of our land is a sin against God and humanity, and that any theology that legitimizes the occupation is far from Christian teachings because true Christian theology is a theology of love and solidarity with the oppressed, a call to justice and equality among peoples.[53]

From the suffering that Nakba and Naksa have created, a call has been given. "We call out as Christians and as Palestinians to our religious and political leaders, to our Palestinian society and to the Israeli society, to the international community, and to our Christian brothers and sisters in the Churches around the world."[54] Quickly, it becomes apparent that this is more than a "call out." Clearly, KP is also an open invitation to all to hear their story and engage in a moral discourse about the Palestinian context of ethnic cleansing and apartheid. It is also plea for a Wesleyan/Methodist engagement through social holiness.

Kairos Palestine: The Text

Kairos Palestine is deliberately connected to *Kairos South Africa* and they are both a part of a larger group of *"kairos"* documents that consist of *Kairos Central America* (1988); *The Road to Damascus: Kairos and Conversion*, (1989), and *Kairos Europa*, (1989).[55] Comparison with these texts to the "The Barmen Declaration" (1934) and King's, "Letter from Birmingham Jail" (1963) are inevitable as

---

Rights," http://www.arabhra.org/hra/Pages/Index. aspx?Language=2 (accessed July 25, 2013).

[52] KP, "Reality on the Ground," 1-1.5.1. See, Rania Al Qass Collings, Rifat Odeh Kassis, and Mitri Raheb, *Palestinian Christians in the West Bank: Facts, Figures and Trends*, second edition (Bethlehem, Diyar Publisher, 2012), 13, where we are told that there is a greater percentage of Christians in Egypt (10%), Lebanon (30%), Syria (5%), Iraq (3%), and Jordan (3%) than in either Israel (1.7%) or the oPt (1.2%).

[53] KP, 2.

[54] KP, "Introduction."

[55] For the texts of the other three see, Robert McAfee Brown, *Kairos: Three Prophetic Challenges to the Church* (Grand Rapids: Eerdman's, 1990). Also see,

well as helpful. All of these are examples of contextual, political, public theology, and the *Kairos* documents are obviously connected to the term *"kairos."*[56]

KP takes *kairos* to mean, "...the moment when we see God's gifts in the midst of our suffering."[57] It is the occasion for a charismatic epiphany, the gift of hope in the midst of suffering, or a moment of revelation when the will of God and the nature of truth are made known prophetically and through this epiphany there is a sense of utter urgency. The alpha point of any kairos moment is ultimately, fundamentally, and inexorably connected to the outrageous hope of the resurrection that results in something far more significant than utopian idealism.[58] It envisions the kingdom of God, even the "beloved community" among us. The kairos call is a kingdom call. Prophetic engagement of social injustice is constitutive to the kairos moment.[59] There is an eschatological vision of the Kingdom of God that is in some sense construed as an ideal state of affairs, and this is radically contrasted with "reality on the ground." It is the prophetic pronouncement that creates the ethical binary between the goodness of a loving God against the evils of an unjust state of affairs. Genuine prophecy is not "foretelling" the future as with Dispensationalism. It is "forth-telling" the word of God. For *KP* this "forth-telling" is constructed around faith, hope, and love.

Faith

There is an obvious Trinitarian connection in *KP* with implications for a theological anthropology. Their faith in one good and just God who is the loving Creator of all things is affirmed, and "every human being is created in God's image and likeness and that everyone's dignity is derived from the dignity of the Almighty One."[60] The connection between the doctrine of God to the image of God and the image of God to human rights is explicitly made. *KP* continues to affirm faith in God's eternal Word as a Christological description and not as a reference to Scripture.[61] To be sure, there is an interchange between this use and referring to Scripture as God's word with the theological interplay between Christ and Scripture. Underlying all this is a vibrant pneumatology, with an affirmation of faith in the Holy Spirit who helps us to understand Holy

---

[56] Kjetil Fretheim, "The Power of Invitation: The Moral Discourse of *Kairos Palestine,*" *Dialog: A Journal of Theology,* 51:2 (June 2012), 137.

[57] *KP*, p. 4.

[58] Dirk J. Smit, "Kairos Documents," *Essays in Public Theology*, Study Guide in Religion and Theology 12 (Stellenbosch: African Sun Media, 2007), 254.

[59] James M. Gustafson, "Varieties of Moral Discourse: Prophetic, Narrative, Ethical and Policy," in *Seeking Understanding: The Stob Lectures, 1986–1998,* ed. Calvin College and Seminary (Grand Rapids, Mich.: Eerdmans, 2001), 43–76.

[60] *KP*, 2.1.

[61] *KP*, 2.1.1.

Scripture, which "makes manifest the revelation of God to humanity, past, present and future."[62] Just as the Holy Spirit made incarnation possible so the Holy Spirit works to make theology contextual. This explicit connection among Scripture and Spirit and Word is the starting point for a post-colonial hermeneutic of liberation that unfolds in the following section, "How do we understand the word of God?" To read, meditate, and interpret results in Scripture becoming a "living Word."[63] At this point the method becomes strikingly similar to Wesley's "searching the Scripture," which consists of reading, meditating and hearing. By "searching the Scripture" it does indeed become a "living Word."

This understanding of faith in the Triune God and the affirmation of the image of God creates a hermeneutic that is put into contrast with a "fundamentalist Biblical interpretation that brings us death and destruction...."[64] What is being called for is indeed a deconstruction of any fundamentalist hermeneutic, and more to the point, a dispensationalist eschatology. But, as we have seen Christian Zionism is not just a problem arising from dispensationalism. Holocaust guilt is another origin of Christian Zionism. In the same way Christian theology was complicit to the construction of a hermeneutic that contributed to the Shoah, so Christian Zionism has been complicit in the creation of a hermeneutic that has contributed to the Nakba and the Naksa.

The essence of the hermeneutics of Christian fundamentalism and dispensationalism is that it was constructed from a colonial perspective and still seeks to maintain it. The colonial hermeneutic is invariably (to borrow Said's phrase) "orientalist" in its understanding.[65] This *essentializes* depictions of Arabs in particular as being antithetical to the West and inferior. Here the hermeneutical assumptions of the British mandate are uncovered. In the same way that the African peoples were racialized in the 19th century by a similar construct, so were Arabs in general and Palestinians in particular. The issue of racialization is why the Palestinian issue is also an African, and more to the point, an African-*American* one.[66] Just as objectification was used against Africans to justify their enslavement, so have the Palestinians been objectified to justify their being ethnically cleansed from the land. It could well be argued that the rationale for Methodists to be against slavery is the same rationale for Methodists to be supportive of the Palestinian cause. Otherwise, and more insidiously, this objectification too easily results in the villainization of Palestinians as "jihadist terrorists" and the rationale for the architecture of apartheid and the denial of human rights as the "lesser of evils." But to be clear, one cannot politically deny

---

[62] *KP*, 2.1.2.
[63] *KP*, 2.2.1, 2.2.2.
[64] *KP*, 2.2.2.
[65] Edward Said, *Orientalism* (New York: Vintage Books, 1978).
[66] Susan Albuhawa, "The Palestinian Struggle is a Black Struggle" *The Electronic Intifada*, http://electronicintifada.net/content/palestinian-struggle-black-struggle/12530 (accessed June 11, 2013).

human rights without explicitly denying the image of God. Much of this is reflected in the struggle of Palestinians for self-identity.[67]

Additionally, Fundamentalism has produced an oppressive and limited reading of what the Biblical concept of "land" means and demonstrates how religion is used to justify political claims on the land.[68] One of the most comprehensive deconstructions of the Zionist hermeneutic and its exploitation of the "holy land" concept has been carried about by Nur Masalha in, *The Zionist Bible: Biblical Precedent, Colonialism and the Erasure of Memory*, where he shows how the focus on the conquest narratives of Joshua have been used to support the occupation and to justify ethnic cleansing.[69] The birth of the state of Israel has done more to shape the Zionist hermeneutic than anything else. Christian and Jewish fundamentalists in particular link the land with the doctrine of election and Israeli "exclusivism" and "exceptionalism." It does not see the land as "the prelude to complete and universal salvation."[70] The argument in *KP* is that the land should be seen as a land of "reconciliation, peace and love" with a Palestinian connection to it that is seen as a "natural right."[71]

Such a view of the land is the result of a fundamentalist/colonialist hermeneutic and, "...any use of the Bible to legitimize or support political options and positions that are based upon injustice, imposed by one person on another, or by one people on another, transform religion into human ideology and strip the Word of God of its holiness, its universality and truth."[72] So that, "...the Israeli occupation of Palestinian land is a sin against God and humanity because it deprives the Palestinians of their basic human rights, bestowed by God. It distorts the image of God in the Israeli who has become an occupier just as it distorts this image in the Palestinian living under occupation."[73]

Hope

Hope consists primarily of faith in God, and faith in God for a better future.[74] The nature of hope requires the

> ...capacity to see God in the midst of trouble, and to be co-workers with the Holy Spirit who is dwelling in us. From this vision derives the strength to be steadfast, remain firm and work to change the reality in which we find ourselves.

---

[67] Jacqueline O'Rourke, *Representing Jihad: The Appearing and Disappearing Radical* (New York: Zed Books, 2012). 6-10.

[68] Jamal Hader (sic), "The Context of Kairos Palestine." *Ecumenical Review* 64, 1 (March 2012): 3-6. *Academic Search Premier*, EBSCO*host* (accessed June 28, 2013).

[69] Nur Masalha, *The Zionist Bible: Biblical Precedent, Colonialism and the Erasure of Memory* (Bristol, CT: Acumen Publishing, 2013).

[70] *KP*, 2.3.
[71] *KP*, 2.3.1, 2.3.4.
[72] *KP*, 2.4.
[73] *KP*, 2.5.
[74] *KP*, 3.2.

Hope means not giving in to evil but rather standing up to it and continuing to resist it.[75]

Theologians of *KP* see several signs of hope beginning with the Church and a vibrant parish life that includes many young people committed to justice and peace. There are local centers of theology that are religious and social in nature. In some quarters there is an active and vigorous interfaith dialogue among Judaism, Christianity, and Islam. "Steadfastness" of spirit and a "continuity of memory which does not forget the Nakba and its significance" have become Palestinian hallmarks.[76]

All of this speaks to Palestinian "steadfastness" and is often symbolized by the olive tree. Steadfastness is life lived out as resistance to both the ethnic cleansing of Nakba and the apartheid of Naksa. It is love as resistance. The correlation of hope with steadfastness is an important one to be made at this point. Steadfastness is driven by a faith in God and a hopeful vision that scans the countryside for evidence that God is at work in the midst of trouble through Spirit-empowered brothers and sisters in Christ, and that this same Spirit is capable of working through people of other faiths and even through world institutions. Steadfastness is the manifestation of an outrageous hope that is rooted and grounded in the belief that God is creator of all, the Spirit is mysteriously at work in all things, and that Christ has been raised from the dead "in victory over death and evil."[77] It is only on this basis that there may arise another sign of hope, "...determination among many to overcome the resentments of the past and to be ready for reconciliation once justice has been restored."[78]

The final section on hope deals with the Church and its mission, which envisions a praying and serving people to be "prophetic, to speak the Word of God courageously, honestly and lovingly in the local context and in the midst of daily events."[79] If there is a side to be taken it is to be the side of the oppressed.[80] This means proclaiming the Kingdom of God as a "kingdom of justice, peace and dignity...which cannot be tied to any earthly kingdom."[81]

Love

Love is without discrimination and includes friends as well as enemies. However, while love may be seen as non-coercive it is bound by an obligation to

---

[75] *KP,* 3.2.
[76] *KP,* 3.3-3.3.3
[77] *KP,* 3.5.
[78] *KP,* 3.3.4. See, Naim Ateek, *A Palestinian Christian Cry for Reconciliation* (Maryknoll, NY: Orbis Books, 2009).
[79] *KP,* 3.4.
[80] *KP,* 3.4.1.
[81] *KP,* 3.4.2, 3.4.3.

"resist evil of whatever kind."[82] Love sees the "face of God' in every human person, but this does not mean that evil and aggression on their part is to be accepted. Instead, "love seeks to correct the evil and stop the aggression."[83] To that end "the occupation is both an evil and a sin that must be resisted and removed."[84] Such a resistance is a "right and a duty for the Christian," however such a resistance must have "love as its logic."[85] In the Christian's imitation of Christ it is clear "that we cannot resist evil with evil."[86] While evil must not be resisted with evil it may be resisted through civil disobedience.[87]

What is stated next is of such importance it should be quoted extensively:

> Palestinian civil organizations, as well as international organizations, NGOs and certain religious institutions call on individuals, companies and states to engage in divestment and in an economic and commercial boycott of everything produced by the occupation. We understand this to integrate the logic of peaceful resistance. These advocacy campaigns must be carried out with courage, openly sincerely proclaiming that their object is not revenge but rather to put an end to the existing evil, liberating both the perpetrators and the victims of injustice. The aim is to free both peoples from extremist positions of the different Israel governments, bringing both to justice and reconciliation. In this spirit and with this dedication we will eventually reach the longed-for resolution to our problems, as indeed happened in South Africa and with many other liberation movements in the world.

The call is to people of faith as well as civil and international organizations to engage in divestment and boycott of those companies that benefit from the occupation. Herein lies the greatest challenge. In that sense there is a clear prophetic announcement made by *KP* that unequivocally declares that the military occupation of Palestine by Israel to be a sin, while at the same time there is a call to Christians to repent for ignoring it.

> We say to our Christian brothers and sisters: This is a time for repentance...Perhaps, as individuals or as heads of Churches, we were silent when we should have raised our voices to condemn the injustice and share in the suffering. This is a time of repentance for our silence, indifference, lack of communion, either because we did not persevere in our mission in this land and abandoned it, or because we did not think and do enough to reach a new and integrated vision remained divided, contradicting our witness and weakening our work.[88]

---

[82] *KP*, 4.2., 4.2.1.
[83] *KP*, 4.2.1.
[84] *KP*, 4.2.1.
[85] *KP*, 4.2.3.
[86] *KP*, 4.2.4.
[87] *KP*, 4.2.5.
[88] *KP*, 5.2.

The source of frustration is the intermingling of good and evil in both human beings and institutions resulting in what calls the "moderation of violence" which is a part of the logic of violence. "Humanitarianism, human rights and international humanitarian law...when abused by state, supra-state and military action, have become the crucial means by which the economy of violence is calculated and managed."[89]

The most one can then hope for is the "least of all possible evils" and, "Indeed, it is through the use of the lesser evil that societies that see themselves as democratic can maintain regimes of occupation and neo-colonization."[90] It is precisely on these tumultuous grounds that prophetic stances are taken and if they are not grounded in love and reaching out in what is outrageous hope, the despair can be overwhelming. This is where Palestinians stand and their story is shared as a direct appeal to empathy and emotion as a prophetic function.

Where the Palestinians are concerned, the dominance of the Zionist narrative has come at the expense of the suppression of the Palestinian one and with that the denial of justice. The narratives of Nakba and Naksa are crucial to Palestinian identity and to their prophetic function. The invitation is not just to be engaged in ethical discourse. It is also one of story sharing. The hope is that their narrative will eventually be heard with empathy and responded to with compassion and justice and this becomes an opportunity for moral pedagogy.

Suffering Nakba and Naksa for years has resulted in a great deal of frustration because the larger Christian community does not seem to be listening, while the remainder of the world does nothing. So the question is raised,

> Why now? Because today we have reached a dead end in the tragedy of the Palestinian people. The decision-makers content themselves with managing the crisis rather than committing themselves to the serious tasking of finding a way to resolve it...What is the international community doing? What are the political leaders in Palestine, in Israel and in the Arab world doing? What is the Church doing?[91]

The direct appeal from *KP* follows next. Cahill's understanding of participatory discourse alludes to a shared sphere of behavior, which is oriented by a cluster of shared concerns and goals. Its function is to constitute relations constructed by empathy and interdependence. At this point, *KP* seeks to directly engage the Church and others to participate, and the concrete action being proposed is a boycott of Israel as an act of non-violence that sees love as resistance to evil. "Palestinian civil organizations, as well as international organizations, NGOs and certain religious institutions call on individuals, companies and states to engage in divestment and in an economic boycott of everything produced by the occupation."[92]

---

[89] Eyal Wizman, *The Least of all Possible Evils: Humanitarian Violence from Arendt to Gaza* (London: Verso, 2011), 3.
[90] Wizman, *Least of all Possible Evils*, 9.
[91] *KP*, Introduction.
[92] *KP*, 4.2.6.

Invitational Discourse

As a concept, invitational discourse is a "form of communication based on a commitment to equality, recognition and self-determination," which "promotes change and transformation [...] through the incorporation of new ideas and perspectives."[93] This is at the heart of *KP*, and is the nature of its appeal. The issues of recognition and self-determination for Palestinians are crucial to a lasting peace.

The WMC has accepted the invitation to discourse and has passed it along to its member groups. So what are the points of opposition to the Palestinian plea for action? There are at least four. First, both kinds of Christian Zionism have gone unchecked and continue to contribute to the subversion of Palestinian justice.[94] This has reinforced a colonial eschatology and has allowed "Holocaust guilt" to succeed in suppressing any criticisms of the Israeli government, thus allowing the architecture of apartheid to continue unabated, tightening up the grip of the matrix of control. Soon that hope for a two state solution must be abandoned and in its place there must be a struggle for Palestinian civil rights. Thirdly, charges of "anti-Semitism" continue to be the response to anti-Zionism. For this reason Christians fail to use our "special relationship" with Jewish people to engage in some serious and difficult discussions around Israel as an apartheid state. There has been a tacit assumption that such matters are not up for discussion. The reason there is such an Israeli fear over being labeled an apartheid state is because being labeled as such would entail a moral mandate from the international community for boycott, divestment, and sanctions (BDS) as a non-violent response to a situation of violence. After all, there is already a historical and political precedent for that with South Africa. Fourthly, we often fail to have the kind of relationships needed with the Muslim community to engage them on the issue of Palestine. There is a huge incentive among Zionists of all stripes to keep the church distrustful of Muslim motivations by promoting Islamophobia.

Social holiness means being hearers and doers of the word. Put another way, talking about something is not the same thing as doing something about it. So what should be done and what should the strategy be? We could certainly begin by accepting the challenge suggested by the WMC to actually read *Kairos Palestine*, pray for the Palestinians, and work toward a sustainable peace. Theologically, I would make some possible areas of connection and exploration. As suggested from the start, having heard a bit of the Palestinian story Wesleyans/Methodists could certainly make connections through the sociality of holiness with the issue through "social holiness," the ethical implications of the "image of God," engaging in "searching the Scripture" by hearing Palestinians read the Bible to us through a post-colonial hermeneutic. Secondly, we should

---

[93] Donald Ellis and Yael Warshel, "The Contribution of Communication and Media Studies to Peace Education," in *Handbook on Peace Education*, ed. G. Salomon and E. Cairns (New York: Psychology Press, 2010), 139.

[94] See, Barry E. Bryant, "Reflections of a Recovered Christian Zionist," *Quarterly Review* 25:1 (Spring 2005), pp. 31-43.

follow the lead of emerging Israeli and Jewish voices, Palestinian Christian leadership, the South Africans who have seen the "facts on the ground" and have been bearing witness in labeling the situation as an apartheid state. Apartheid is surely an "execrable villainy." Omar Barghouti, Noam Chomsky, and others have argued that because it is apartheid the international community should organize boycotts, divestment, and sanctions against the Israeli government, just as it has done before with South Africa.[95] Christian theologians could also pay more attention to the post-Zionist scholarship that has emerged in recent years, particularly the work of Ilan Pappe, who has labeled the situation, not just apartheid, but "ethnic cleansing." It is the hope of post-Zionism that a truly democratic Israel can be imagined and realized.

Finally, Americans have an additional role to play that goes one step further. We should be engaged in a campaign to end military aid to Israel. But, dealing with this issue is a two-headed monster. To deal with this in congress one has to deal with American Israel Public Affairs Committee (AIPAC) and the lobbying power of the military industrial complex. The reason being, the US gives Israel money and they come shopping for arms in the US, the world's largest distributor of military armaments.[1] Nonetheless, Stop US Tax Aid to Israel Now (SUSTAIN) argues that one way to end apartheid and the occupation is to end US tax aid.[2] Not only does our tax money help to finance apartheid and the occupation, the military equipment purchased in the US with US money is often used against civilians.[3]

Rather than contributing to the subversion of Palestinian justice, Wesleyans/Methodists in particular have the theological resources in the idea of "social holiness" to justify our standing with Palestinian Christians over the objections of Christian Zionists. In this *kairos* moment Wesleyans/Methodists have an opportunity to respond to World Methodist Council's resolution and join the kingdom call being issued by Palestinian Christians in, *Kairos Palestine: A moment of truth- a word of faith, hope, and love from the heart of Palestinian suffering.*

---

[95] Omar Barghouti, *Boycott, Divestment, Sanctions: The Global Struggle for Palestinian Rights* (Chicago: Haymarket Books, 2011); Noam Chomsky and Ilan Pappe, *Gaza in Crisis: Reflections on Israel's War against the Palestinians* (Chicago: Haymarket Books, 2010).

[1] For the statistics see, http://endtheoccupation.org/section.php?id=451 (accessed August 6, 2013).

[2] See, http://www.aidtoisrael.org/section.php?id=379; http://stop30billion.org/;http://www.amnesty.org/en/news-and-updates/foreign-supplied-weapons-used-against-civilians-israel-and-hamas-20090220 (accessed August 4, 2013).

[3] See, "Israel Misuses U.S. Weapons against Palestinians: Case Study of F-16 Fighter Jets" *US Campaign to End the Israel Occupation*, http://www.endtheoccupation.org/article.php?id=3352 (accessed August 6, 2013).

Chapter 10

"In the City, for the City": Re-Membering Roots and Discovering What it Means to be Our Full Selves and Good Neighbors in Southeast Portland

By Cassie J. E. H. Trentaz

"Nestled on Mt. Tabor's bosom..."[1] This opening line of Warner Pacific College's alma mater always gets its fair share of snickers and giggles (by both students and members of the faculty and staff) when sung at ceremonial occasions such as commencement or convocation. However, besides inciting giggles, it may also be revealing about the relationship between location/place and the college's sense of identity. This becomes an even greater possibility when paired with the next line, "Glorious Hood in view."

These two lines set the tone for the song sung by those moving from student to alumnus of this Portland, OR, liberal arts college. As such, what do they tell us about this place? Do they reveal a school rooted in its Pacific Northwest location? Do they speak of the proverbial flight from nest-ling student out into the big, wide world? Do they refer to mountainous aspirations? Or, do they begin to paint the picture of a school that has, at least for key portions of its history, looked upward and outward for principle sources of inspiration rather than within, perhaps as reflection of perceived identity, perhaps also longing to get out beyond the city boundaries?

The city has been a source of discomfort and strangeness for many institutions affiliated with "Holiness" Christianity in the twentieth and twenty-first century United States. This discomfort with location led WPC as recently as the middle of the last decade to consider (not for the first time) whether they might be able to move locations to somewhere outside the city, somewhere more suburban perhaps, with proximity to the resources of the city, but with physical room to accommodate the need to sprawl a bit more and perhaps also

---

[1] Lyrics from *Hail Pacific* by Albert F. Gray.

because the communal makeup of the college felt more comfortable in that environment. Many were raised in such environments. Many knew the language and the culture of those spaces. Many also had primarily heard notions of "holiness" that were associated with separation from things that cities often carry in their reputations. Gone would be the ability to nestle in the bosom of Mt. Tabor. However, the college community would also no longer be nestled among the dirt and the grit and the complexities of the urban space around it. For awhile, this felt like an attractive option (although finances did not seem to be cooperating). Then, something changed.

The "Other" Portland

Kyra Butler '12 wasn't sure what she would say as she approached the two homeless 17-year-olds sitting on a bench in downtown Portland on a frigid Tuesday night last winter.

The Warner Pacific Christian Ministries major was attending an outdoor church gathering as part of an internship with Home PDX, a ministry that reaches out to (and is comprised primarily of) ["our friends who live outdoors"]. One of the male church leaders had approached the apparent runaways, a boy and a girl, but they refused to talk to him, so he asked Butler to give it a try. She quickly learned of the dire straits [of these two].

"They opened up to me in five minutes about how they [had] run away from a group home and had nowhere to go and nothing to help support them, and my heart broke," Butler later wrote in a personal reflection about the experience. "...they were stranded in Portland when it was 28 degrees outside, and I was scared for them. That night, I learned how to call for assistance... I also learned how to provide them with the resources they needed to survive, at least for the night, and was able to get them to a shelter safely. That night was the most real, engaging, and growing thing I have faced in a really long time. And I feel like I am better equipped for youth ministry because of it."[2]

Portland has a reputation in the "wider world" of being a progressive, left-leaning, ecologically responsible, open-minded, young, hipster/hippie urban center. That Portland exists at least in pockets and serves sometimes as a thoughtful and beautiful model of urban life. However, as with all cities, there is another Portland, an "other" Portland—one that does not get the kind of attention the previously described Portland gets and, therefore, often goes unnoticed, even to parts of Portlandia itself. This Portland does not luxuriate in being able to walk or bike to grocery stores, green spaces, or cultural centers. This Portland is not the "foodie" Portland, but marked by "food deserts" and few recreational spaces, where access to public transportation is often spotty and lower income apartment complexes and adult care homes abound. This Portland does not look like the young hipster/hippie leftists of inner Portland, but like those who used to live in some of those Portlandia-ish hotspots but can no longer afford it. This Portland is diverse (in some respects). It is alive (in

---

[2] Scott A. Thompson, "Ministry PDX" in *Experience*, Summer 2011 issue, p. 8.

some respects). It is full of people who are creative and resourceful but often struggling.

Warner Pacific College is located in Southeast Portland on the border of and sometimes in the midst of this "other" Portland. So what does location have to do with institutional identity? What does location have to do with institutional responsibility? As WPC began to realize that once again they were, indeed, "stuck" in their current location, something began to stir among the college community that shifted the lens away from "stuck-ness" toward a serious consideration of identity, mission, place, responsibility, and possibility. We are and have been concerned about what, why, how, and who we teach. We are and have been concerned about who we are inviting students to become as a part of learning in our community and thoughtful consideration of why they are participating in higher education. We now began to pay attention to questions of "where" as a component just as vital to that process of educational and vocational formation. As an institution with Wesleyan-Holiness roots, I contend this shift is not simply making the best out of a complicated situation, but deeply rooted in and representative of digging deep into the institution's foundational theo-ethical identity.

Roots: Social Holiness

Some Basics:

If we go way back, WPC is associated with the broad religious traditions known as Christianity. According to communal memory, these traditions, although holding diverse interpretations of what it all means, arose from a community gathered around a central figure: Jesus—a lower-economic, colonized, Palestinian of Jewish religious and ethnic heritage. And according to the communal memory and central text, the biblical canon, we find a story of someone coming to this central figure and asking him, "what is central?" As the story goes, Jesus responded by referring to his religious heritage and giving what we know as the great commandments: love God with everything you are and have and love your neighbor and/as yourself. Everything hinges upon these loves. If we read the notion of "neighbor" through the lens of the rest of the canon, we see also the call for Jesus-followers to love our so-called enemies (our not-yet-recognized-as-neighbors) and the world (our eco-neighbors). We might call these five loves the operative characteristics of faithful Jesus-following and the path to the reality when "all will be well."

That does not solve everything, however. Each group since has then had the responsibility to ask the questions of what it means to be faithful, responsible lovers "here" and "now." Warner Pacific College's particular roots stem from a movement in the late 1800s that looked at the results of colonization, burgeoning industrialization, and rise of U.S. urbanization and said "wait—there are folks on the streets becoming poorer, sicker, and exhausted and folks in the churches are getting comfortable and disconnected from that reality and from each other. What does it mean to be faithful and responsible real Jesus-following lovers in these contexts?" That movement, which gave birth to the Church of God (Anderson, IN), led by a man named Warner (sound familiar?) understood the basics of love through two theo-ethically loaded words—holiness and unity.

What the Church of God Reformation Movement (Anderson, IN) has been saying for generations in articulating the vitality of holiness is simple: behaviors matter. How we use our resources and treat ourselves, each other, and the earth matters. And, because we are a part of a tradition that's a particular kind of holiness—a Wesleyan-Holiness—we assert a "social holiness." Our behaviors have implications for ourselves and those around us.

This is not primarily an isolated, protective "I don't drink, smoke or chew or go with girls who do" kind of holiness. It is a holiness, as I will explore more below, directly connected to the five loves, a holiness that says we are not holy if we are not ever-increasing in love for God, self, neighbor, enemy, and world. And, says this kind of holiness: love is not love if it is not practical, rooted in the contexts of those with need, and directly addressing that need toward participating in the creation of the "all will be well" or the Kingdom/Kin-dom of the God who loves in the world.

WPC comes from a people who said that our holiness actually depends on, is defined by this ever-increasing love of God, self, neighbor, enemy, and world. As such, our goal is not to remain "clean," unafraid to touch the "unclean" for fear of becoming "unclean" ourselves, but we hold to the stories of Jesus who had the courage to be and be with the "unclean" hoping that together we might create "a new clean." Social holiness theo-ethically challenges personalized, individual, formulaic notions of "me + Jesus and that's all I need" kind of thinking. As such, the goal is also not just to address the needs of one's soul, but that of the entire person and community.

The Church of God (Anderson, IN), WPC's founding church, is also a part of a people who recognized that we are neither alone in the world nor self-sufficient in this. This is the unity piece, necessarily interconnected with the holiness piece. We need each other and there is something holy about leaning on one another in being the image of the communal (Trinitarian) and incarnate (embodied in time and place) God that we love and who loves us and calls us to love. There is something revolutionary in modeling interconnectedness, mutuality, communality among cultural threads that lean toward individualism, self-sufficiency, competition. Being with others is actually an essential component to living a life ever-increasing in love and that lines that intentionally divide people from one another destroy the one-ness of the body of Christ in the world. Our one-ness, our being-with one another, our resistance of "us" and "them" toward only "us" is part of the proof of our Christ-following. We cannot love what we do not know and we cannot know what we don't make space to hear and learn. This begins not with where we wish we were, but where we are.

So, asked WPC, what does any of this have to do with looking somewhere "out there" for the context of our work? What does it mean to be who we are in this time and in this place? Does it not make sense to open our eyes and pay attention to our real live neighbors in our real live neighborhood who happen to be both engaging in beautiful transformative work and experiencing some painful, complicated need? This sounds very Wesley-ish. Let's say more about the "Wesleyan" part of Wesleyan-Holiness.

The Wesleyan Part of Wesleyan-Holiness: Social, Economic, and Political Dimensions.[3]

Living and ministering in eighteenth century England, John Wesley was no stranger to the particular concerns and complexities of his time as evidenced by his responses in sermons and writings to the real concrete conditions of his hearers and readers. In order to respond to those real concrete conditions, he had to have known something about them. This is a testament of his travels along with his beloved horse from place to place across the British land, paying attention to neighbors known and yet-to-be-known and the possibilities and limitations of their lives in the midst of changing economic structures and conditions. During his decades of itinerant ministry, Wesley noticed that many people were living in conditions of poverty and need. He began to ask the questions of why so many were hungry, why so many were ill. These questions became the foundation for his social critique as well as his theological reflections on what it meant to be responsible people of faith, holy living, and love in that time and place.[4] In these travels, he discovered an "other" England and it troubled him. He was sure that there was something about his own salvation that was tied up into the lives and conditions of these neighbors and he was concerned about salvation—his own and others'.

Throughout his life Wesley outlined his ideas about the way of salvation. Although there are steps or stages in the process, there was also a sense for Wesley that one is not necessarily finished with a step after it has been experienced once, but that many stops along the way are experienced or enacted several times. Salvation is not a "one and done" experience, but a process, a path, and a way of healing throughout life. The way of salvation is not a one-way street of God's actions on and for humankind, either. Rather, it requires human cooperation. Humans are empowered to participate with God. We are not alone in our process of "growing in grace," but we have an important role.

Grace is a key for Wesley and, according to him, grace actually works. It causes real change in real lives in the real world. Before one is even aware of it, grace is at work. Grace is the condition of life. It pervades creation as evidence of God's love, calling and enabling response.

In awakening to/by this grace, one becomes aware of one's need for healing and accepts it as something that one cannot do for oneself and is led to begin

---

[3] Portions of this section are adapted from Cassie J. E. H. Trentaz, *Theology in the Age of HIV & AIDS: Complicity and Possibility* (New York: Palgrave Macmillan, 2012).

[4] See works such as Manfred Marquardt, *John Wesley's Social Ethics: Praxis and Principles* (Nashville: Abingdon Press, 1997) and Theodore W. Jennings, Jr., *Good News to the Poor: John Wesley's Evangelical Economics* (Nashville: Abingdon Press, 1990).

the life-long process of repentance. Once one has responded to grace's awakening and repented, Wesley was confident that God is ready to forgive. This forgiveness is known as justification and the mark of justification is faith. For Wesley, the whole process is a matter of salvation by grace through faith grounded in an ethic of love. The complement to justification is the new birth. Justification is seen as something that God does to the believer. The new birth is the response that occurs within her or him. The new birth begins the process of sanctification, a process that continues throughout the life of the believer as she or he grows in grace.

So why chronicle these steps here? What does this have to do with the story I am telling? Here is a significant piece that sets Wesley's way of salvation apart from many interpretations that stop at justification or see forgiveness as the end of the process. Wesley did not believe that one could rest after he or she had repented and been forgiven. Rather, he argued, it is the forgiven one's responsibility to continue to cooperate with God in the process of striving toward increasing holiness defined as increasing in love. In other words, it is the faithful, responsible, forgiven one's job to be attentive to what is going on within and around her or him. Knowing who you are, where you are, and who is there with you is part of the work of continued salvation.

This process is what Wesley referred to as going on toward "Christian perfection" or entire sanctification. According to Wesley, this does not mean one is perfect in knowledge or free from temptation or mistakes. It means that one is so full of love that there is simply no more room for non-love. As with salvation, sanctification is not a state but a continued way of life. We simply do not stop learning, growing, healing. And we need each other to help along the way. Holiness is communal. And our community upon which it depends is not simply the folks that we choose, but those who we find ourselves nestled (if I may) among. This has implications for the story of WPC.

When considering these pieces, holiness is simply not possible in isolation but requires thick engagement with and for the diversity within our world. Wesley argued for "the inappropriateness of any model of spirituality that relied on the individual pursuit of holiness. As he once put it: 'The gospel of Christ knows no religion, but social; no holiness but social holiness.'"[5]

Wesley was first and foremost a functional, pastoral theologian. He studied hard and read widely, but his theological interpretations and articulations came largely out of his observations of the real lived lives of the "Methodist" people, their neighbors, and their communities. He articulated his ideas with the goal of helping those people and their communities live holy, healthy, happy, and fully human lives pleasing to God and empowered to transform the broken places in the world. This concern, rooted in the enduring claims of Christianity, empowering people to participate in and with the work of God in

---

[5] Randy L. Maddox, *Responsible Grace: John Wesley's Practical Theology* (Nashville, TN: Kingswood Books, 1994), 209, referring to Wesley's statements introducing *Hymns and Sacred Poems* (1739) and explained further in his sermon "Upon Our Lord's Sermon on the Mount: Disocurse IV." See vol. 5 of *The Works of John Wesley* for that series.

the world, and with concrete implications for lived life in and with others is part of what was so compelling for theo-ethical descendents of Wesley in other times and places—the Church of God in the industrializing, urbanizing late nineteenth century U.S. and its descendents in postcolonial, post-Christian, postmodern, post-post Portland.

In our twenty-first century U.S. Pacific Northwest context, the word "holiness" feels a little awkward, ill-fitting, perhaps too tight with buckles and hooks in strange places like something from another time and place altogether. And yet, when digging in our own soil to discover our roots, there is still something richly compelling about that basic conviction that behaviors matter and that we need each other to become our fullest, healthiest, happiest, holiest, most human selves. We are learning to recognize our far-reaching interconnectedness. For many of a Wesleyan stripe, holiness is, indeed, about attending to this in our path of becoming fully alive and responsible humans.[6]

It is also about transformation of the entire world here and now into a loved, fully alive, and loving place. Wesley was not satisfied with those who preached the justification of sinners without then engaging in meeting the needs of the community. He was concerned not only with inward transformation but also material, not only individual transformation but also social, and not only transformation of the soul but also of the body. He was concerned not for that perfection sought during the Enlightenment and beyond, which ignores the messiness of bodies and communities, but "Christian perfection" representing the possibility of transformation in the here and now marked by ever-increasing need-meeting love. "[G]race that allegedly saves my soul while leaving the concrete and visible relations of my life unaffected is merely illusory."[7] Rather, Wesley admonished, "Let our conveniences give way to our neighbour's necessities."[8] A Christian life is marked primarily by love demonstrated by the lessening of sorrows and increasing of joys.[9] Christ followers are to be actively responsible for the health, holiness, happiness, and full humanness—or, perhaps to draw upon WPC's latest slogan—the "flourishing" of ourselves and each other.

Therefore, those taking their cues from Wesley were to order their lives out of the interests of the daily lived conditions of their neighbors in need. It is precisely because there were poor and hungry people in the community and in the world that Wesley asserted that anyone who accumulated wealth was a thief. His experience taught him that accumulation of wealth leads to the protection of money rather than care for one's neighbor. What was perhaps the worst consequence for Wesley is that wealth leads to a disconnection of the

---

[6] Maddox, *Responsible Grace*, 146. Emphasis Maddox'.

[7] Jennings, *Good News to the Poor* , 155.

[8] John Wesley, "On Visiting the Sick," in *The Works of John Wesley*, ed. Thomas Jackson, vol. 7 (London: Wesleyan Methodist Book Room, 1872; reprint. Grand Rapids, MI: Baker Books, 2007), 124 (page citations are to the reprint edition and will be noted as volume: page for the remainder of this paper).

[9] Wesley, "Serious Thoughts occasioned by the late Earthquake at Lisbon," 11:11.

wealthy from the conditions of their neighbors in need. One part of the world—even within the same city—does not know how the other part lives and dies. Anonymous charity is insufficient. One must not simply send aid to the neighbors in need but to carry it to them, to get to know them and their conditions of living, and to see how things are. As a prolific as he was, Wesley was strikingly consistent.

Wesley did not blame those in need for their conditions and admonished those who moved too quickly to that position. Rather, in encountering a set of difficult circumstances, Wesley asked how his own way of life contributed to those conditions. He was not too proud to beg in order to gain resources to help meet those needs. And resources that came in to him, flowed right back out.

Wesley carried his analysis beyond his own lifestyle, however. He also critiqued people and professions of power for their contributions to the changing economic conditions affecting so many. Wesley chastised doctors, lawyers, merchants, and distillers for unfair prices, ignoring the needs of the poor, wasting materials that could be used to feed the hungry, and removing their services from the reach of those who most needed them, all for the sake of profit. Wesley also occasionally critiqued practices of the government about the prison system, wasting food and money on luxury items, and racking up an irresponsible national debt due to inhumane imperialist/colonialist exploits.[10] All of these critiques were because there were poor, hungry, and sick people in the land who were being ignored and who could benefit if the government, church, and people in powerful positions and professions acted responsibly to care for their neighbors. All of these critiques arose out of a desire to know his neighbor in order to love his neighbor in ways that his neighbors would actually receive as love.

Wesley and the Methodists did not wait for the people in power to come around and act responsibly. Instead, they organized help themselves by creating systems to provide for tangible needs through various services to those in need. They regularly visited the under-served in their communities, bringing food or resources as available, and assessed the basic needs in order to seek the resources still lacking. They offered small business loans to help get families economically back on their feet. They helped others to find and secure employment. They built schools and provided training and education for under-resourced children and adults. Wesley even studied and performed some medical practices in order to provide inexpensive, accessible, reliable, and easily understood remedies for those in need of physical healing and relief.[11]

As the Methodist communities grew, the resourcefulness and assets among them increased. When there was a need they often figured out ways to meet it

---

[10] See Wesley's "Thoughts on the Present Scarcity of Provisions," 11:53-58.

[11] See Wesley's famous tract *Primitive Physic: An Easy and Natural Method of Curing Most Diseases*, 22nd ed. (Eugene, OR: Wipf and Stock Publishers, 2003).

regardless of whether the person in need was a member of the Methodist society or not. Wesley was concerned about the souls of his neighbors but he was concerned about their concrete material conditions as well. What is more, if one did not tend to their neighbor, Wesley argued, one's own soul was in jeopardy.[12] The socio-economic and political ethic grounded in a concern for and solidarity with the neighbor in need was the natural outgrowth of a personally transformed life, a life responding to love in love. The inward work necessarily brought forth outward works. Concern for and solidarity with the neighbor in need were, for Wesley, the fruits of the healing way of salvation. Without them one was simply not truly transformed. A holy life could not be lived in isolation. There is no real holiness that is not social holiness. And that holiness could not be social without attending to the community in which one lives with the resources that one has.

There were weaknesses in Wesley's socio-political-economic ethic. In eighteenth century England the Anglican Church was tied to the constitutional monarchy and the monarchy had been fairly good to the church. Likewise, all other attempts at different types of government had proven unsuccessful and not more humane for the people. Democracy seemed like mob rule to Wesley, something he was familiar with. So Wesley and the church were nervous about too much criticism of the monarchy, preferring an "apolitical" conservative approach instead. This greatly inhibited the success of Wesley's socio-economic ethic and praxis because he was approaching individual issues within an overall political system that was riddled with injustices.

Wesley and his community had great impact on the communities in which they lived and worked. However, without the broader structural political critique of their times and places, they often worked against themselves. This, combined with a number of other threads in the midst of the heyday of British colonialism and the birth of the USA, led to the weakening of Wesley's socio-economic and political ethic as it was passed, or not passed, through the following generations of Wesleyans. This is perhaps also why Wesley is often more famous for his emphasis on personal transformation than his social ethic.

That may also be a significant contributing factor to why institutions like WPC have struggled in their past to find their places within their cities and neighborhoods or to see value in that as part of institutional identity and responsibility. The Church of God (Anderson, IN), although Wesleyan in roots, had some twentieth century wanderings through the post WWs and "Church Growth" eras, framing and re-framing, and struggling to find identity in contexts and through questions not unlike many U.S. American Protestant churches. Somewhere along the way, we began to lose the sense of rooted engagement with our geo-cultural location as an outgrowth of our theo-ethical location. In the first decade of the twenty-first century, WPC sought to re-engage these roots and the questions of what it means to be Wesleyan-Holiness in our time and place.

---

[12] Maddox, *Responsible Grace*, 242.

Bringing it Home

I am not sure that institutions are concerned about their salvation, per se. However, I do think, even if some would claim it as naïve, that most institutions are peopled by those concerned about living responsible and meaningful lives. I am certain this is the case with WPC. We make up the soul of our institution. We do not live and work for ourselves alone. This, we know. We do not work simply to climb up the ladder of the academy. We are concerned for cultivating our own sense of meaning and purpose and thoughtful formation as much as we are concerned for cultivating those things in the lives of our students.

When faced with the decision to choose to look outward for some other place to be or to figure out how to be here, now, WPC began to live into its Wesleyan-Holiness roots by taking its cues from Wesley's understandings of our humanness and holiness connected directly to the health, happiness, holiness, and full humanness of the others with whom we share space and time. In this view, holiness does not allow us to achieve or maintain separation or "purity." Rather, holiness makes us "dirty" with the stuff of life around us. There is something ancient about this:

> In the New Testament it is by touching the "damaged" and "polluted" in the name of Christ that we express our holiness ... Holiness gets us dirty ... it means that we feed the hungry and give water to the thirsty and welcome the stranger and clothe the naked and visit the sick. That's dirty work ... Being the holy people of God is not to be unplugged from the world. It is to be plugged in.[13]

In changing the lens from looking outward for a new location to rooting within the possibilities of our historic/current location, WPC began to reconsider what it means to be holy in this time and place. This necessitated a reimagining of some dominant theo-ethical understandings of holiness moving away from isolationism and individualism and toward the relational connection that Wesley calls for in the pursuit of full humanness and love for those in Southeast Portland. In essence, we decided to get to know our neighbors in order to love them. This is compelling for multiple reasons, practical and theological. And the great news is, these are our roots.

Wesley was convinced that "the way of love" could bring wellness to the soul, mind, and body.[14] This is not cheap sentimental love but empowering, accountable, justice-making love. It is love that takes seriously the call of the divine and the needs of the neighbor, love that resists the accumulation of riches and the sense of entitlement they bring with them,[15] love that considers

---

[13] Gilbert W. Stafford, "Holy Cow! Or Holy God; Holy Moses! Or Holy People; Holy Rollers! Or Holy Life," sermon delivered 27 November 2007, Anderson School of Theology, Anderson, IN.

[14] E. Brooks Holifield, *Health and Medicine in the Methodist Tradition* (New York: Crossroad, 1986), 20.

[15] See Wesley's sermon on "The Danger of Riches," 7:12.

both the spiritual and physical conditions of individual human lives and communities, love that recognizes that holiness is connected with real embodied concrete historical contexts. In our branch of the wider tradition of Christianity, holiness is not a state of removal from the real world nor is Christian perfection an achievement over those who are "less perfect." Rather, the pursuit of holiness, the going on toward "perfection," is increasing in love for those who share this world.

Wesley's understanding of holiness emphasizes the "divine goal not just of reconciliation and a new status in the eyes of God, but the gracious re-creation of both individuals and the social world through the renewal of the image of God in humanity"[16]—an image defined by relationality. "If love is the imitation of God" and "if God is the one who hears the distress of the afflicted, then the imitation of God will likewise respond concretely to human affliction in whatever form . . . The visible and dramatic realization of love in the everyday world is the only proof that there is a God who is love."[17] By being here, now, with our beautiful and sometimes struggling neighbors, we participate in demonstrating evidence that God cares about the world.

WPC is a community that is descended from people who believe and have staked their lives on the belief that love works. It affects change in real people and real things in real embodied contexts. Those effects are visible in the ways that people care for one another, themselves, and the world in responding to the free love of God and others by offering that love freely and relationally in the world. "Love provokes love,"[18] if it is not abstract or disinterested love but love that earns respect by giving it, that gains power by empowering others, that seeks justice and wellness as a component of holiness, that strives to lessen the sorrows and increase the joys of its neighbors. We do not always choose our neighbors, but we can choose what kind of neighbors we will be.

Sometimes we assert that we love our neighbors without actually knowing anything about them. This is not love. As the people of WPC began to look around, we began to take notice of who our neighbors are and began to ask the difficult and important question of what it means, then, to be good neighbors to those particular neighbors in Southeast Portland. Love, asserts the life and teachings of Wesley, is practical, particular, and concrete. One cannot offer practical love without knowing the beloved and his or her needs. One cannot offer practical love when one is looking for somewhere else to be.

So we are here, nestled in the bosom of Mt. Tabor. We have decided to be here. Now our question is, how do we love our neighbors in an area that hovers near the top in the nation in homelessness, food insecurity, unemployment, sex trafficking and that is also rich in natural resources, open to innovation, and creativity? There is great potential here. And great need. This sounds like

---

[16] Theodore Runyon, *The New Creation: John Wesley's Theology Today* (Nashville: Abingdon Press, 1998), 231.
[17] Jennings, *Good News to the Poor*, 151.
[18] Ibid., 146.

something Wesley would be all over. It sounds like we have a place to participate here.

As the college community has begun seriously exploring what it means to live into and out of our geo-cultural, historical, and theo-ethical locations, we are finding ourselves moving in deepening circles of engagement. We took early steps by lowering tuition rates, actively recruiting students from our home place, and increasing access to higher education to many first generation college students and others who may simply have not had access to higher education at a private institution or at all. In this, we hoped to open our doors wider, not only to grow enrollment, but as an outgrowth of our social holiness—making our resources available to those with an associated need. This is leading the community deeper into engaging class analysis, racial/ethnic diversity, and confronting our current and historical "whiteness" as well as the unique and complicated issues and story of race within the Portland metro area.

This also is leading the community deeper into engaging other neighbors. We are beginning to engage the complexities of religious diversity in our neighborhoods, striving to get to know and love those neighbors of different religious traditions and backgrounds and those who stand outside of all traditional religious institutions but continue to creatively and thoughtfully make meaning in their own lives and the life of the community we share. The people of WPC continue to tap into the resources and commitment within Portland toward engaging ecological responsibility and love of our world and non-humans neighbors we share it with by auditing our "waste" and exploring (albeit sometimes slow) opportunities to steward ecological resources thoughtfully. And, this pursuit of getting to know and finding out how to actively, practically, and concretely love our particular neighbors has led the community to dive deeper into engaging the questions of sexual diversity, to become a community where all people can be safe and loved—a topic that Wesleyan-Holiness churches and institutions have sometimes been reputed to handle in less than kind ways, if at all.

In recent years, we have seen students impacting local legislation on human trafficking. We have put in thousands of hours of direct service hours as well as sought training in asset based community development to work with the community and not simply "at" or "for" our neighbors. We have begun to resist anonymous or harmful "charity" but are trying to work alongside our neighbors who have been helping other neighbors with great care to fill in their needed gaps. We have begun gathering and listening to stories of our neighbors and included these as part of our course "texts." We have begun to listen to our neighbors who live outdoors, our neighbors who are hungry, our neighbors who are wildly resourceful and creative to dream and hope together about the future of our shared neighborhood. We have begun to participate in knitting together our part of community-based support networks, offering up the unique resources that our community has. We have begun to try to cultivate a kind of community culture that welcomes new students in to a long and continuing story in which they are invited to participate and then to offer their hard-earned counsel to those who will come behind. In essence, we are trying to know in order to love, to recognize that our health, our happiness, our holiness, and our full humanness are intricately woven together with the health, happiness, and holiness of our neighbors, enemies, and world, choosing to be here in this place at this time with these people for this work.

This has not always been smooth. All is not yet well. It has been complicated. It has been gritty. We do not always have the resources to create the kinds of support systems required of a community like this. We have also not always had the models to look to in order to plan well what those are. We have not always "counted the cost" well. There is much more work to be done. However, the neighborhood is beginning to know that we are grateful to be here, that we want to share in its real life, that we want to contribute our assets to meet the needs those can meet and to gratefully accept help in the places we need it. We still have much to do but we are learning what parts of the work are ours to contribute and who we are here, now.

In the tradition of which WPC is a part, we try to hold together both of our foundational pillars—holiness and unity. This means that being-with is an essential component. We cannot do it by ourselves and we are not alone in the world. That is not always the dominant story in academia. We need to hear from each other and there is something holy about leaning on one another in being the image of the communal (Trinitarian) and incarnate (enfleshed—body and soul in time and place) God that we love and to know and love each other and ourselves. This is not an amorphous unity that discounts the value of each unique person. The love of each self is balanced with love of each neighbor. WPC is a part of a people who looked around and said "there are people missing from the table—are they exhausted? Voiceless? Why are some of our neighbors not here? We are not complete without them."

But our goal, like our ancestors, is not togetherness alone. It is a particular type we call the Kin-dom of God. As we learn from Wesley, this is not for another time and place but has real implications and expectations for our real decisions and our real participation here and now. It is not solely a spiritual kin-dom but a body and soul kin-dom—a kin-dom of enough bread for hungry bellies as well as salvation for hungry souls. It is not an exclusive and protective kin-dom but an inclusive kin-dom of just peace—of love for even our enemies with a big enough table where all know themselves loved and can know and love themselves and neighbors and, in so doing, God. To figure out the role of a Christ-centered, urban, liberal arts college in that work is what forms our identity and what calls us toward our next seventy-five years. At least.

WPC is "in the city, for the city," as one of the school's recent slogans proclaims, because it is in the city. In some ways, it is as simple as that. But for us to embrace the fact that we are in this city in this moment is to root ourselves in the concrete contexts and concerns of our neighborhood, drawing on our rich heritage to love our neighbors who we do not always choose, to recognize that our behaviors matter and that we need each other to live into the kingdom/kin-dom of the God who is known in and through practical, particular, pain-addressing, justice-making, gift offering and receiving, unafraid, life-giving love.

Participating in this work is hard. Remembering who we are is hard. Good neighboring is hard. Real love is hard. Social-holiness is hard. None of these things come thoughtlessly, but with attention, intention, and care.

So, here (and now) we are. We are nestled in and by this city not only because that is where we are, but because that is who we are. This is our homeplace—physically and theo-ethically. Living into our role as loving neighbors in Southeast Portland is not a new marketing campaign nor is it an act of simple resignation. It is our way of continuing our heritage and responsibility to love in our here and now, to do the work that is ours, and to not do it alone.

About the Contributors

Bryant, Barry E. is Associate Professor of United Methodist and Wesleyan Studies and the Director of the Center for Applied United Methodist Studies at Garrett-Evangelical Theological Seminary. His most recent publication is *"Know Your Disease": John Wesley's Doctrine of Sin*.

Crawford, Nathan is Director of Youth and Young Adults at Trinity United Methodist Church in Plymouth, Indiana. He has published numerous articles and is the author of *Theology as Improvisation: A Study in the Musical Nature of Theological Thinking* as well as editor of *The Continuing Relevance of Wesleyan Theology: Essays in Honor of Laurence W. Wood*.

Dodrill, Jonathan is a Ph.D. candidate in Historical and Theological Studies at Garrett-Evangelical Theological Seminary. His research focuses on Wesleyan/holiness communities and urban religious expressions. He teaches Wesleyan/Methodist Studies and Christian history courses at Garrett-Evangelical and in the Course of Study School at Wesley Theological Seminary.

Green, Roger is the department chair and Professor of Biblical Studies at Gordon College. His has written extensively on the history and theology of the Salvation Army, including *The Life and Ministry of William Booth: Founder of the Salvation Army* and *Catherine Booth: A Biography of the Cofounder of the Salvation Army*.

Joseph, Abson Prédestin is Associate Professor of New Testament at Indiana Wesleyan University. He previously served as Dean of Academic Affairs at Caribbean Wesleyan College, Jamaica (2005-2011). Dr. Joseph is an ordained minister from the Wesleyan Church of Haiti. He is also the author of *A Narratological Reading of 1 Peter*.

Maddox, Randy is William Kellon Quick Professor of Wesleyan and Methodist Studies Duke University. He is the author of *Responsible Grace: John Wesley's Practical Theology*, as well as editor of *Aldersgate Reconsidered*, *Rethinking Wesley's Theology for Contemporary Methodism*, *The Cambridge Companion to John Wesley*, and Volume 12 of *The Bicentennial Edition of the Works of John Wesley*.

Rieger, Joerg is Wendland-Cook Endowed Professor of Constructive Theology at Southern Methodist University. He has published extensively in the intersection of theology and empire, including his recent books *Occupy Religion: Theology of the Multitude* and *No Rising Tide: Theology, Economics, and the Future*.

Swoboda, A.J. is a pastor, writer, and professor in Portland, Oregon. He pastors Theophilus church and teaches at a number of universities. His most recent publication is *Introducing Evangelical Ecotheology* (Baker Academic).

Trentaz, Cassie is Assistant Professor of Theology, Ethics, and Church History at Warner Pacific College in Portland, OR. Her research and activism explore how religious communities can speak life and enact social transformation in the midst of the complex contexts in which we live. She is the author of *Theology in the Age of Global AIDS & HIV: Complicity and Possibility* (Palgrave Macmillan, publisher).

Wilson, David teaches Christian history and theology at George Fox Evangelical Seminary and Warner Pacific College, and is Co-Senior Pastor of Mt. Scott Church, in Portland, Oregon. David's recent publications include an article with R. L. Shelton on Wesleyan Hermeneutics in the *Oxford Encyclopedia of Biblical Interpretation* (2013) and a chapter with Phyllis Mack on Mary Bosanquet Fletcher's use of the Bible in *Dissent and the Bible in Britain: 1650-1950* (Oxford, 2013). David is currently editing a collection of Mary Bosanquet Fletcher's sermons with critical articles and commentary. David is also the director of "The Fletcher Page," a website dedicated to the scholarly study of John and Mary Fletcher, at www.thefletcherpage.org.

Winslow, Karen is Professor of Biblical Studies and Chair of the Biblical Studies Department at Azusa Pacific Seminary in Azusa, California. She is Co-editor of *Relational Theology: Issues and Implications* and Associate Editor of *Global Wesleyan Theological Dictionary*. She has written the book, *Early Jewish and Christian Memories of Moses' Wives: Exogamist Marriage and Ethnic Identity* and is currently writing a commentary on 1-2 Kings for the New Beacon Bible Commentary series. Her chapter, "Recovering Redemption for Women: Feminist Exegesis in North American Evangelicalism," will be published fall 2014 in Volume 2 of *Feminist Interpretation of the Hebrew Bible in Retrospect*.

www.ingramcontent.com/pod-product-compliance
Lightning Source LLC
Chambersburg PA
CBHW021811220426
43662CB00006B/264